Microsoft Dynamics GP 2010 Cookbook

Solve real-world Dynamics GP problems with over 100 immediately usable and incredibly effective recipes

Mark Polino

[PACKT] enterprise

PUBLISHING

professional expertise distilled

BIRMINGHAM - MUMBAI

Microsoft Dynamics GP 2010 Cookbook

First published: July 2010

Production Reference: 1290610

Published by Packt Publishing Ltd.
32 Lincoln Road
Olton
Birmingham, B27 6PA, UK.

ISBN 978-1-849680-42-4

www.packtpub.com

Cover Image by Tina Negus (tina_manthorpe@sky.com)

Credits

Author

Mark Polino

Reviewers

Frank Hamelly

Leslie Vail

Acquisition Editor

Kerry George

Development Editor

Dhwani Devater

Technical Editor

Chris Rodrigues

Indexer

Rekha Nair

Editorial Team Leader

Akshara Aware

Project Team Leader

Priya Mukherji

Project Coordinator

Zainab Bagasrawala

Proofreader

Jeff Orloff

Production Coordinator

Adline Swetha Jesuthas

Cover Work

Adline Swetha Jesuthas

About the Author

Mark Polino is a Microsoft MVP for Dynamics GP, a Certified Public Accountant, and a Microsoft Certified Business Management Solutions Professional. He is the author of the premier Dynamics GP related blog, DynamicAccounting.net and the creator and presenter of the successful series "Getting More Out of Microsoft Dynamics GP: 50 Tips in 50 minutes". Mark has worked with Dynamics GP and its predecessor, Great Plains, for more than 10 years.

He works as a Principal Consultant with I.B.I.S., Inc. and spends his days helping clients implement Microsoft Dynamics GP.

Acknowledgement

To my wife Dara and my children, Micah and Angelina, thank you for your support of this project. You've patiently endured this obsession without complaining or killing me in my sleep. To mom and dad, thanks for the cheerleading even though you had no idea what this book is about.

Thank you to Andy Vabulas, Dwight Specht, and Clinton Weldon at I.B.I.S. for your support of this book. Without your openness to this project it never would have happened. To Abby, Troy, Ross, and all the other I.B.I.S. consultants who listened to me drone on about how the book was progressing, you have both my apologies and my thanks for your encouragement.

I owe a debt of gratitude to the kind folks at the Hampton Inn in Mt. Airy, NC. The majority of this book was written there while working on a Dynamics GP project. The hotel is staffed with some of the nicest people that you will ever meet and they were happy to fuel this book with great rooms and Diet Mt. Dew.

Much of this book was written on an Acer netbook. Without the small size and long battery life of the netbook the Dynamics GP 2010 Cookbook would never have been finished on time.

To everyone else who has offered encouragement throughout this project, you have my thanks. To those who have been less than encouraging, I hope you someday decide to write a book.

About the Reviewers

Frank Hamelly, founder and CEO of East Coast Dynamics, is a Microsoft Certified Business Professional - GP, Microsoft Certified Trainer, and Microsoft MVP. Frank holds certifications in Financials, Distribution, Report Writer, and FRx and has over 10 years experience in Financials, Distribution, Sales Order Processing, Manufacturing, Project Accounting, Field Service, and the Payroll and Human Resources series of GP. He also has project management and implementation experience with SAP, Baan, Fourth Shift, and MAS90/200.

A graduate of the University of Pittsburgh with a degree in Business Administration, his 20+ years industry experience includes manufacturing, aerospace, telecommunications, utilities, and professional services organizations.

Leslie Vail is a CPA and has been working as a Microsoft Dynamics GP consultant for 17 years. She began with version 1.0 in 1993. During this period she has completed numerous implementations, conversions, and custom development projects. She presents at many partner and customer technical conferences and conducts training classes throughout North and Central America.

Leslie is recognized throughout the industry for her product expertise and contributions to the Dynamics community. She is the principal of ASCI, Inc., a consulting firm located in Dallas, TX.

As a Microsoft Certified Trainer (MCT) she serves as a Subject Matter Expert (SME) for the Microsoft Assessments and Certification Exams (ACE) Team. She is a member of the US MCT Advisory Council and has been named a Microsoft Most Valuable Professional (MVP) since 2007. She was listed as one of the Microsoft Dynamics Top 100 Most Influential People in 2009 by DynamicsWorld. She is one of the top contributors to the Microsoft Dynamics GP Newsgroup and the Microsoft Dynamics GP Community forum and she maintains the popular Dynamics Confessor BlogSpot (http://dynamicsconfessions.blogspot.com/).

She has reviewed and developed Microsoft Courseware, co-authored the book "Confessions of a Dynamics GP Consultant", and is the Technical Editor of several books dedicated to Microsoft Dynamics GP. Leslie also provides some content for the Dynamics Confessions newsletter.

She provides implementation and consulting services for companies ranging from a high-net-worth individual to a multi-national manufacturing firm. She is certified as a Microsoft Certified IT Professional in Microsoft Dynamics GP Applications and Microsoft Dynamics GP Installation & Configuration. She holds a Microsoft Certified Technology Specialist certification in: Dexterity, Modifier with VBA, Integration Manager, Report Writer, HR/Payroll, Financials, Inventory and Order Processing, FRx Report Designer, SQL Server 2000, and Microsoft XP Professional.

A skilled developer, Leslie uses Dexterity, Modifier with VBA, Integration Manager, and eConnect to provide custom solutions to her clients. She is a Certified Integration Developer (CID), a Dexterity CID, a Dynamics Tools CID, and a Dexterity Certified Systems Engineer.

Her training expertise spans the entire Microsoft Dynamics GP product line. She is an experienced trainer and teaches classes for Dexterity, Financials, Inventory and Order Processing, HR/Payroll, Integration Manager, Modifier with VBA, FRx Report Designer, SQL Server Reporting Services, Report Writer, Crystal Reports, SmartList Builder, Excel Report Builder, Integrated Excel Reports, Extender, and System Manager.

Prior to working with Microsoft Dynamics GP, Leslie was the tax director for a large financial institution; before that, she worked for one of the original 'Big Eight' accounting firms as a senior tax accountant.

Table of Contents

Preface

Tens of thousands of Microsoft Dynamics GP users keep the accounting functions of their firms running day in and day out. They ensure that vendors get paid, customer payments are tracked, and the financial statements balance in the end. In short, they provide the information critical to corporate decision making.

Although thousands of people use Dynamics GP, many of them only use a subset of the functionality. They figure out just enough to do their job but never delve into ways to do it better. Many users also start with a particular version of Dynamics GP but don't update their skills for new features in updated versions. Employers generally offer little or no training after the initial implementation. The work gets done, but users are left with a feeling that there must be a better way. This book is designed to remove that nagging feeling and provide ways to get more from Dynamics GP.

Why a Dynamics GP Cookbook

Although users manage to get the job done, usually there is a better way. In countless consulting and speaking engagements I find users who simply don't know about the simple features or techniques that can make using Dynamics GP easier.

These features don't require extensive knowledge of Dynamics GP, simply a desire to make using Dynamics GP easier, faster, and simpler. These features, tips, and techniques have been compiled into a set of recipes designed to let Dynamics GP users cook up solutions to their problems.

Like your grandmother's cookbooks, these recipes are laid out in simple steps designed to make them easy to follow and get right the first time. The recipes outlined here are optimized for quick application. Users can put these recipes to work the day they read them. This instant gratification is designed to draw users deeper into more recipes with the goal of improving efficiency. The time saved by these recipes can be put back into other finance activities or the simple pleasure of going home on time.

Spreading these recipes to a few people just wasn't enough. Great recipes are made to be shared and that's what this book is designed to do.

What this book covers

Chapter 1, Personalizing Dynamics GP includes recipes designed to enhance the usefulness of Microsoft Dynamics GP by personalizing the look and feel of the application.

Chapter 2, Organizing Dynamics GP includes recipes that are designed to help administrators get more out of Dynamics GP for their users by changing the way Dynamics GP is organized.

Chapter 3, Automating Dynamics GP includes recipes that focus on efficiency and automation and are designed to be time savers across the system.

Chapter 4, Harnessing the Power of SmartLists includes recipes used to harness the power of Dynamics GP's Ad hoc reporting tool and ways to leverage the reporting power of SmartLists.

Chapter 5, Connecting Dynamics GP to Microsoft Office 2010 includes recipes that help connect Dynamics GP with Microsoft Office 2010 and ways to use Office to improve processes in Dynamics GP.

Chapter 6, Exposing Hidden Features in Dynamics GP includes techniques that are well known to consultants but often missed by users. It contains hidden settings that can help save a lot of time.

Chapter 7, Improving Dynamics GP with Hacks includes recipes that are used to hack existing features in Dynamics GP so as to improve its usability.

Chapter 8, Preventing Errors in Dynamics GP includes recipes for administrators and users to help prevent errors in Dynamics GP. It also includes ways to fix erroneous transactions that managed to make it to the general ledger.

Chapter 9, Maintaining Dynamics GP includes recipes for an administrator or power user to help maintain Dynamics GP.

Chapter 10, Extending Dynamics GP with Free Software includes recipes that make use of third-party applications to provide additional functionality, address industry-specific requirements, and improve efficiency in Dynamics GP.

What you need for this book

Although this book is divided into chapters arranged around a common theme, the book can be consumed in a variety of ways. One approach is to walk through the table of contents, applying recipes with the most promise for a reader's firm. The recipes are typically not dependent on each other but do refer back to related items to build on lessons learned. Alternatively, working through a chapter at a time, in any order, can help a firm improve their processes around a common theme such as Personalizing or Automating Dynamics GP.

There is no requirement to work through the book in order. Feel free to pick it up and start anywhere.

Though the book is designed for Microsoft Dynamics GP 2010, the evolutionary nature of the system means that most of these recipes will work just fine in earlier versions.

With version 10 Microsoft introduced new navigation options with the creation of a Home page and Area Pages. This navigation design is not only continued, but extended in Dynamics GP 2010. With Microsoft's heavy focus on role tailoring and improved navigation, the conventions in this book follow the improved navigation options. This may be new to long time Dynamics GP users used to the familiar **Transactions | Financial | General** nomenclature. The new navigation options cluster all of the activities together for a single module, reducing the number of steps required for multiple actions.

To help users understand the new conventions I've included examples of the new layouts.

The Microsoft Dynamics GP Home page opens by default or when **Home** is selected from the Navigation Pane on the lower left. Above the Navigation Pane is the Shortcut Bar and in the center is the Home page with customizable navigation and information options:

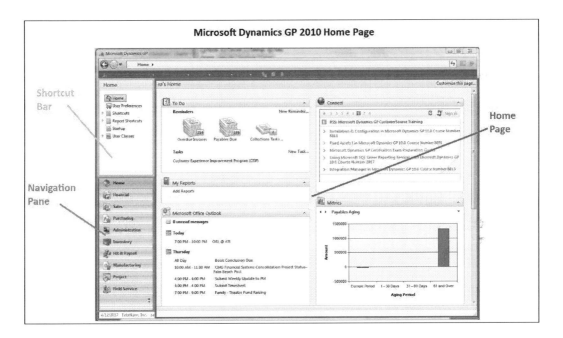

When anything other than **Home** is selected on the Navigation Pane the screen displays a List Pane in place of the Shortcut Bar on the left. The Home page is replaced with an Area Page. The Area Page contains menu items specifically related to the functional item selected on the Navigation Pane:

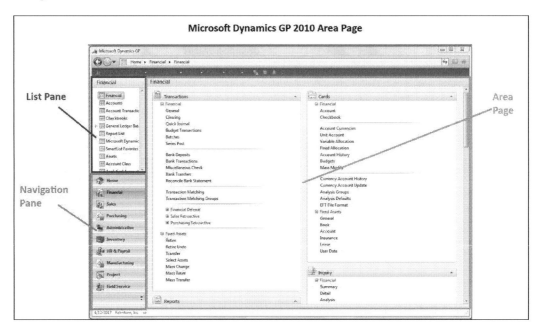

I hope you enjoy these Dynamics GP recipes and that the time you save by using these recipes gets you home in time for dinner and dessert.

Who this book is for

This book is for Dynamics GP users and Microsoft Dynamics GP partners and is primarily focused on delivering time-proven application modifications. This book assumes that you have a basic understanding of business management systems and a basic knowledge of Microsoft Dynamics GP. All of these recipes are real-world tested and designed to be used immediately.

Conventions

In this book you will find a number of styles of text that distinguish between different kinds of information. Here are some examples of these styles and an explanation of their meaning.

Code words in text are shown as follows: "Save the sheet to the desktop as `Segment3Import`."

A block of code is set as follows:

```
Update Dynamics..sy01402
Set syUSERDFSTR='TRUE-60-1000'
Where syDefaultType=30
```

New terms and **important words** are shown in bold. Words that you see on the screen, in menus or dialog boxes for example, appear in the text like this: "Click on **OK** to accept the changes and close the window."

Reader feedback

Feedback from our readers is always welcome. Let us know what you think about this book—what you liked or may have disliked. Reader feedback is important for us to develop titles that you really get the most out of.

To send us general feedback, simply send an e-mail to `feedback@packtpub.com`, and mention the book title via the subject of your message.

If there is a book that you need and would like to see us publish, please send us a note in the **SUGGEST A TITLE** form on `www.packtpub.com` or e-mail `suggest@packtpub.com`.

If there is a topic that you have expertise in and you are interested in either writing or contributing to a book on, see our author guide on `www.packtpub.com/authors`.

Customer support

Now that you are the proud owner of a Packt book, we have a number of things to help you to get the most from your purchase.

Errata

Although we have taken every care to ensure the accuracy of our content, mistakes do happen. If you find a mistake in one of our books—maybe a mistake in the text or the code—we would be grateful if you would report this to us. By doing so, you can save other readers from frustration and help us improve subsequent versions of this book. If you find any errata, please report them by visiting `http://www.packtpub.com/support`, selecting your book, clicking on the **let us know** link, and entering the details of your errata. Once your errata are verified, your submission will be accepted and the errata will be uploaded on our website, or added to any list of existing errata, under the Errata section of that title. Any existing errata can be viewed by selecting your title from `http://www.packtpub.com/support`.

Piracy

Piracy of copyright material on the Internet is an ongoing problem across all media. At Packt, we take the protection of our copyright and licenses very seriously. If you come across any illegal copies of our works, in any form, on the Internet, please provide us with the location address or website name immediately so that we can pursue a remedy.

Please contact us at copyright@packtpub.com with a link to the suspected pirated material.

We appreciate your help in protecting our authors, and our ability to bring you valuable content.

Questions

You can contact us at questions@packtpub.com if you are having a problem with any aspect of the book, and we will do our best to address it.

1
Personalizing Dynamics GP

In this chapter, we start with recipes for users of Microsoft Dynamics GP. After all, that's who this book is for. This chapter is designed to improve a user's productivity from day one. In this chapter we will look at ways of:

- Improving visibility by setting Required Fields to bold and red
- Getting faster access to data with the Shortcut Bar
- Reducing clicks with Startup shortcuts
- Personalizing the Home page by selecting the right role
- Speeding up access to data with Quick Links
- Rearranging Navigation to make it easier
- Jumping to the right location with Breadcrumbs
- Managing personal reports with My Reports
- Viewing open items with the Task List
- Visualizing information with Home page Metrics
- Accessing accounts faster with Favorites in Lookups
- Cleaning up the mess by fixing AutoComplete errors

Introduction

This chapter explores recipes designed to enhance the usefulness of Microsoft Dynamics GP by personalizing the look and feel of the application. These recipes provide the initial steps in harnessing the full power of Dynamics GP. They are designed to improve productivity today so don't wait to put them to use.

In almost all cases the recipes in this chapter do not require administrative privileges and are available to the average user. The ability of each user to tailor these items to their own needs is what makes these recipes so powerful.

By personalizing Dynamics GP users get the opportunity to fine tune the system to the way that they work. There is something incredibly satisfying about tailoring a system to make it more efficient, and we'll cover some of those personalizing options here.

Although the nature of these recipes makes them useful right away, it is strongly recommended that these items be attempted in a test environment first.

Improving visibility by setting Required Fields to bold and red

Microsoft Dynamics GP provides an option for each user to identify required fields on any form. By activating this setting, users can get an obvious visual cue indicating the minimum required fields on any form. This recipe shows how to set required fields to bold red and what the end result will look like.

Getting ready

Prior to changing the appearance of required fields the feature Show Required Fields needs to be turned on. To activate this feature:

1. Click on the Help icon (the white question mark on a blue background in the upper-right corner) on the Home page of Dynamics GP.
2. Ensure that **Show Required Fields** has a checkmark next to it. If it does not, click on the **Show Required Fields** item to turn this option on.

How to do it...

To improve visibility of required fields, follow these steps:

1. The Shortcut Bar is the vertical bar on the top left-hand side of the screen and appears when the **Home** button is selected on the left. From the Shortcut Bar, click on **User Preferences**. Then, click on the **Display** button to open the **User Display Preferences** window.
2. In the bottom right, under the heading **Required Fields**, set **Font Color** to **Red** and **Font Style** to **Bold**:

3. Click on **OK** to accept the changes and close the window. Then, click on **OK** to close the **User Preferences** window. Now, any window that allows data entry will show the required fields in bold red, such as the one in the following screenshot:

How it works...

Dynamics GP contains identifiers behind the scenes to mark fields as required. Dynamics GP uses these identifiers to change the color of the field label. Highlighting required fields provides a quick visual cue to ensure that at least the minimum amount of data is entered prior to saving a form. This will save hours of time by preventing annoying messages indicating that required fields have not been completed, especially as there is no indicator as to what field is missing.

There's more...

By default, activating **Show Required Fields** simply sets the required fields to black and regular font. That is, it doesn't distinguish these at all. This is important because if **Show Required Fields** is off completely, Dynamics GP 2010 will prompt users to turn it on. However, it won't appear to have any effect:

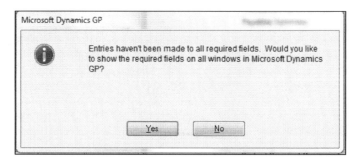

There are some areas in Dynamics GP where required fields are not marked in red and bold despite this feature being enabled. In almost all cases these fields occur in the grid section of a transaction entry form. This area of a form has a heading at the top and a grid that allows multiple entries under one heading. The nature of the programming behind the grid format prevents Dynamics GP from properly highlighting these fields.

When a user receives a warning that a required field is missing, but all required fields appear to be correctly filled in, they should examine the fields in the grid for missing information. The most common culprits are the Unit of Measure (U of M) and Site ID fields.

Modifier with VBA

With the available Modifier with VBA utility for Dynamics GP, an administrator or developer can mark additional fields as required; and in most cases Dynamics GP will apply the red and bold formatting automatically. More information on Modifier with VBA is available from the manuals in Dynamics GP or from an authorized Microsoft Dynamics partner.

Getting faster access to data with the Shortcut Bar

The Shortcut Bar provides fast access to Dynamics GP's windows and SmartLists along with web pages and external applications. Often, external shortcuts are used for quick access to currency websites, budget spreadsheets, shipping sites, or any other applications. Almost anything used to improve a user's productivity can be linked via the Shortcut Bar. In this recipe, we'll spend some time looking at how to get the most out of it.

Getting ready

The vertical area to the left of the Dynamics GP home page is known as the Navigation Pane. Click on **Home** on the Navigation Pane to make the Shortcut Bar visible in the top left.

Clicking on other Navigation Pane sections makes other navigation options available. Only the **Home** selection makes the Shortcut Bar available.

There are six types of items that can be added to the Shortcut Bar:

- ▸ Dynamics GP windows
- ▸ SmartLists
- ▸ Macros
- ▸ Web pages
- ▸ External files
- ▸ Folders

How to do it...

The most common use of the Shortcut Bar is to add a Dynamics GP window for fast access. The simplest way to do this is to:

1. Select **Financial** from the Navigation Pane on the left. In the **Financial** Area Page, select **General**. This opens the **Transaction Entry** window.

2. In the **Transaction Entry** window, click on **File**, then click on **Add to Shortcuts**:

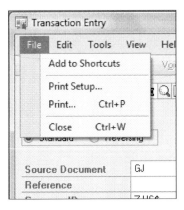

3. Click on the **Home** button to see the **Transaction Entry** window added to the Shortcut Bar:

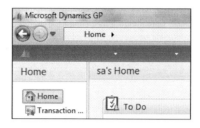

How it works...

The Shortcut Bar in Microsoft Dynamics GP works a lot like shortcuts on the Microsoft Windows desktop. Dynamics GP places a pointer to the window or file inside the shortcut and launches the appropriate selection when the shortcut is clicked on.

There's more...

Typically, users simply accumulate shortcuts on the Shortcut Bar. However, getting the most out of the Shortcut Bar requires a few extra techniques.

Using external shortcuts for greater flexibility

In order to add web pages and external shortcuts, right-click on the Shortcut Bar. Then, select **Add** followed by **Add Web Page** or **Add External Shortcut**.

Selecting **Add Web Page** provides the option to enter the location (URL) along with a button to test that the link works correctly.

Selecting **Add External Shortcut** provides an option to browse for the external file on your system. This can be an application file such as an Excel spreadsheet (as shown in the following screenshot) or a Microsoft Word document. It can also be a link to an application such as Microsoft CRM budgeting software or even Solitaire for a much needed break.

Setting a keyboard shortcut allows the use of a set of keystrokes to launch a shortcut. For example, *Ctrl + Shift + J* could be pressed to launch the **Transaction Entry** window for a journal entry.

Organizing with folders

Right-clicking on the Shortcut Bar and selecting **Add | Folder** provides the option to add a folder to the Shortcut Bar that can be used to organize entries. For example, a Month End folder can be used to hold links to windows, routines, and reports that are used as part of the month-end closing process. This is a great place to start organizing shortcuts.

Complex shortcuts

Microsoft's 'Developing for Dynamics GP' blog provides additional information on dealing with complex shortcuts for scenarios such as launching an application and opening a specific file. More information on this is available at `http://blogs.msdn.com/ developingfordynamicsgp/archive/2009/08/24/creating-external -shortcuts-with-parameters.aspx`.

See also

▸ *Reducing clicks with Startup shortcuts*

▸ *Remembering processes with an Ad hoc workflow*

Reducing clicks with Startup shortcuts

For users who want the same set of features available every time Dynamics GP opens, the Shortcut Bar supports automatically opening a: window, SmartList Favorite, web page, macro, or external file when Dynamics GP starts.

For example, someone with heavy Accounts Payable responsibilities would regularly use the **Payables Transaction Entry** window. Adding this window as a startup shortcut would open this window immediately after Dynamics GP starts without the user having to do anything. In this recipe, we'll look at how to activate a shortcut automatically when Dynamics GP starts.

Getting ready

To use this recipe, users need a basic familiarity with shortcuts. As that was covered in the last recipe, everyone should be in good shape.

How to do it...

To set shortcuts to open automatically, complete the following steps:

1. Open the **Payables Transaction** window in Dynamics GP by selecting **Purchasing** from the Navigation Pane and clicking on **Transaction Entry**.
2. Select **File | Add as a Shortcut** to add the shortcut to the Shortcut Bar.
3. Select **Home** to see the shortcut that was just added.

4. Right-click on the shortcut that was just created and select **Cut**. Right-click on the **Startup** folder and select **Paste**. Once Dynamics GP is restarted, the window represented by the shortcut will start automatically:

How it works...

The **Startup** folder on the Shortcut Bar is designed to open items when Dynamics GP starts to provide consistent and quick access to regularly used items in the system. These are unique to each user.

There's more...

The **Startup** shortcut folder is designed for more than just windows in Dynamics GP.

File example

Another option to add items to the **Startup** folder on the Shortcut Bar is to right-click on the folder and select **Add | Add External Shortcut**. Name the shortcut and select **Browse**. Find the external file in the menu system and click on **Open**.

Optionally, add a **Keyboard Shortcut** and click on **Add**.

Drag and Drop

Experienced users will comment that it is also possible to select the shortcut with the left mouse button and drag it to the **Startup** folder. That works as well, except for a bug in Dynamics GP that prevents dragging and dropping the first shortcut into the **Startup** folder. If there is already a shortcut in the folder, dragging and dropping works fine. However, until the first one has been created, dragging and dropping a shortcut into a folder is impossible.

Interestingly, dragging shortcuts to folders worked correctly in version 9 and seems to have broken with version 10.

See also

 ▸ *Getting faster access to data with the Shortcut Bar*
 ▸ *Improving consistency with Shortcuts and User Classes*

Personalizing the Home page by selecting the right role

With version 2010 of Dynamics GP, Microsoft has placed a strong emphasis on a user's role in both the organization and the software. Selecting the right role in the system presents many of the best Home page options by default.

A role is usually selected by default when a user is created and it's often wrong because at setup, the focus is placed on job titles, not on the tasks the user performs. Additionally, user's roles evolve and change over time. Fortunately, changing a user's role is easy so we'll look at how to do that in this recipe.

How to do it...

To change a user's Home page role, complete the following steps:

1. On the Home page click on the **Customize this Page** link.
2. Click on the **Change Role** button on the bottom right-hand side. Changing the role resets any customizations that a user has made to their Quick Links, Metrics, or Microsoft Outlook settings on the Home page.
3. Click on **OK** to indicate an understanding of the consequences of changing a role.
4. In the **Select Home Page** window, select an industry at the top. Changing an industry simply adds or removes available role options below. Selecting **Other** as the industry provides all of the role options.
5. On the left, select the role closest to a user's responsibilities. As a role is highlighted, a description of that role's tasks is included on the right-hand side of the window. Click on **OK** to accept the role:

See also

▶ *Managing personal reports with My Reports*

▶ *Visualizing information with Home page Metrics*

Speeding up access to data with Quick Links

Like the Shortcut Bar, Quick Links provide fast access to data both inside and outside of Dynamics GP. Though there is some overlap with shortcuts, Quick Links provide some unique features. For starters, related Quick Links are provided based on the user's Home page role. Additionally, Quick Links also provide fast access to Navigation Lists, something that shortcuts can't do. In this recipe, we'll select an included Navigation list and then add it as a Quick Link.

Getting ready

Navigation Lists provide another way to work with data in Dynamics GP, and these aren't available to add to the Shortcut Bar. For our Quick Links example we will look at adding a Navigation list as a Quick Link.

How to do it...

To add a Navigation list as a Quick Link:

1. Click on the **Home** button on the Navigation Pane to the left. On the main Home screen, find the section labeled **Quick Links**.

2. Place the cursor in the **Quick Links** section and a pencil icon will appear on the upper right-hand side. Click on the small pencil icon and select **Add | Dynamics GP Navigation List**:

3. Click on the plus (**+**) sign next to **Sales** to expand the list.

4. Click on the plus (**+**) sign next to **Accounts** and select **Customers**. Click on **OK** to finish.

5. In the open **Quick Links Details** box, find and select the **Customers** link. Click on the **Move Up** button repeatedly until **Customers** is at the top of the list and then click on **OK**:

How it works...

This process puts the **Customers** Quick Link at the top of the **Quick Links** area. Now, clicking on the **Customers** Quick Link will immediately open that Navigation list. Without this Quick Link a user would need to select **Sales** from the Home page and find the **Customers** Quick Link every time they needed to add a customer. Simply selecting a Quick Link is a much faster way to get deep into Dynamics GP.

See also

▸ *Personalizing the Home page by selecting the right role*

Rearranging Navigation to make it easier

The Navigation Pane on the left-hand side of Dynamics GP is full of useful functions. Sometimes it is too full! For many users it's beneficial to rearrange items on the Navigation Pane to better suit their role. We'll look at how to do that in this recipe.

Getting ready

Most users quickly discover that left-clicking and dragging the separator above the **Home** button on the left allows them to shrink and expand the space available for Navigation Pane buttons. This expands the room for lists and shortcuts above by transforming the large buttons into smaller, but less intuitive, icons. However, there is so much more that can be done to personalize the Navigation Pane.

How to do it...

Cleaning up the Navigation Pane can provide faster and simpler navigation options. Let's see how by completing the following steps:

1. On the Navigation Pane select **Navigation Pane Options** from the bottom-right corner of the pane.

2. In the **Navigation Pane Options** window select **Purchasing** and move it to the top using the **Move Up** button at the right.

3. Then select the **Sales** module and deselect its checkbox. Click on **OK**:

Now the **Purchasing** choice has been moved to the top where a user can easily get at it and the **Sales** option not required for this user has been removed.

How it works...

In our example, a heavy user of the Purchasing module now has the Navigation Pane button immediately below the **Home** button making it easily accessible. The **Sales** button that wouldn't be used by a typical Purchasing employee has been removed to clean up the interface.

Jumping to the right location with Breadcrumbs

Dynamics GP 2010 has embraced the concept of Breadcrumbs. Breadcrumbs provide a fantastic opportunity to ease system navigation. By showing the path through the system, new users gain an understanding of how to navigate within Dynamics GP. Experienced users learn that it's a fast way to hop through the system without accessing menus. In this recipe, we'll look at how to use breadcrumbs to improve navigation through Dynamics GP.

Getting ready

In Dynamics GP, select **Financial** from the Navigation Pane. On the **Financial** Area Page select **Transaction Entry** in the **Transactions** area. This will open the **Transaction Entry** window for a general journal entry.

How to do it...

Let's now look at how breadcrumbs can improve navigation for a user by completing the following steps:

1. On the upper left of the screen is the breadcrumb trail. It shows **Home | Financial | Financial**:

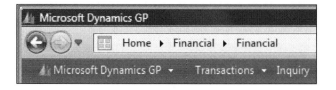

2. This is the path through the system to this window. It indicates that from the Home page, the user has navigated to the **Financial** Area Page.

3. On the Navigation Pane to the left select **Accounts**. This opens the **Accounts** Navigation List and changes the breadcrumb to show **Home | Financial | Accounts**. Select **Financial** from *inside* the breadcrumb trail to go back one step and return to the **Financial** Area Page.

Managing personal reports with My Reports

My Reports is a section of the Dynamics GP Home page designed to provide fast access to reporting options in Dynamics GP. Similar to the Quick Links functionality, My Reports provides single-click access to reports, replacing multiple clicks and drill-downs with a direct connection.

In Dynamics GP, every prebuilt report (also known as a Report Writer report) requires an option. An option is simply a named group of settings for a particular report. For example, a user may have a Receivables Aged Trial Balance report with date and selection criteria designed for month-end reporting. The report name is always Receivables Aged Trial Balance, but the option name to describe those particular month-end settings might be Month End.

The My Reports feature provides one-click access to reports with saved options. In this recipe we'll look at how to add a report to My Reports.

How to do it...

To add a report to My Reports, we will need to complete the following steps:

1. Select the **Sales** button from the Navigation Pane on the left. From the list on the left, select **Report List**.

2. In the center section, scroll down to the report named **Aged Trial Balance** with the **Option** as **demo** and select the checkbox to the left.

   demo is a prebuilt, saved report option. Report options are saved report settings for items such as dates and restrictions.

3. Click on **Add to** to add this to the **My Reports** section of the Home page. Accept the default name for the report by clicking on **OK**:

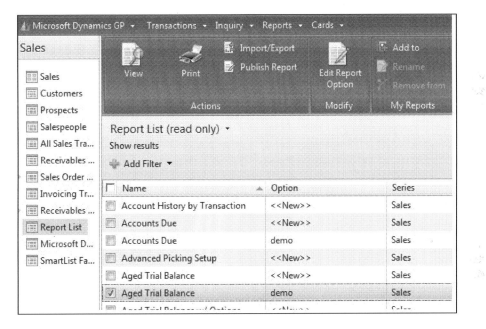

4. Click on the **Home** button on the Navigation Pane to return to the Home page. The **Aged Trial Balance-demo** report now appears on the Home page under **My Reports**:

> My Reports
>
> Aged Trial Balance-demo

5. Click on the **Aged Trial Balance-demo** link under **My Reports** to run the report automatically.

There's more...

Other features and options are available to assist with managing reports in Dynamics GP.

Reports without options

Reports without options cannot be added to the **My Reports** section of the Home page. Consequently, users need to create and save report options to make those reports available to the Home page.

Better dates in report options

A technique for setting up report dates for automatic reporting is covered in detail in the Chapter 3 recipe, *Controlling reporting dates with Beginning and Ending Periods*.

See also

▸ *Personalizing the Home page by selecting the right role*

▸ *Speeding up access to data with Quick Links*

▸ *Viewing open items with the Task List*

▸ *Controlling reporting dates with Beginning and Ending Periods*

Viewing open items with the Task List

Dynamics GP provides a Task List for managing items to be accomplished within the system. Although it is not quite as powerful as say Outlook's tasks, the Task List in Dynamics GP can provide direct links to the appropriate window, web page, or external file needed to accomplish a task. Even Outlook can't provide a direct link to the right window in Dynamics GP. Additionally, tasks can be assigned to other users in the system to better delegate the workload. In this recipe, let's look at how to use the Task List in Dynamics GP.

Getting ready

Open tasks are displayed on the Home page in Dynamics GP under the **To Do** heading.

To get started, select **New Task** from the Home page to see the full task list. An example is shown in the following screenshot. Yes, that's not particularly intuitive, but that is how it works:

How to do it...

As an example, we'll look at adding a month-end bank reconciliation task by completing the following steps:

1. To create a new task, select **New Task** from the **To Do** section on the Home page to open the full task list.

2. Select **New Task** on the **Task List** window. In the **Task** field, enter **Reconcile Bank Statement**. Set the due date to the 5th of May and the **Status** to **Pending**:

3. From the **Task Assigned To** drop-down menu select a user to assign this task to. From the **Link To** drop-down menu select **Microsoft Dynamics GP window**.

4. To attach the **Reconcile Bank Statement** window, click on the blue arrow next to the **Name** field.

5. In the new **Add Command** window that opens select **Transactions** on the left. Then click on the plus (**+**) sign next to **Financial** on the right.

6. In the right-hand side pane select **Reconcile Bank Statement** and click on **OK**:

7. Click on **Save** to save the task. If the task was assigned to another user it will now appear in their task list.

How it works...

The new task now appears in the **Tasks** area on the Home page. Selecting the checkbox next to a task marks it as complete and sets the user who completed the task as well as the date the task was marked as completed.

There's more...

Even better, tasks can be repeated. This means that they work great for regular processes such as month-end or quarter-end tasks.

Recurring tasks

To set a task as recurring:

1. Select the **Recurrence** button during task creation or double-click on an existing task and select **Recurrence**.

2. From the previous example select the **Reconcile Bank Statement** task and double-click on the line.

3. Click on the **Recurrence** button. Set the **Recurrence Pattern** to **Monthly** on Day **5** of every **1** month. This means the task will recur on the 5th of every month. That's about five days after a typical bank statement cutoff.

4. Leave the **Range of recurrence** set to **No End Date** and click on **OK**.

   Now this task will repeat on the 5th day of every month, perfect for a calendar month-end bank cutoff. Obviously, if a company's bank statement cuts off at some other time during the month these settings can be easily changed:

See also

▸ *Using Reminders to remember important events*

Visualizing information with Home page Metrics

On the Home page Dynamics GP provides a default set of metrics via charts and graphs designed to provide better visualization of data based on a user's role. Individual users can include or exclude various charts from their Home page and select a default chart. In this recipe, we'll look at ways to tailor the Home page metrics for each user.

How to do it...

Home page metrics provide charts for additional analysis. Let's see how to put these to use by completing the following steps:

1. On the Home page in the **Metrics** section move the mouse over the title **Metrics** to expose additional options on the right. Click on the pencil icon that now appears on the title bar to the right.

2. The left-hand side shows all of the metrics available to a particular user. Selecting a metric on the left and clicking on **Insert** moves that metric to the right and makes it available on the user's Home page. Selecting a chart on the right and clicking on **Remove** eliminates that chart from the Home page:

How it works...

The Metric functionality was significantly expanded in version 2010. In Dynamics GP 2010, users can add multiple metrics to their Home page. Additionally, users can create their own metrics using **SQL Server Reporting Services** (**SSRS**) and apply those metrics to their Home page. The creation of new metrics is beyond the scope of this book. However, more information on this is available via the Dynamics GP manuals.

There's more...

Dynamics GP 2010 provides an option to view multiple metrics on the Home screen, open metrics in a browser window, and drill back for more information.

Multiple metrics

Inserting multiple metrics in the **Metrics to display** box will place all of those metrics on the Home page:

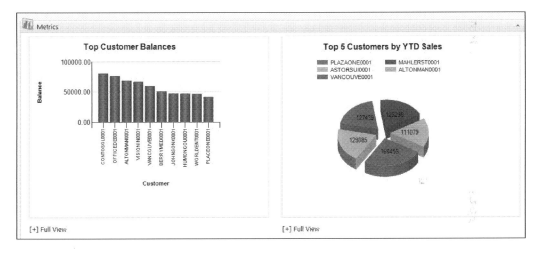

The option to display all of the selected metrics is controlled by the **Customize this Page** selection on the Home page. Once opened, the **Show All** checkbox under the **Metrics** selection of the **Customize Home Page** window controls how many metrics are shown on the Home page. If the **Show All** checkbox is selected, all of the metrics will appear. If it is not selected, one metric will show on the Home page with an option to scroll through all of the available metrics:

![Customize Home Page window showing "Customize your home page" with options to mark content to display including To Do, Microsoft Office Outlook, Connect, Metrics, Show All, My Reports, and Quick Links]

Full View

Clicking on the **Full View** option below a metric opens the SSRS report behind that metric in a web browser. Selecting individual items in the metric drills back to reports with more information. For example, clicking on **Full View** below the **Top Customer Balances** metric and then clicking on the **CONTOSOL0001** column drills down into that customer's balance detail:

![Report Viewer - Windows Internet Explorer window showing Top Customer Balances Detail report]

Top Customer Balances Detail

Customer Number	Customer Name	Customer Balance	Current	31 - 60 Days	61 - 90 Days	91 - 120 Days	121 - 150 Day
CONTOSOL0001	Contoso, Ltd.	80714.12	68447.65	0.00	0.00	0.00	0
Customer: CONTOSOL0001							
Number of Customers Displayed: 10							

See also

▸ *Personalizing the Home page by selecting the right role*

▸ *Speeding up access to data with Quick Links*

▸ *Managing personal reports with My Reports*

Accessing accounts faster with Favorites in Lookups

In larger organizations it is common for users to only work with a subset of the chart of accounts. Often these accounts are limited to a certain division or department. To find a set of accounts fast, Dynamics GP provides a mechanism to look up a more limited set of accounts and save these as Favorites. This provides faster access when selecting accounts in transactions. In this recipe, we'll look at using Favorites in Lookups. Favorites are actually part of SmartLists, which are covered in detail in *Chapter 4, Harnessing the Power of SmartLists*.

This recipe showcases the power of integrating SmartLists into the application interface. It provides an unlimited number of ways to target account selection including selection based on department, company, account type, financial statement type, and more, all with just a few clicks.

Getting ready

To begin this recipe we are required to set up a simple SmartList to set up the account limits. To do so, complete the following steps:

1. Select the **Microsoft Dynamics GP** menu and click on **SmartList** to open the **SmartList** window.

2. Click on the plus sign (**+**) next to **Financial** and select **Accounts**:

3. Now, click on the **Search** button. In the **Column Name** field, click on the lookup button (it looks like a magnifying glass) and select **Account Number**.

4. Set **Filter** to **begins with** and enter the **Value** as **000**. Click on **OK** to close
    the window:

5. Click on the **Favorites** button. In the **Name** field, enter **Segment 000** and click on
    Add. Then select **Add Favorite**:

This process creates a specialized list based on a segment in the chart of accounts, and
then saves it to make it available for account selection.

How to do it...

The Favorites list only needs to be built once. After that, the real fun starts. Complete the
following steps:

1. First, select **Financial** from the Navigation Pane on the left and select **General**
    from the **Transactions** section of the **Financial** Area Page.

2. Click on the **Accounts** field and then click on the lookup button.

3. Click on the arrow next to **View** and hover over **Favorites**.

4. Select **Segment 000**, the Favorite created previously:

This presents a specialized list to users giving them a more targeted list of accounts to select from when creating a transaction.

There's more...

There are more options than just this recipe for limiting the selections from the chart of accounts.

Set as Default View

The new feature in Dynamics GP 2010 is the ability to save a Favorite as the default view. Once a Favorite has been selected in the view, simply click on **Set as Default View** from the **View** menu. Default views are per user and only available for master record lookup, not transactions.

Restricted List

If users only need to restrict the available accounts occasionally, there is a temporary option. After clicking on the lookup button and then on the arrow next to **View**, users should select **Restricted List** instead of **Favorites**. The **Restricted List** option provides similar functionality to Favorites, but the search is not saved and Restricted lists cannot be set as the default view.

Resetting

Selecting **All Accounts** resets the list, removing all restrictions.

Account Security

Account Security is a feature in Dynamics GP that limits a user's access to certain accounts in the chart. A user cannot even see an account that they don't have access to. This is another option to limit the selection of accounts available to a user. However, it requires an administrator and quite a bit of thought to set up correctly. Setting up Account Security is less like a recipe and more like a seven-course meal, so it's not covered here.

Activating Account Security without proper setup makes it appear as if the chart of accounts has been deleted. Deactivating Account Security returns users' access to the chart but not before triggering a gut-wrenching fear that it's time to find a new job.

See also

   ▶   *Chapter 4, Harnessing the Power of SmartLists*

Cleaning up the mess by fixing AutoComplete errors

Dynamics GP includes a fantastic feature known as AutoComplete that remembers what a user has typed in a field and later makes data entry suggestions based on that information. This can significantly reduce repetitive data entry. However, if a user makes an error during data entry, such as a misspelled or incorrect word, that error will continue to be suggested over and over again.

There is a simple way to remove erroneous entries, and we'll look at how this is done in this recipe.

Getting ready

To demonstrate this feature we first need to intentionally create an AutoComplete error:

1.   Select **Sales** from the Navigation Pane on the left.
2.   On the **Sales** Area Page select **Customer** under **Cards** on the right to open up the **Customer Maintenance** window:

![Customer Maintenance window showing File, Edit, Tools, Additional, Help menus with Save, Clear, Delete, Write Letters buttons; Customer ID and Name fields with Hold and Inactive checkboxes]

3. With the **Customer Maintenance** window open, type **MISPELL** in the **Customer ID** field and press *Tab*. Click on the **Clear** button to remove this customer entry.

How to do it...

Now that we have an error, let's see how to fix it:

1. Back in the **Customer ID** field, type **MIS**. Dynamics GP will suggest **MISPELL**. Right-click on the suggested word **MISPELL** and select **Remove From List**:

2. Now, typing **MIS** in the **Customer ID** field doesn't provide the **MISPELL** suggestion.

How it works...

AutoComplete is controlled in **User Preferences**, which is accessed via the Shortcut Bar. The AutoComplete settings are defined for each user. This means that each user has a different set of AutoComplete entries, so removing an errant entry doesn't affect other users.

There's more...

To better manage AutoComplete, there are some other settings that can be adjusted on a per-user basis.

Removing unused entries

The AutoComplete cache of entries can grow quite large and unwieldy leading to a significant number of entries to sort through, thus reducing the effectiveness of this feature. A consistent way to manage the size of the AutoComplete list is by letting AutoComplete remove unused entries automatically. To set this up:

1. Select **User Preferences** from the Shortcut Bar and click on **AutoComplete**.

2. In the **Remove Unused Entries After** field enter **90** and click on **OK**. This means any AutoComplete entries that have not been used for 90 days will be removed.

Reducing the number of AutoComplete entries

Another option for managing the size of the AutoComplete cache is to limit the maximum number of AutoComplete entries. To accomplish this:

1. Select **User Preferences** from the Shortcut Bar and click on **AutoComplete**.

2. For the **Max. Number of Entries to Store per Field** entry the default is 10,000. Think about it: 10,000 entries per field, per user is a huge limit. This limit can safely be lowered by changing the value to **1,000** in the **Max. Number of Entries to Store per Field** field.

Resetting AutoComplete

If significant changes are made to a system, users can get a fresh start by completely resetting their AutoComplete entries. This is accomplished via the **Remove Entries** button, which is made available after clicking on **User Preferences** and then on the **AutoComplete** button.

2
Organizing Dynamics GP

In this chapter, we move from recipes designed for a typical user to recipes fit for the head chef. These recipes are designed to help administrators get more out of Dynamics GP for their users by organizing Dynamics GP.

In this chapter, we will look at:

- Speeding up account entry with Account Aliases
- Gaining visibility with Horizontal Scroll Arrows
- Streamlining payables processing by prioritizing vendors
- Getting clarity with User Defined fields
- Developing connections with Internet User Defined fields
- Gaining additional reporting control with Account Rollups
- Remembering processes with an Ad hoc workflow
- Improving financial reporting clarity by splitting purchasing accounts
- Speeding up lookups with Advanced Lookups
- Going straight to the site with Web Links

Introduction

Dynamics GP provides a number of features to better organize the overall system and improve its usefulness for all users. This chapter is designed to demonstrate how to implement and fine tune these features to provide the most benefit.

Speeding up account entry with Account Aliases

As organizations grow the chart of accounts tends to grow larger and more complex as well. Companies want to segment their business by departments, locations, or divisions. All of this means that more and more accounts get added to the chart. As the chart of accounts grows it gets more difficult to select the right account. Dynamics GP provides the Account Alias feature as a way to quickly select the right account. The account aliases provide a way to create shortcuts to specific accounts. This can dramatically speed up the process of selecting the correct account. We'll look at how this works in this recipe.

Getting ready

Setting up Account Aliases requires a user with access to the **Account Maintenance** window. To get to this window:

1. Select **Financial** from the Navigation Pane on the left. In the **Cards** section of the **Financial** Area Page click on **Accounts**. This will open the **Account Maintenance** window.

2. Click on the lookup button (indicated by a magnifying glass) next to the **Account** field.

3. Find and select Account No. **000-2100-00**.

4. Enter **AP** in the **Alias** field, which is in the middle of the **Account Maintenance** window. This associates the letters AP with the Accounts Payable account selected. This means that the user now only has to enter AP instead of the full account number to use the Accounts Payable account:

```
Account Maintenance                                    ☐ ☐ ✕

 File    Edit    Tools    Help              sa Fabrikam, Inc. 4/12/2017

 💾 Save   ✎ Clear   ✕ Delete                                    🖨

 Account      ◄ 000 -2100 -00      ► 🔍 🗋 → 🔁   ☐ Inactive
 Description   Accounts Payable
 Alias         AP                         ☑ Allow Account Entry

 Category      Accounts Payable                              🔍
```

How to do it...

Once aliases have been set up, let's see how the user can quickly select an account using the alias.

1. To demonstrate how this works, click on **Financial** from the Navigation Pane on the left. Select **Transaction Entry** from the **Financial** Area Page under **Transactions**.

2. In the **Transaction Entry** window select the top line in the grid area on the lower half of the window.

3. Click on the blue arrow next to the **Account** heading to open the **Account Entry** window.

4. In the **Alias** field type **AP** and press *Enter*:

Account Entry	▭ ▢ ✕
File Edit Tools Help	sa Fabrikam, Inc. 4/12/2017
Alias	AP
Account	◄ 000 -2100 -00 ►
Description	Accounts Payable

5. The **Account Entry** window will close and the account represented by the alias will appear in the **Transaction Entry** window:

Co. ID	Account	Debit	Credit	⌃
Description			Exchange Rate	⌄
Distribution Reference			Corresp Co. ID	
TWO	◄ 000 -2100 -00 ►	$0.00	$0.00	

How it works...

Account Aliases provide quick shortcuts for account entry. Keeping them short and obvious makes them easy to use. Aliases are less useful if users have to think about them. Limiting them to the most commonly used accounts make these more useful. Most users don't mind occasionally looking up the odd account. However, they wouldn't want to memorize long account strings for regularly used account numbers.

It's counter-productive to put an alias on every account as that would make finding the right alias as difficult as finding the right account number. The setup process should be performed on the most commonly used accounts to provide easy access.

See also

▸ *Gaining visibility with Horizontal Scroll Arrows*

Gaining visibility with Horizontal Scroll Arrows

A consequence of company growth is that not only does the chart of accounts grow larger and less intuitive, but the actual lengths of account numbers tend to grow longer as well. Companies want to be able to report by account, department, location, and so on. This results in a proliferation of segments added to the main account number and can create very long account names. Dynamics GP can accommodate an account number as long as 66 characters. The longest I've seen used in practice was 27 characters and even that was unwieldy. Most users only need a portion of that length for their day-to-day work.

This presents a problem because very long account numbers won't fit into the account number field on most screens. For this recipe, we'll look at how Dynamics GP provides a solution to this in the **User Preferences** window.

How to do it...

Here we'll see how to increase the visibility of long account numbers:

1. On the Navigation Pane on the left select **Home.**
2. Click on **User Preferences** on the Shortcut Bar.
3. Select the checkbox for **Horizontal Scroll Arrows**:

This turns on the functionality to allow users to scroll horizontally within the **Account** field and lets them see the full account number:

Co. ID	Account			Debit	Credit	
Description					Exchange Rate	
Distribution Reference					Corresp Co. ID	
TWO	◄ 000 -2100 -00		►	$0.00	$100.00	▲
TWO	◄ - -		►	$0.00	$0.00	

How it works...

Once Horizontal Scroll Arrows are activated small arrows appear at the left-hand and right-hand side of the **Account** field letting users scroll right and left to see the full account number.

There's more...

Horizontal Scroll Arrows are implemented on a per-user basis, meaning each user has to turn this on individually. Administrators can make this active for all users with an SQL script.

Additionally, for companies using alphanumeric characters in their chart of accounts, wide letters such as **M** or **W** are often difficult to see. There is also an option to increase the visible width of a particular segment.

Activating Horizontal Scroll Arrows for all users

Horizontal Scroll Arrows are activated by the user. However, an administrator can turn this feature on for all users in all companies by running the following SQL script against the Dynamics database:

```
Update SY01400
Set HSCRLARW=1
```

Widening segments for better visibility

When companies use alphanumeric characters in their chart of accounts wide letters, such as M or W, are often cut off. Horizontal scroll arrows don't help because the problem is that the segment field is too narrow, not the entire account field. To resolve this problem Dynamics GP provides an option to widen the segment fields as well.

On the Navigation Pane click on **Administration**. Select **Account Format**. For each segment that needs to be wider, select the field under the **Display Width** column and change it from **Standard** to **Expansion 1**, **Expansion 2**, or **Expansion 3** to widen the field. **Expansion 3** represents the widest option.

Companies using only numbers in their chart of accounts won't need to widen the segment field. However, firms that include letters as part of their chart will need to increase the width. Following is a list of the expansion options and the letters these are designed to accommodate:

- Expansion 1: A,B,E,K,P,S,V,X, and Y
- Expansion 2: C,D,G,H,M,N,O, Q,R, and U
- Expansion 3: W

Streamlining payables processing by prioritizing vendors

Management of vendor payments is a critical activity for any firm. It's even more critical in difficult economic times. Companies need to understand and control payments. A key component of that is prioritizing vendors. Every firm has both critical and expendable vendors. Paying critical vendors on time is a key business driver.

For example, a newspaper company that doesn't pay their newsprint supplier won't be in business for long. However, they can safely delay payments to their janitorial vendor without worrying about going under.

Dynamics GP provides a mechanism to prioritize vendors and apply those priorities when selecting which checks to print. That is the focus of this recipe.

Getting ready

Setting this up first requires that the company figure out who the priority vendors are. That part is beyond the scope of this book. The **Vendor Priority** field in Dynamics GP is a 3-character field. Users shouldn't be tempted by the possibilities of 3 characters. A best practice is to keep the priorities simple by using 1, 2, and 3 or A, B, and C. Anything more complicated than this tends to confuse users and actually makes it harder to prioritize vendors.

Once the vendor priorities have been determined the priority needs to be set in Dynamics GP. Attaching a priority to a vendor is the first step. To do that:

1. Select **Purchasing** from the Navigation Pane. In the **Purchasing** Area Page, under **Cards**, click on **Vendor Maintenance**.
2. Once the **Vendor Maintenance** window opens, click on the lookup button (indicated by a magnifying glass) next to **Vendor ID**.
3. Select a vendor and click on **OK**.
4. Once the vendor information is populated, click on the **Options** button. This opens the **Vendor Maintenance Options** window.

5. In the center left is the **Payment Priority** field. Enter **1** in the **Payment Priority** field and click on **Save**:

How to do it...

Now that a vendor has been set up with a priority let's see how to apply that information when selecting checks to print:

1. To use vendor priorities to select invoices for payment, click on **Select Checks** from the **Purchasing** Area Page.

2. In the **Select Payables Checks** window enter **TEST** to name the check batch. Press *Tab* to move off the **Batch ID** field and click on **Add** to add the batch.

3. Select a **Checkbook ID** and click on **Save** to save the batch.

4. In the **Select** field click on the drop-down box and select **Payment Priority**. Enter **1** in both the **From** and **To** fields.

5. Click on the **Insert** button to lock in **Payment Priority** as an option:

6. Click on **Build Batch** at the top of the **Select Payables Checks** window. If there are any transactions where the vendor is set to a priority of 1, this will populate a batch of checks based on the vendor priority:

Select Payables Checks	☐ ☐ ✕
File Edit Tools Options Additional Help	sa Fabrikam, Inc. 4/12/2017
Add to Batch Clear	
Batch ID TEST	Checkbook ID UPTOWN TRUST
Batch Total $1,258,369.64	Currency ID Z-US$

How it works...

Since priority is one of the built-in options for selecting checks it's easy to ensure that high-priority vendors get selected to be paid first. All of this is easily accomplished with basic Dynamics GP functionality that most people miss.

Getting clarity with User Defined fields

Throughout Dynamics GP maintenance cards typically include at least two user defined fields. User defined fields can be renamed in the setup screen for the related module. This provides a great mechanism to add in special information. We'll take a look at a typical use of a user defined field in this recipe.

How to do it...

For our example, we'll look at using a user defined field to rename the **User-Defined 1** field to **Region** in the **Customer Maintenance** window.

1. From the Navigation Pane select **Sales**. In the **Sales** Area Page click on **Setup**, then **Receivables**, and finally **Options**.

2. In the **User-Defined 1** field type **Region** and click on **OK** to close each window:

Default Tax Schedule IDs:		
Sales	ALL DETAILS	🔍
Freight	ALL DETAILS	🔍
Miscellaneous	ALL DETAILS	🔍
User-Defined 1	Region	
User-Defined 2	User-Defined 2	
☐ Miscellaneous	☐ Tax	
	OK	

3. Back on the **Sales** Area Page click on **Customer** under the **Cards** area. On the bottom left above **User-Defined 2** is the newly named **Region** field ready to be filled in:

Ship To		
Bill To		
Statement To		
Salesperson ID		
Territory ID		
Region		
User-Defined 2		

How it works...

Changing the field name only changes the display field. It doesn't change the underlying field name in the database. SmartLists are smart enough to show the new name. In our example the description **Region** would appear in a SmartList, not **User-Defined 1**.

User defined fields such as these are present for Customers, Vendors, Accounts, Sales Orders, Fixed Assets, Inventory Items, and Purchase Receipts among others. These can each be renamed in their respective setup screens.

There's more...

All user defined fields are not the same. Some have special features.

Special User Defined 1 features

User Defined 1 has special features inside of Dynamics GP. Most of the built-in reports inside of Dynamics GP allow sorting and selection by the User Defined 1 field. These options aren't provided for User Defined 2. Consequently, administrators should carefully consider what information belongs in User Defined 1 before changing its name as the effects of this selection will be felt throughout the system.

Company Setup user defined fields

On the **Company Setup** window there are two user defined fields at the top right. There is no option in Dynamics GP to rename these fields. The **Company Setup** window is accessed by clicking on **Administration** on the Navigation Pane, then clicking on **Company** under the **Setup** and **Company** headers.

Expanded user defined fields

Certain areas such as Fixed Assets, Inventory Items, and Purchase Receipts have more complex types of user defined fields that can include dates, list selections, and currency.

- ▶ *Renaming Fields for clarity*
- ▶ *Developing connections with Internet User Defined fields*
- ▶ *Going straight to the site with Web Links*

Developing connections with Internet User Defined fields

Dynamics GP provides a built-in set of Internet fields for users to enter information such as web pages, e-mail addresses, and FTP sites. What many people don't know is that these are actually user defined fields and can be changed by an administrator. This allows a firm to add a second e-mail address or remove the FTP link if they want to. In this recipe, we'll look at how to customize these fields.

It is important to keep in mind when setting up Internet User Defined fields that these settings affect all of the Internet User Defined field names attached to address IDs assigned to a Company, Customers, Employees, Items, Salespeople, and Vendors.

How to do it...

Customizing the Internet User Defined fields is easy. Let's look at how it is done. For our example, we'll add the social networking service Twitter as a new label:

1. Select **Administration** from the Navigation Pane. Under the **Setup** and **Company** headers in the **Administration** Area Page select **Company**.

2. Click on the **Internet User Defined** button and change the description in the **Label 4** field to **Twitter**. Click on **OK**:

3. Back on the **Company Setup** screen click on the blue italic letter (**I**) to the right of the Address ID to open the **Internet Information** window. In the **Twitter** field type `http://www.twitter.com/mpolino`.

4. Click on the link associated with the **Twitter** field on the left. This opens a web browser and navigates to my Twitter account so that you can follow me. Click on **Save** to update the record:

Internet Information	
E-mail	
Home Page	http://www.dynamicaccounting.net
FTP Site	
Twitter	http://www.twitter.com/mpolino
Login	
Password	
User Defined 1	http
User Defined 2	

How it works...

The secret to Internet User Defined fields is how the data is entered. Internet items use a prefix in the field to identify the type of Internet transaction to be used with the link. `http://` is used for web pages, `mailto://` for e-mail, and `ftp://` for FTP sites. These prefixes tell Dynamics GP what to do when a link is clicked on. If no prefix is entered, GP will try to figure out what to do and may or may not succeed.

If `http://www.microsoft.com` is entered in the **Home Page** field, clicking on the link to the left will start the default browser and open the Microsoft web page. If `http://` is not included but www is, GP figures out that it should open a web page. Just putting in `microsoft.com` isn't enough for GP to understand that the link corresponds to a web page. Similarly, if a user enters `mailto://mpolino@gmail.com` in the **E-mail** field and clicks on the corresponding link the default e-mail client opens up ready to send an e-mail to me. If no prefix is used on an e-mail address, GP will respond with a "File Not Found" error when the link is clicked on. It's not smart enough to know that the @ symbol means that this is an e-mail account.

Using a prefix in the Internet User Defined fields explicitly defines how this link should work and provides the most consistency to users.

There's more...

Some Internet User Defined fields look special but aren't, and some really are special.

Login and password

By default **Label 5** is set to **Login** and **Label 6** is set to **Password**. These fields are supposed to represent the login and password for one of the associated web pages or FTP sites. However, these fields are not encrypted and there is limited security control. So, it may not be appropriate to leave these fields named **Login** and **Password** if a company doesn't want users entering that information here.

Labels 7 and 8

Label 7 and **Label 8** in the **Internet User Defined Setup** window are special fields that allow a user to look up and attach links to files located on the computer or the network. Clicking on the label name on the left opens the associated file. Any of the user defined fields can hold a filename, not just text. However, the special ability of labels 7 and 8 to allow users to look up filenames means that administrators should reserve these fields for file attachments.

See also

> ▸ *Renaming Fields for clarity*

> ▸ *Going straight to the site with Web Links*

> ▸ *Getting clarity with User Defined fields*

Gaining additional reporting control with Account Rollups

Microsoft Dynamics GP provides great functionality for analyzing and reviewing individual accounts and sequential groups of accounts. Many users don't know that it also provides impressive functionality for analyzing non-sequential groups of accounts via a feature known as Account Rollup.

Account Rollups are inquiries built to allow users to see different GP accounts rolled up together and to provide drill back capability to the details. Additionally, these queries can include calculations for things such as budget versus actual comparisons and calculations.

FRx Reporter provides similar functionality and Account Rollup allows users to access this functionality without the wait time of starting up FRx. Let's see how to mix up some account rollups in this recipe.

Getting ready

Before using Account Rollups it's important to understand how to set them up.

1. To set up Account Rollups, select **Financial** from the Navigation Pane. Then select **Account Rollup** in the **Inquiry** section to open the **Account Rollup Inquiry Options** window.

2. In the **Option ID** field enter the name **Actual vs. Budget** and press _Tab_. Select **Yes** to add the option. On the right, set the number of columns to **3**.

3. In the first row type **Actual** in the **Column Heading** field and set the **Type** to **Actuals**.

4. In the second row type **Budget** in the **Column Heading** field and set the **Type** to **Budget**. In the **Selection** column click on the lookup button (indicated by a magnifying glass) and select **BUDGET 2008**.

5. In the third row type **Difference** in the **Column Heading** field. Set the **Type** to **Calculated**. Click on the blue arrow next to **Selection** to open up the **Account Rollup Inquiry Calculated Column** window.

6. In the **Column** field select **Actual** and click on the double arrow (**>>**). Then click on the minus (**-**) button. Back in the **Column** field select **Budget** and click on the double arrow (**>>**). Click on **OK**.

7. Back on the **Account Rollup Inquiry Options** window, select the **Segment** field, and then select **Segment2**. Use the lookup buttons (indicated by a magnifying glass) in the **From** and **To** fields to add account **4130** and click on **Insert**. Repeat this process to insert **4120** and then **4100** into the **Restrictions** box below. Click on **Save** and close the window:

Notice when looking up these accounts for selection that these numbers are not sequential; there are a number of accounts in between.

How to do it...

Now that we've built an account rollup let's see how to make it work:

1. Select **Account Rollup** under **Inquiry** on the **Financial** Area Page.

2. In the **Option ID** field look up **Actual vs. Budget** with the help of the lookup button (indicated by a magnifying glass).

3. The screen will show **Actual**, **Budget**, and **Difference** for each period in this year. The year can be changed at the top and the **Display** can be changed to show either **Net Change** or the **Period Balance** for each period in the year along with a **Total** at the bottom, using the controls next to the **Year**. The **Difference** field is the Actual minus Budget calculation that we created when setting up the rollup:

Period	Actual	Budget	Difference
Beginning Balance	$0.00	$0.00	$0.00
Period 1	$0.00	$30,000.00	($30,000.00)
Period 2	$0.00	$30,000.00	($30,000.00)
Period 3	($539.55)	$30,000.00	($30,539.55)
Period 4	($8,792.14)	$30,000.00	($38,792.14)
Period 5	$0.00	$30,000.00	($30,000.00)
Period 6	$0.00	$30,000.00	($30,000.00)
Period 7	$0.00	$30,000.00	($30,000.00)
Period 8	($5,755.50)	$30,000.00	($35,755.50)
Period 9	$0.00	$30,000.00	($30,000.00)
Period 10	($864.19)	$30,000.00	($30,864.19)
Period 11	($364.32)	$30,000.00	($30,364.32)
Period 12	$0.00	$30,000.00	($30,000.00)
Total	($16,315.70)	$360,000.00	($376,315.70)

(Account Rollup Inquiry window — Option ID: Actual vs Budget, Year: 2017, Display: Net Change / Period Balances — sa Fabrikam, Inc. 4/12/2017)

4. Click on a period with an amount in the **Actual** column and select the blue **Actual** link at the top. A new window will open with the included accounts and the actual amounts for each account.

5. On drilling down to the **Account Rollup Detail Inquiry Zoom** window, Dynamics GP provides a checkbox option to show accounts even if these have zero balance. Additionally, an option at the top controls the printing of Account Rollup information. The rollup can be printed in **Summary** or in **Detail**.

6. Selecting a line and clicking on **Balance** from the **Account Rollup Detail Inquiry Zoom** window drills back to the detailed transactions behind the balance:

How it works...

Account Rollups combine the account totals from disparate accounts for reporting. This is great for tying back multiple accounts that roll up into a single line on the financial statements. Account Rollups also work well for analyzing a single segment, such as a department, across multiple accounts. In the past, I've used this for easy comparisons of Fixed Asset general ledger accounts to the subledger and for rolling up full-time equivalent of unit accounts to get the number of employees across the company with drill back to the employees in each department.

See also

Chapter 4, Harnessing the Power of SmartLists

Remembering processes with an Ad hoc workflow

Dynamics GP provides options for robust workflow functionality integrated with **Microsoft Office SharePoint Server** (**MOSS**) or **Windows SharePoint Services** (**WSS**). However, for many users this is more functionality than they need. Additionally, many organizations don't feel they are ready for the cost and complexity of MOSS. For users who only need a simple workflow to ensure that they remember the steps for a particular task, a basic workflow can be built using shortcuts and folders.

This process works well for irregular tasks such as month-end or quarter-end processes where tasks are performed infrequently enough, thus making it easy to forget the steps. For this recipe, we'll look at setting up a basic month-end workflow.

Getting ready

The basic steps of this task are to create a folder to hold the workflow and then to add the steps in order to that folder. For our example, we will assume that a month-end financial closing workflow includes posting a Quick Journal, processing a Clearing Entry, and closing the month.

How to do it...

Here are the steps to create a basic Ad hoc workflow:

1. Click on the **Home** button from the Navigation Pane on the left. This makes the Shortcut Bar available on the top left.

2. Right-click on the Shortcut Bar and select **Add | Folder** to add a folder to the Shortcut Bar that can be used to organize entries. Name the folder **Month End** and press the *Enter* key. Now, there is a folder to hold month-end entries.

3. The next step is to add our three sample entries. Select the **Month End** folder on the Shortcut Bar. Right-click on the folder and select **Add | Add Window**:

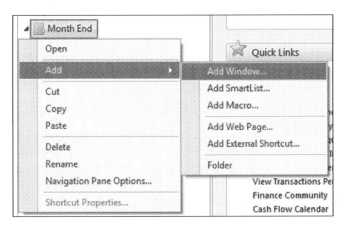

4. Click on the plus sign (**+**) next to **Microsoft Dynamics GP**. Click on the plus sign (**+**) next to **Financial** and select the window named **Quick Journal Entry**. Change the name at the top to **1) Quick Journal Entry**. Click on **Add**. Putting a number in front of the text prevents this shortcut from interfering if the same shortcut appears somewhere else on the Shortcut Bar:

5. Next, select **Clearing Entry** also under **Microsoft Dynamics GP** and **Financial**. Rename it to **2) Clearing Entry** in the **Name** field and click on **Add**.

6. Finally, click on the plus sign (**+**) next to **Company** under **Microsoft Dynamics GP** and select **Fiscal Periods Setup**. Rename this to **3) Close Period** and click on **Add**. Select **Done** to finish.

7. These items will now appear on the Shortcut Bar on the left under the **Month End** folder. Selecting an item with the left mouse button will allow moving of these items around to adjust the order if necessary.

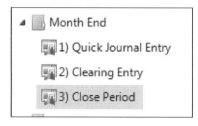

How it works...

Ad hoc workflows provide an option to group a set of steps together and make these all available in one place. Clicking on the arrow to the left of the folder closes it up and keeps the steps out of the way until these are needed. Clicking on the arrow again reopens the folder to run the steps. Some common uses include creating a basic set of steps for new users, month-end and quarter-end processes, and any other process where it is important to ensure that all of the steps are followed.

See also

> ▸ *Improving consistency with Shortcuts and User Classes*

> ▸ *Getting faster access to data with the Shortcut Bar*

Improving financial reporting clarity by splitting purchasing accounts

By default, in Dynamics GP, when a payables invoice is fully or partially paid, the payment portion of the transaction doesn't flow through the payables account. This can make it more difficult to trace a transaction as the transaction could skip the payables account altogether by crediting cash and debiting an expense.

GP provides an optional setting to force transactions to flow through the payables account and that's what we'll look at in this recipe.

How to do it...

Setting up GP to pass voucher payments through payables is as easy as following these steps:

1. Select the **Administration** button from the Navigation Pane on the left. In the **Administration** Area Page click on **Company** under the **Setup** and **Company** headers.

2. Click on the **Options** button. In the **Company Setup Options** window scroll down to the setting marked **Separate Payment Distributions** and select the checkbox next to it:

Company Setup Options						☐ ☐ ☒
File	Edit	Tools	Additional	Help		sa Fabrikam, Inc. 4/12/2017

☐	Calculate Terms Discount Before Taxes
☐	Enable Intrastat Tracking
☑	Separate Payment Distributions
☐	Merge Trade Discount and Markdown Distributions in Sales
☐	Merge Trade Discount Distributions in Purchasing
☐	Calculate Tax Rebates
☐	Enable Posting Numbers in General Ledger
☐	Enable GST for Australia
☐	Enable Tax Date
☐	Enable Reverse Charge Taxes

3. Click on **OK** to close the window and accept the changes.

How it works...

Let's assume a $100 purchase transaction where $20 is paid in cash and the remaining $80 would go to accounts payable. By default, GP will create a transaction distribution that looks similar to the following screenshot:

Account	Debit	Credit
Account A (Purch)	100	
Account B (Cash)		20
Account C (Payable)		80

After the **Separate Payment Distributions** checkbox is selected, GP will create a transaction that looks similar to the following screenshot:

Account	Debit	Credit
Account A (Purch)	100	
Account B (Cash)		20
Account C (Payable)		100
Account D (Payable)	20	

Notice that the full $100 is credited to payables and then the $20 payment is debited to reduce accounts payable to the amount due.

Speeding up lookups with Advanced Lookups

Dynamics GP provides a very robust functionality in lookup windows for finding data such as accounts, vendors, customers, items, and more. Various fields can be used for sorting or searching and some additional fields are always provided by default. However, if all of that is not enough, Dynamics GP provides an option for administrators to add additional fields to lookups. This recipe demonstrates how to accomplish that.

Getting ready

Before using Advanced Lookups they need to be set up. Up to four custom lookups can be created for each type in the system. We will do this as follows:

1. Select **Administration** on the Navigation Pane, and under the **Company** heading select **Advanced Lookups**.
2. On the **Advanced Lookups Setup** window use the drop-down menu to select a **Lookup Name**.
3. For our example, select **Customers**. In the first **Sort by Field** drop-down menu scroll down and select **Zip**.
4. Change the **Description** to **Zip Code**.
5. Click on **Save** to save the lookup and close the window.

These setup steps add a lookup based on zip code to any place where **Customers** are selected in the system:

How to do it...

Once an advanced lookup has been set up, let's look at how to use it by completing the following steps:

1. Select **Sales** from the Navigation Pane on the left. Select **Customer** on the **Sales Area Page**.

2. In the **Customer ID** field click on the lookup button (indicated by a magnifying glass) and click on the arrow next to **Additional Sorts**. A predefined set of lookups is shown at the top of the drop-down menu and customer lookups are at the bottom. In the middle is the **Zip Code** lookup created previously.

3. Click on **Zip Code** and the Zip codes will appear on the right-hand side of the window. The search box at the top also changes to allow searching by selected lookup. In this case, will be Zip code:

How it works...

Administrators get the chance to set up four extra lookups for each of the lookup options. Lookup options include:

- ▸ Accounts
- ▸ Addresses
- ▸ Customers
- ▸ Employees
- ▸ Items
- ▸ Open documents
- ▸ Open Payables documents
- ▸ Prospects
- ▸ Purchase orders
- ▸ Sales Document Numbers
- ▸ Sales documents
- ▸ Vendor addresses
- ▸ Vendors
- ▸ Vouchers

This provides users with more opportunities to ensure that they are selecting the right information with a minimum amount of work.

See also

- ▸ *Speeding up account entry with Account Aliases*
- ▸ *Accessing accounts faster with Favorites in Lookups*

Going straight to the site with Web Links

Dynamics GP provides a great feature to tie web page links to specific values in Dynamics GP. For example, when a bank account is selected a link is made available to that bank's website. The link is contextual, meaning that it is tied to the value in the field. In this recipe, we'll look at setting up and using the Custom Link feature.

Getting ready

Before users can benefit from this recipe, an administrator needs to set up the custom links. To set up the links:

1. Select **Administration** from the Navigation Pane on the left. Then click on **Custom Link** under the **Company** heading.

2. Click on **New** on the bottom left.

3. In the **Prompt** field select **Checkbook**. In the **Custom Link Label** field type **Website**.

4. In the **Field Value** box click on the lookup button (indicated by a magnifying glass) and select the **FIRST BANK** checkbook.

5. Type www.firstbank.com into the **Internet Address** field as the bank's website and then click on **Save** to save the record.

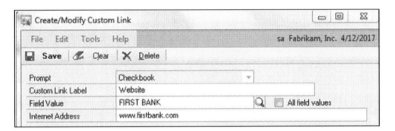

Congratulations, that's all there is to setting up a custom link.

How to do it...

Now we'll see how to use a custom link by completing the following steps:

1. To demonstrate how the custom link works for users, click on **Financial** on the Navigation Pane. Select **Bank Deposits** from the **Financial** Area Page under **Transactions**.

2. In the **Checkbook ID** field use the lookup button (indicated by a magnifying glass) to select the checkbook used in the previous setup. Once the checkbook shows in the **Checkbook ID** field click on the **Checkbook ID** label.

3. A field will drop down with two options. One, marked **Checkbook Maintenance**, leads back to the **Checkbook Maintenance** window. This is the typical behavior if Custom Links have not been set up:

4. Select the second link, **Website**, to open up a web browser and navigate to the website set up in the link.

How it works...

This process associates website links with values in specific fields. This allows contextual drill through to web pages for more information. Custom links can be created for Checkbooks, Credit cards, Currency, Customers, Employees, Exchange Rates, Items, Salespeople, Tracking Numbers, and Vendors providing plenty of options to link to more information on the Internet.

There's more...

A single site can be made available for all of the choices or multiple choices can be applied to a single value.

All field values

Selecting the **All field values** checkbox means that the website entered will be used for all values in this field. For example, if a single currency website is used for all currencies, selecting the **All field values** checkbox points all currency values to that one website. This option is available for prompts named:

- ▸ Checkbook
- ▸ Credit Card
- ▸ Currency
- ▸ Exchange Rate
- ▸ Tracking Number

Multiple values

For Custom Links the **Prompt** field is the key identifier. There can be multiple prompts for a single value, creating more than one link for a value. For example, a bank might have a website used to check balances and a completely different one for processing ACH transactions. By creating two links, one named Balances and one named ACH, both links can be available for a single checkbook.

See also

- ▸ *Developing connections with Internet User Defined fields*
- ▸ *Getting faster access to data with the Shortcut Bar*

3
Automating Dynamics GP

The recipes in this chapter are designed to be time savers across the system; they focus on efficiency and automation. In this chapter, we will look at ways to automate Dynamics GP including:

- Using Reminders to remember important events
- Controlling reporting dates with Beginning and Ending Periods
- Automating reporting with Report Groups
- Speeding up entry by copying an Inventory Item
- Improving consistency with Shortcuts and User Classes
- Speeding up month-end close by Reconciling Bank Accounts daily
- Automating processes with Macros
- Getting early warnings with Business Alerts
- Splitting AP across departments automatically with Control Account Management
- Getting control of accruals and deferrals with Recurring GL batches
- Speeding up document delivery with e-mail

Introduction

Up to this point we've looked at recipes for personalizing Microsoft Dynamics GP for users and ways in which administrators can organize GP for smoother operation. In this chapter, we'll take these themes even further and look at recipes to automate Dynamics GP, allowing users and administrators to focus on value-adding tasks.

Using Reminders to remember important events

It's always nice to be reminded when you're bound to forget something important. It's even better to get an automatic reminder triggered by certain events. Well, Microsoft Dynamics GP has prebuilt functionality to remind users when certain thresholds are approaching or met. For example, GP can provide a reminder when invoices are overdue or payables are due.

In this recipe, we'll look at how to set up the built-in Reminders.

How to do it...

To set up a Reminder:

1. Click on **Home** on the Navigation Pane on the left to open the Home page. In the **To Do** section click on **New Reminder**. The **Predefined Reminders** section is at the top. It contains a set of commonly used reminders and the ability to set the number of days around which a reminder is given.

2. For our example, select the **Remind Me** checkbox next to **Overdue Invoices** and **Payables Due**. In the **Remind Me** days field enter **5** next to **days after due date** on the **Overdue Invoices** line.

3. Select the **Display as a Cue** checkbox for each of the options selected:

4. On the **Payables Due** line key in **3** next to **days before due date** and click on **OK**.

Reminders are refreshed when the Home page is refreshed. Click on the two swirling arrows on the top right next to the breadcrumbs to refresh the page:

How it works...

After the prebuilt reminders are set up a reminder will appear in the **Reminders** section of the Home page when an invoice is 5 days past the due date. This is great for following up after a 5-day payment grace period.

Similarly, the **Payables Due** option from our example would provide a reminder 3 days before payment is due.

Prebuilt reminders are available for Overdue Invoices, Payables Due, Recurring General Ledger Batches, Recurring Receivables Batches, Recurring Payables Batches, Items Due for Stock Count, Collection Tasks Due, and Lots Due to Expire.

There's more...

Just getting a reminder is nice, being able to drill down into the reminder is even better.

Drill down into Reminders

Clicking on a reminder opens a window that lists each individual reminder. For the prebuilt reminders, each item gets a line of its own. So each overdue invoice and each upcoming payable in our example gets its own line. Clicking on a line drills back into the actual transaction. The Reminder details can be sorted and the **Open** button on the right provides additional drill back options beyond the default drill back from clicking on a line:

Due Date	User	Description	Amount (functional)
8/20/2013		Payable Due: Business Equipment Center - 1001	$75.89
8/21/2013		Payable Due: Superior Telephone Systems - 6000	$914.79
8/22/2013		Payable Due: Office Design Systems, Ltd - 4000	$313.54
8/23/2013		Overdue Invoice: Computers Unlimited - SLS2026	$954.73
8/23/2013		Overdue Invoice: Manchester Suites - SLS9001	$1,165.00
8/26/2013		Overdue Invoice: Northern State College - SLS17000	$1,671.13
8/26/2013		Overdue Invoice: Vista Travel - SLS5016	$823.28
8/28/2013		Payable Due: Vision Advertising Inc. - 7000	$128.68
8/28/2013		Payable Due: PageMaster - 9000	$424.28
9/4/2013		Overdue Invoice: Holling Communications Inc. - SLS1000	$129.91
9/6/2013		Payable Due: Lindell Brokerage - 2000	$495.00

(454) Document(s)

Change Reminder Preferences

For example, for an overdue payable transaction the **Open** button includes a link to **Select Checks** where this voucher can be added to a check batch for payment.

See also

▶ *Getting warnings with SmartList Alerts*

▶ *Getting early warnings with Business Alerts*

Controlling reporting dates with Beginning and Ending Periods

Dynamics GP provides a number of features to improve and simplify reporting. One of the most overlooked features is the ability to automatically control dates when running reports. That functionality is the juicy goodness covered in this recipe.

Dynamics GP contains a large number of built-in reports. These reports were created with the included Report Writer tool and are often referred to as Report Writer reports to distinguish them from other report types such as SmartLists or SQL Server Reporting Services reports.

Report Writer reports have several common elements, one of which is an Option name. A report option is simply a named collection of settings for a particular report. For example, Historical Aged Trial Balance is the name of a report. Prior to running it a user might name an option for that report such as "072009 North" to indicate that the report settings have been limited to information from July 2009 and the North region.

Since many reports are run at regular intervals the same option can be reused to avoid recreating the report settings each time. This works fine except for dates. Most users set the dates in a report option to a fixed period such as "From: 1/1/2009 To: 1/31/2009". This works until it's necessary to report on February. Then, users have to manually change the date again. Dynamics GP provides beginning and ending date controls for both fiscal periods and calendar months to eliminate manual adjustment of dates. Let's see how it works.

Getting ready

Beginning and ending date options can greatly simplify reporting. To set up a report option using the beginning and end of previous periods:

1. Select **Sales** from the Navigation Pane on the left.

2. Select **Posting Journals** under the **Reports** section and select **New**.

3. In the **Option** field type **Last Period**.

4. In the **Ranges** field select **Posting Date** from the drop-down menu.

5. In the **From** date field use the drop-down menu to select **Beginning of Previous Period**. Repeat this with the **To** date field and select **End of Previous Period**:

6. Click on **Insert** to update the range and click on **Save** at the top to save this report option:

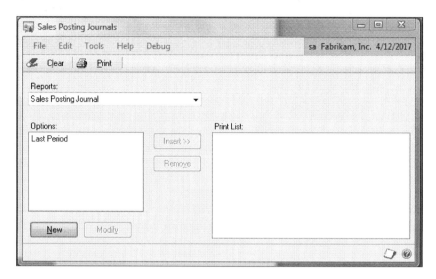

How to do it...

Once these report options are set up, running a report is incredibly simple.

1. Select **Posting Journals** from the **Sales** Area Page again.

2. Select the **Last Period** option and click on the **Insert** button in the center.

3. Click on **Print**:

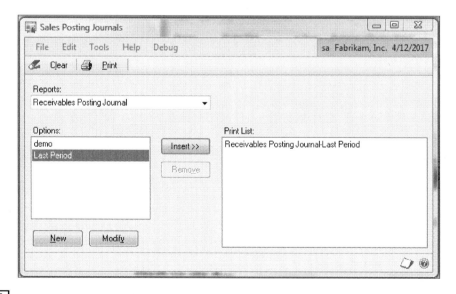

How it works...

Using beginning and end of previous period for report dates makes use of the Fiscal Period setup in Dynamics GP to control report dates. Since much of accounting is backward looking this provides a fast way to print reports for the last fiscal month right after month end. Dynamics GP also provides an option to use the beginning and ending dates of the current period for in-period reporting.

There's more...

In addition to Periods Dynamics GP provides an option to use beginning and end dates for the previous and current month. Since month means something different than period, this is often confusing to users.

Fiscal period versus Month

In Dynamics GP a period is a fiscal period as defined in the Fiscal Period setup. A month is a calendar month. For companies reporting on a calendar basis the two are interchangeable. For most companies using period is the better option because it ties reporting to the company's fiscal period in GP. Even for calendar-based firms using periods instead of months provides some insurance in case the firm decides to change to a different fiscal calendar later.

Where Beginning and End of Previous Month settings are often useful is for tax-based reporting. Certain taxes, including sales tax, use tax, and payroll tax, are typically calendar based. These require calendar-year reporting even if a firm reports financial results based on a fiscal year.

Beyond the period

The focus of this recipe has been on using beginning and ending period or months to simplify repetitive reporting. In addition to period and month reporting Dynamics GP offers beginning and ending fiscal year and calendar year choices as well.

See also

- ▶ *Automating reporting with Report Groups*

Automating reporting with Report Groups

Built-in reports in Dynamics GP are also known as Report Writer reports after the tool used to modify these reports. Each report needs a saved set of parameters known as an Option. Options allow reports to be run over and over again with the same group of settings. Even better, multiple report options can be combined into a group of reports. Running a Report Group runs each report in the group in sequence. Consequently, Report Groups can significantly reduce the amount of work required to run multiple reports. In this recipe, we'll cover creating and using Report Groups.

Getting ready

The first step to using Report Groups is creating them. Before adding reports to groups users should check the report options to ensure that they don't require user interaction. Report options should not be set to "Ask Each Time" or "Print to the Screen".

1. Select **Purchasing** from the Navigation Pane. Select **Groups** under **Reports**.

2. In the **Purchasing Reports** field select **Aged Trial Balance** and in **Reports** select **Historical Aged Trial Balance**:

3. Select the first report option and click on **Insert**.

4. In the **Purchasing Reports** field select **Analysis** and in **Reports** select **Received/Not Invoiced**.

5. Select the first report option and click on **Insert**:

6. Click on **Save**. When prompted, name the group **Last Period** and click on **Save** to close the window.

How to do it...

Once a report group has been set up, running multiple reports is extremely easy:

1. Back on the **Purchasing** page select **Groups** under **Reporting**.

2. On the **Purchasing Report Groups** page select **Last Period** from the **Purchasing Group** drop-down menu (the group you set up previously).

3. Click on **Print**:

How it works...

Report Groups are an absolute life saver at month end and year end. These are times when a consistent set of reports is typically printed for archiving purposes. Being able to fire off a Report Group, go to a meeting, and come back to a pile of completed reports is just really cool.

Another great use of Report Groups is building a list of reports for fixed assets. Because of limited historical-reporting functionally in the Fixed Asset module it is important to print and save year-end fixed asset reports. Building a list of reports into a Report Group means that users don't have to remember which reports to run from year to year. They can simply run the appropriate Report Group.

There's more...

Report Groups are provided for each of the module areas in Dynamics GP. However, for companies that want to go even further, Report Groups can even be combined into groups.

Groups of groups

Reports bundled into groups by module are great. However, for even greater efficiency, Report Groups can be bundled into Combined Groups allowing cross-module report printing in one step. To build Combined Groups select **Reports | Combined Groups** from the menu at the top of Dynamics GP.

The **Combined Groups** window works just like the regular report group window except that all of the selections are Report Groups, not individual report options.

▸ *Controlling reporting dates with Beginning and Ending Periods*

Speeding up entry by copying an Inventory Item

When entering master records it's always a challenge to ensure that records are entered consistently. This is especially true for inventory items as there are a large number of potential settings. Using inventory classes can provide some help but even classes have their limits.

It's also common for a new inventory item to be very similar to an existing inventory item. Vendors often make small but key changes resulting in the need for a new item to allow proper tracking.

Dynamics GP provides a great feature that allows copying an inventory item when creating a new one. Since that's the focus of this recipe let's take a look at how to use it.

How to do it...

To copy an inventory item to a new item number:

1. From the Navigation Pane select **Inventory**. In the **Inventory** Area Page click on **Item** under **Cards**.

2. The new item number goes in the **Item Number** field. Enter **NEW123** for our example and click on the **Copy** button above:

3. Use the lookup button (indicated by a magnifying glass) to select an item to copy from. Select item **1-A3261A** if using the Fabrikam sample company. Otherwise, any item will do.

4. Notice that there are a number of attributes available to copy to the new item. We'll leave these all selected. Click on **Copy** to create the new item:

5. When done, there is a new item with the new item number. Changes can still be made. To illustrate this, change the **Description** to **New Copied Items** and click on **Save**:

How it works...

By using an existing inventory item as a base, Dynamics GP provides a mechanism to copy an inventory item to a new item number. The process is extremely flexible, allowing fine grain control over which settings are copied and changes after the copy is created.

Users need to remember that they can choose not to copy all of the information from one item to another. For example, users might not want to copy vendor assignment if a different vendor will be used for the copied item. Additionally, users may never want to copy cost information from an original item to its copy. The key is to use the copy feature to get only what is required in the new item.

Improving consistency with Shortcuts and User Classes

Throughout this book we look at various ways that shortcuts and the Shortcut Bar can improve the usefulness of Dynamics GP. In this recipe, we take a look at how administrators can control shortcuts by assigning specific shortcuts to specific user classes.

This feature allows an administrator to assign a shortcut to a class of users. Every user in the class gets the shortcut automatically and they can't remove it. For example, this is a great way to ensure that all payables users have a shortcut to Payables Transaction Entry. It is also useful for attaching a currency website shortcut to a class of senior accountants. The focus of this recipe is assigning shortcuts to user classes.

Getting ready

Assigning shortcuts to user classes requires that the user be logged in as 'sa'. This is the SQL Server system administrator account, otherwise known as the head chef in this cookbook. For this action, other accounts with system administrator access, even those who can create users, won't work. It must be the 'sa' account.

User classes are created in the **Administration** Area Page. To set up a user class:

1. Select **Administration** from the Navigation Pane on the left.
2. On the **Administration** Area Page click on **User Classes** under **Setup**.
3. Enter **AP USER** in the **Class ID** field and **AP User** in the **Description** field.

4. Click on **Save**:

Users also need to be assigned to user classes. If users are not assigned to classes, they can be added with these steps:

1. Select **Administration** from the Navigation Pane and select **User**.

2. Enter the system password if prompted to do so and click on **OK**.

3. Use the lookup button (indicated by a magnifying glass) next to **User ID** to select a user.

4. Use the lookup button (indicated by a magnifying glass) next to **Class ID** to select the **AP USER** class and click on **Save** to apply the class:

How to do it...

Now that classes are set up and attached to users we can apply a shortcut to a class of users:

1. Select **Purchasing** from the Navigation Pane.

2. Click on **Transaction Entry** to open the **Payables Transaction Entry** window.

3. Click on **File | Add to Shortcuts** to add a shortcut to this window on the Shortcut Bar:

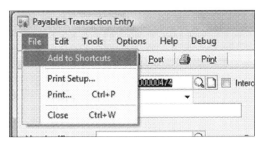

4. Select **Home** on the Navigation Pane to activate the Shortcut Bar.
5. Right-click on the **Payables Transaction Entry** shortcut and select **Cut**.
6. Right-click on the **AP User** class created previously and select **Paste** to move the shortcut to the AP User class. It is important to note that for a newly created user class to show up in the Shortcut Bar the 'sa' user will need to log out and then log back in:

How it works...

Moving a shortcut into a user class folder provides a degree of shortcut control to administrators. It provides a way to ensure that a minimum set of shortcuts is passed down to a set of users. In Dynamics GP 2010 user classes have been disconnected from security, making these even more useful for shortcuts. The user classes used for shortcuts don't have to be tied to security at all. This means that classes can be designed to support groups of shortcuts.

As an added bonus, the system administrator can assign keystrokes to those shortcuts and shortcuts added to a class by an administrator can't be changed or removed.

See also

▸ *Getting faster access to data with the Shortcut Bar*
▸ *Reducing clicks with Startup shortcuts*

Speeding up month-end close by Reconciling Bank Accounts daily

Month-end bank reconciliation is one of the most common time-consuming activities when trying to close the month. With a few process changes bank reconciliation can be performed daily. Month-end bank reconciliations simply become one more daily activity.

Describing the process to accomplish daily bank reconciliations is the focus of this recipe.

Getting ready

Before a company can perform daily bank reconciliations, bank reconciliations need to be current. If a company's reconciliations are out of balance the accounts will need to be balanced to the last statement before moving to daily reconciliations.

Additionally, companies will need access to the daily transactions from their bank. In most cases this information can be easily downloaded from the bank's website for transactions through the previous day.

How to do it...

Daily bank reconciliations do a great job of spreading the work. Let's see how:

1. Download and print the company's bank transactions from the bank's website for the period since the last reconciliation.

2. Select **Financial** from the Navigation Pane and click on **Reconcile Bank Statements** on the **Financial** Area Page.

3. Use the lookup button (indicated by a magnifying glass) to select a bank account to reconcile.

4. In the **Bank Statement Ending Balance** field, enter the ending bank balance for the previous day from the bank's website printout. Use yesterday's date for the **Bank Statement Ending Date** and today's date as the **Cutoff Date**:

Reconcile Bank Statements						□ ◻ ✕
File	Edit	Tools	View	Range	Help	4/12/2017 »

💾 Save ✕ Delete

Checkbook ID	UPTOWN TRUST 🔍 🗋
Description	Computer-Uptown Trust
Currency ID	Z-US$

Bank Statement Ending Balance		$322,357.42
Bank Statement Ending Date	3/31/2017 ▦	
Cutoff Date	4/1/2017 ▦	Transactions

◀◀ ◀ ▶ ▶▶

5. Click on **Transactions** to start the reconciliation.

6. Select the checkboxes for completed transactions and complete a typical bank reconciliation, but DO NOT press **Reconcile** once the difference reaches zero (0). Select the checkboxes for matched transactions on the website printout and save that for tomorrow. This helps avoid confusion about which checkboxes were selected and which weren't:

Select Bank Transactions							□ ◻ ✕
File	Edit	Tools	View	Range	Help	Debug	sa Fabrikam, Inc. 4/12/2017

Checkbook ID UPTOWN TRUST Display: All ▾ Sort: by Type ▾

Select Range ▾ Redisplay

	Type	Number	Date	C	Payment	→ Deposit	→
	DEP	20001	1/9/2014	☐	$0.00	$130,368.25	
	DEP	20002	1/16/2014	☐	$0.00	$228,576.73	
	DEP	20003	1/23/2014	☐	$0.00	$161,252.58	
	DEP	20004	1/23/2014	☐	$0.00	$460,357.76	
	DEP	20005	1/31/2014	☐	$0.00	$17,567.11	
	DEP	20006	1/31/2014	☐	$0.00	$16,956.84	
	DEP	20007	1/31/2014	☑	$0.00	$46,477.47	
	DEP	20008	1/31/2014	☑	$0.00	$100,939.66	
	CHK	031702	3/17/2017	☐	$6,927.46	$0.00	
	CHK	1000.1	8/1/2013	☐	($395.59)	$0.00	
	CHK	1000.2	7/25/2013	☐	($1,000.00)	$0.00	

Cleared Transactions

	No. of	Total Amount			
Payments	8	$339,574.56	Adjusted Bank Balance	$65,694.14
Deposits	2	$147,417.13	Adjusted Book Balance	$65,694.14
			Difference	$0.00 →

Adjustments

🖨 🗋 ⓘ   OK   Reconcile

7. Click on **OK** to return to the **Reconcile Bank Statements** window and click on **Save** to save the partial reconciliation.

8. Each day repeat these steps until the bank statement arrives at month end.

9. When the bank statement arrives review the statement against the bank reconciliation in Dynamics GP. I have seen a few situations where the website and the paper statement differ. Only then should the **Reconcile** button be clicked on and reconciliation reports printed for storage. The following image is a printout of one such reconciliation report:

```
System:       6/5/2010    12:40:00 PM                    Fabrikam, Inc.                          Page:     1
User Date:    4/12/2017                          RECONCILIATION POSTING JOURNAL                   User ID: sa
                                                    Bank Reconciliation


Audit Trail Code: CMADJ00000001                                    Bank Statement Ending Balance: $322,357.42
Checkbook ID:     UPTOWN TRUST                                     Bank Statement Ending Date:    3/31/2017
Description:      Computer-Uptown Trust                            Cutoff Date:                   4/1/2017


Statement Ending Balance                              $322,357.42
Outstanding Checks (-)                                $885,306.61
Deposits in Transit (+)                            $1,032,616.69
                                                 ----------------------
Adjusted Bank Balance                                $469,667.50
                                                 ----------------------
Checkbook Balance as of Cutoff                       $469,667.50
Adjustments                                                $0.00
                                                 ----------------------
Adjusted Book Balance                                $469,667.50
                                                 ----------------------
Difference                                                $0.00
                                                 ======================
```

How it works...

Daily bank reconciliation is really just the disciplined application of basic bank reconciliation principles. The easy availability of bank information via the bank's website combined with Dynamics GP's ability to save incomplete bank reconciliations makes this an easy recipe to apply. Additionally, other benefits include a better understanding of the company's bank float, faster identification of fraudulent transactions, and an up-to-date cash position.

There's more...

A common objection is that this is still time consuming for larger organizations and high-volume accounts but this is a hollow excuse as options are available for larger transaction volumes as well. There is, however, one little hiccup when dealing with the bank statement cutoff.

High Transaction Volume Accounts

For high transaction volume bank accounts Microsoft provides an optional electronic bank reconciliation module. This allows companies to take a file from the bank and electronically match it to the bank statement. Where most companies go wrong is that they only get the file on a monthly basis. If there is an error it's even harder to find in a high volume account at month end.

Companies in this situation should work to get a daily electronic reconciliation file from the bank. Often, firms chafe at the extra costs from their bank but rarely do they take a hard look at the returns provided by not having employees chasing bank transactions during month end. The stress of month-end closing is also reduced because errors are found earlier in the month, providing time for resolution before a month-end deadline.

Bank statement cutoff

Typically, there are a few days of mailing delay between the bank statement cutoff and delivery. For this period of a few days daily bank reconciliation can't be completed. The problem is that reconciliations would go beyond the end of the statement period making it impossible to print bank reconciliation reports that match the statement.

There are a couple of options to deal with this issue. The simplest is to just wait for a couple of days and catch up after the statement arrives and the final month-end reconciliation is processed. Another option is to process the reconciliation against the website data only and attach the daily website printout along with the bank statement and balance reports as evidence for auditors.

Automating processes with Macros

Macros provide a way to automate processes within Dynamics GP. These are actually very easy to create and use. Macros are perfect for moderately complex but repetitive processes. For example, a cash transfer between bank accounts is a common repetitive task but there is some complexity to it because the amount is usually different. This example provides a practical lesson in Macros so we'll look at it in this recipe.

How to do it...

To create a macro for a bank transfer follow these steps:

1. Select **Financial** on the Navigation Pane and select **Bank Transfers** from the **Financial** Area Page under **Transactions**.

2. In the **Bank Transfer Entry** window select **Tools | Macro | Record**.

3. Note where the macro is being saved and name the macro **Bank Xfer**. Click on **Save**:

4. Tab to the **Description** field and type **Bank Transfer**.

5. Use the lookup button (indicated by a magnifying glass) to select a Checkbook ID to transfer from. Leave the amount set to zero **($0.00)**.

6. Use the lookup button to select a CheckBook ID to transfer to:

7. From the **Tools** menu select **Macro | Stop Record**. Click on **Clear** and close the **Bank Transfer Entry** window.

8. Now, select the **Microsoft Dynamics GP** menu item and then select **Tools | Macro | Play**.

9. Find and select the **Bank Xfer** macro saved earlier and click on **Open**:

10. The macro will run. As the macro runs, the **Bank Transfer Entry** window will open and the **Description**, **Transfer To**, and **Transfer From** accounts will fill in automatically. The window will then be left open for a user to add the transfer amount. Click on **Post** when finished to complete the transfer.

How it works...

Recording a macro is easy. Macros can be recorded by any user with proper security and because these are stored as a file they can be shared among users. There are an infinite number of uses for macros. These can be reused or built only for a specific scenario. Learning to create and run macros provides a terrific opportunity to automate any number of functions in Dynamics GP.

There's more...

Macros can be attached to the Shortcut Bar and run from there. They can also be run with a keystroke combination. Finally, users can insert pauses in Macros or string these together into a set of steps.

Macros and the Shortcut Bar

Macros can be added to the Shortcut Bar making them easy to run with a single click. Adding items such as Macros to the Shortcut Bar is covered in detail in the Chapter 1 recipe *Getting faster access to data with the Shortcut Bar*.

Running macros with a keystroke combination

Once a macro has been added to the Shortcut Bar, a keystroke combination can be added allowing it to be run from the keyboard. Setting up keystroke combinations for Macros is also covered in the Chapter 1 recipe *Getting faster access to data with the Shortcut Bar*.

Macro pauses

Pauses can be inserted into Macros to allow for data entry in the middle of a macro. To insert a pause click on **Tools | Macro | Insert Pause** while recording a macro. A window will open allowing the creation of instructions for the user. The problem with pausing macros is that the process to restart a macro is not intuitive. When a user executes a macro, the macro pauses at the selected point and waits for user input. After user input, the user must select **Tools | Macro | Continue** to resume the macro.

This set of steps is not obvious to a user. Also, there is not enough room to reasonably enter instructions and restart steps in the instruction box. Nor is there a keystroke combination to resume a macro after a pause.

Sequential Macros

An alternative to pausing macros is to create more than one macro. Create the first macro up to the point where a pause would be inserted. Then create a second macro for the next portion of the process. Add the macros to the Shortcut Bar in a folder in the order these should be executed. After the first macro finishes the user simply needs to insert any data required and click on the second macro to continue the process.

Information on adding items to the Shortcut Bar and Shortcut Bar folders are covered in the Chapter 1 recipe *Getting faster access to data with the Shortcut Bar* and the *Remembering processes with an Ad hoc workflow* recipe in Chapter 2.

See also

- ▸ *Getting faster access to data with the Shortcut Bar*
- ▸ *Remembering processes with an Ad hoc workflow*

Getting early warnings with Business Alerts

It's always nice to find out about problems early. Early notification usually means that there is still time to fix the issue. Dynamics GP provides a great mechanism for early warnings in the form of Business Alerts. Business Alerts allow companies to build a criteria for notification and then to get notified via e-mail or within the application. Additionally, a report of information related to the alert can be sent as a part of the e-mail. A wizard-like interface is used to set up alerts but these can get very complex.

For this recipe, we'll build a basic Business Alert with all of the foundational pieces for a more complicated alert. For our sample business alert we'll assume that a company would like to be notified when their bank balance falls below $10,000 to allow them to transfer cash from another account.

Getting ready

Users must be logged in as 'sa' (the SQL Server system administrator, otherwise known as the head chef in this cookbook) to create business alerts. Log in as 'sa' prior to starting this recipe.

How to do it...

Let's look at how to build a Business Alert:

1. On the Navigation Pane select **Administration**. Select **Business Alerts** under **System**. In the **System Password** field enter the system password and click on **OK**.

2. Leave the **Create New Alert** option selected and click on **Next** to start an alert:

3. Select a company database. The company database for the sample company is **TWO**.

4. Name this alert **BANK BAL <10K** in the **Business Alert ID** field.

5. In the **Description** field type **Bank Bal <10k**. Click on **Next** to move on:

6. In the **Series** field select **Financial**. Find the **CM Checkbook Master** table in the **Tables** menu. Click on it and click on **Insert** to add this table. Then click on **Next** to continue:

7. After selecting the appropriate table it's time to define the alert formula. In the **Define Alert Formula** window select **CM00100_T1 - CM Checkbook Master** under **Table**. Select **Current Balance** in the **Column Name** field and click on **Add Column**:

8. Click on the less than (**<**) button. Type **10000** in the **Constant** field and click on **Add Constant**. Click on **Next**.

9. After the alert criteria have been established it's time to set up the alerts. Click on the **E-mail** selection next to **Send To**. Select **Message and Report** in the **Send** selection. Enter your e-mail address and click on **Insert**. In the **Message Text** area type **Bank Account Balance is below $10,000** and click on **Next**:

10. Finally, we'll lay out the report to accompany the alert. Select the **CM00100_T1 - CM Checkbook Master** table in the **Table** field. Scroll down to **Checkbook ID** in the **Columns** menu. Select it and click on **Insert**. Scroll down to **Current Balance**. Select it and click on **Insert**. Click on **Next** to move on:

11. Click on **Next** past the **Select Report Sorting Options** window.

12. The **Schedule Alert** window can be used to adjust the timing of alert deliveries. We'll leave the defaults and click on **Finish** to wrap up:

How it works...

This process creates a Business Alert that checks the bank balance in Dynamics GP at every midnight and e-mails an alert and detailed report if the balance drops below $10,000. A manager will then get this alert via email or on their phone and be prepared to move cash even before they leave for the office in the morning. Business Alerts are extremely useful for checking items against a threshold. This includes scenarios such as accounts over budget, checkbook balances below a limit, customers over their credit limit, inventory items at their reorder point, and payments past due. This is just a sample of the scenarios that can be created.

There's more...

A great place to start working with Business Alerts is with the included prebuilt alerts.

Prebuilt alerts

Microsoft Dynamics GP comes with a prebuilt set of common Business Alerts, including alerts for many of the scenarios described previously and more. Modifying an existing Business Alert is a great way to learn about the process and move into creating more complex alerts. When creating a Business Alert simply select **Modify Existing Alert** instead of **Create New Alert** and walk through the wizard.

See also

- ▸ *Getting warnings with SmartList Alerts*
- ▸ *Using Reminders to remember important events*

Splitting AP across departments automatically with Control Account Management

Often companies say that they want to see each division reported as if it was a standalone business. Even though all divisions may be part of a single legal entity, companies frequently need to make decisions based on who is under or over performing. Treating each division as a separate business can provide measurements to consistently compare divisions. Frequently, balance sheet accounts such as Fixed Assets and Accounts Payable are included to provide a measure of the capital required to run each division.

However, providing an infrastructure to actually allow each division to function as a business is both expensive and inefficient. Most companies find that using a consolidated payables department for accounts payable is much more effective than providing an AP department for each division. They struggle however, with reconciling that effectiveness with the benefits of divisional reporting.

Dynamics GP provides a solution for both Accounts Payable and Accounts Receivable in a feature known as Control Account Management.

In Control Account Management payables are processed centrally. At month end a routine is run to allocate open payables from the payables GL account to divisional payable accounts. The allocation is based on a segment of the chart of accounts that corresponds to the company's divisions. This provides a mechanism for financial reporting of payables at the divisional level. At the beginning of the next month an automatically created reversing entry is processed to repopulate central accounts payable and allow the normal payables process to continue. In this recipe, we'll see how to make it all work seamlessly.

Getting ready

Before using Control Account Management, the divisional payable accounts need to be associated with the appropriate general ledger segment. For our example, we'll be using the sample company:

1. Select **Financial** on the Navigation Pane. Under the **Setup** heading select **Control Account Management**.

2. Ensure that **Activate Control Account Management** is selected at the top. In **Account Segment** select **Segment 3** to represent the divisions. Click on **Account Type** to continue.

3. Set the **Account Type** to **Payables**. Set the **Batch ID** to **AP CONTROL** and set both **Batch Comment** and **Reference** to **Control Account**:

4. Next to each Segment ID look up or enter the corresponding divisional payable account and click on **Save** when finished. For the sample company, use the Control Accounts shown in the following screenshot. Click on **Save** when done:

How to do it...

Once the divisional AP accounts have been mapped it's time to see how this process works each month:

1. Select **Financial** from the Navigation Pane on the left. Select **Control Account Management** under **Transactions**.

2. Click on **Report** to load the payables distribution data. Review the payables distributions at the bottom of the window:

3. Select the double arrow on the right below the printer icon (shown in the following screenshot) to see more information. From this screen, the batch and date information can be changed. Click on the **Doc Info** and **Dist Info** tabs to see more information about how the payables will be distributed:

4. Click on **Generate** to create the non-posted GL transaction and associated reversing transaction:

			Transaction Entry			

The month-end routine examines open accounts payable transactions and sums the open amounts by the divisional segment of the purchase. GP then uses this information to calculate the outstanding percentage for each division. From there, a reversing transaction is created to move the accounts payable balance out to the divisional payable accounts.

By providing a GL segment to identify the division and then mapping it to a corresponding payables account GP provides a best-of-both-worlds solution. This allows centralized AP management with decentralized reporting at month, quarter, and year end. The fact that the process resets automatically at the start of the next month makes this a first-class solution to an otherwise difficult process.

How it works...

There's more...

This process is so exciting that many people want to see if it will meet similar needs for multi-company scenarios.

Multi-company

When people see this process for the first time it often registers as a potential solution to related multi-company issues. This process will work for splitting centralized AP across multiple companies if the companies are all stored in a single GP company with an identifying GL segment. If the companies are split across multiple GP databases, this process will not work because it can't post across company databases.

See also

> ▸ *Improving financial reporting clarity by splitting purchasing accounts*

Getting control of accruals and deferrals with Recurring GL batches

Most companies have a need for some minimal level of deferrals and accruals. This could be insurance prepaid for the year that needs to be expensed over 12 months. It could be prepaid revenue that is earned in the first half of the year but not billable until year end or any number of similar transactions. For straightforward accruals and deferrals Dynamics GP's recurring batch functionality can be used to manage, track, and post these types of transactions. In this recipe, we'll look at how to set up and process accruals and deferrals using recurring batches.

Getting ready

For our example, assume that corporate insurance is due and paid on January 1, and the payment covers January through December of that year. For simplicity sake, corporate insurance is $12,000 a year and the company is going to recognize $1,000 per month until the full amount is used up.

The payables transaction for $12,000 debited Prepaid Expenses, a balance sheet account, not insurance expense. That's the key setup piece.

How to do it...

Now that we understand the background we'll look at how to set up recognition of the monthly expense:

1. On the Navigation Pane select **Financial**. Click on the **Batches** option on the **Financial** Area Page under **Transactions**.

2. Enter **Z INSUR DEFER** in the **Batch ID** field and set the **Origin** to **General Entry**.

3. In the **Frequency** field select **Monthly**. Enter **12** in the **Recurring Posting** field and click on the **Transactions** button:

4. Set the **Transaction Date** to January 15 to process the first month's expense and set up the recurring transaction.

5. Type **Recognize Insurance** in the **Reference** field:

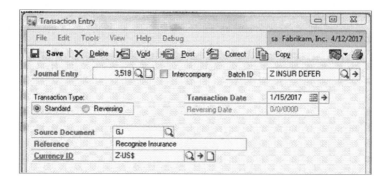

6. Use the lookup button (indicated by a magnifying glass) to find the Insurance Expense account and enter a debit for $1,000. On the line above use the lookup button to find the Prepaid Expenses account and process a credit for $1,000:

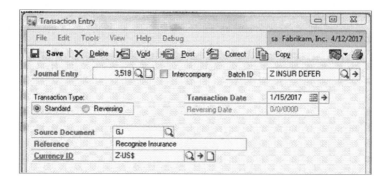

7. Click on **Save** to save the transaction. Close the **Transaction Entry** window and reopen the **Batch Entry** window. Use the lookup button (indicated by a magnifying glass) to reopen the **Z INSUR DEFER** batch and click on **Post**:

8. Use the lookup button (indicated by a magnifying glass) to find the **Z INSUR DEFER** batch again. Unlike single-use batches, the batch doesn't disappear after posting. The batch now contains the **Last Date Posted** and the number of times it has been posted (as shown in the following screenshot). When the number of times posted equals the **Recurring Posting** number, the batch will then disappear:

How it works...

Recurring batches provide an opportunity to slowly use up deferral or build up an accrual amount. Posting these recurring batches is easy. The batches provide information about when these were last posted. This process can be added as a reminder to ensure that posting is completed on time. The ability to date the transaction means that the actual posting process can occur any time during the month and the transaction will post as of the date set in the transaction. This provides another opportunity to reduce month-end work since this month's accruals and deferrals can be posted at the beginning of the month.

There's more...

A few simple best practices can make recurring batches even more effective.

Recurring batch best practices

A couple of simple best practices can provide even more value to recurring batches. Recurring batches are mixed in with other batches in the batch window. Naming recurring batches to start with an underscore (_) will put these batches at the top. Starting the batch name with a 'z' will put these at the bottom.

Since batches will typically be posted multiple times covering several months it's important to date the batch with a date that will appear in each month. For example, batches dated for the 30th will cause the posting in February to revert to the last day of the month and never move back to the 30th. This gets even more important when using fiscal months that can end on odd dates. When using a 4-4-5 fiscal period I've seen months end as early as the 20th. Typically, using the 15th of the month is a great option that will work in all situations.

For those companies that need to manage more than a few accruals or deferrals Microsoft provides additional options.

Revenue/Expense Deferral module

For companies with a large number of deferrals to track Microsoft provides an available Revenue/Expense Deferral module. This module is designed for processing accrual and deferral transactions and is a great option when recurring batches aren't enough.

Field Service Contracts module

For companies that need to track revenue deferrals related to customer contracts a better option is the Contracts module, part of the Field Service suite, also available from Microsoft.

Speeding up document delivery with e-mail

Dynamics GP 2010 adds the ability to directly e-mail documents either individually or in bulk. This feature provides a number of options for e-mailing:

- ▶ Sales Quotes, Orders, Fulfillment Orders, and Invoices
- ▶ Receivables Invoices, Returns, Debit Memos, Credit Memos, Finance Charges, Warranties, and Service/Repair documents
- ▶ Standard Purchase Order, Blanket Purchase Order, Drop Ship Purchase Orders, and Drop Ship Blanket Purchase Orders
- ▶ Vendor Remittances

Documents can be e-mailed in HTML, DOCX, XPS, or PDF formats. E-mailing HTML and DOCX formatted attachments does NOT require that Word 2007 or higher be installed on the client computer. E-mailing documents in XPS and PDF formats does require Word 2007 or higher on the client computer, but Adobe Acrobat is not necessary.

In this recipe, we will look at e-mailing documents individually or in bulk along with some setup items using the sample company.

Getting ready

Before we start we need to add an e-mail address to a few customers to demonstrate how this feature works.

To add e-mail addresses:

1. Select **Sales** from the Navigation Pane. On the **Sales** Area Page click on **Customer** under **Cards**.

2. Use the lookup button (indicated by a magnifying glass) to select customer **CENTRALC0001**. Click on the italic letter 'i' next to the **Address ID** field.

3. Enter your e-mail address in the **To** field and click on **Save**. Close the window:

4. On the **Customer Maintenance** window click on **Save** and close the window.

5. Repeat this process with customers **AARONFIT0001** and **ASTORSUI001**.

How to do it...

Now that some customers have e-mail addresses we will look at how to e-mail invoices to them. To e-mail individual invoices:

1. Select **Sales** from the Navigation Pane. Click on **Sales Transaction Entry** under **Transactions** on the **Sales** Area Page.

2. Set the **Type** to **Invoice**. Use the lookup button (indicated by a magnifying glass) to select invoice **STDINV2261**.

3. Click on the e-mail icon in the upper right under the company name. Dynamics GP will indicate that an e-mail has been sent:

To e-mail multiple invoices at once:

1. Select **Sales** from the Navigation Pane. Click on the **Sales Order Transactions** Navigation list at the top of the Navigation Pane.

2. On the Navigation list click on the **Document Number** header twice to sort by document number in descending order.

3. Select the checkboxes next to invoices **STDINV2259**, **STDINV2260**, and **STDINV2261**:

4. Click on **Send in E-mail** on the Navigation menu. Then click on **Send**.

5. Dynamics GP will e-mail the selected invoices.

How it works...

E-mailing documents is a fantastic way to speed up communication with customers and vendors. Dynamics GP 2010 provides fast, easy, and flexible ways to e-mail documents.

There's more...

Dynamics GP provides a number of setup options to control e-mailing documents.

Setup

1. The setup of e-mails is controlled primarily by the **Company E-Mail Setup** window. It is reached by selecting **Administration** from the Navigation Pane and then clicking on **E-mail Setup** under **Setup** and **Company**.

2. The **Company E-Mail Setup** window controls whether or not documents are embedded in the e-mail body and the formats of those attachments:

Selecting either **Sales Series** or **Purchasing Series** under **Enable E-mail** opens the related e-mail setup window allowing a user to set the **Message ID,** which controls the message included in the e-mail. This window also allows a company to set a central return address for these e-mails:

3. Finally, the content in a Message ID is set up by selecting **Administration** from the Navigation Pane and then clicking on **E-mail Message Setup** under **Setup** and **Company**:

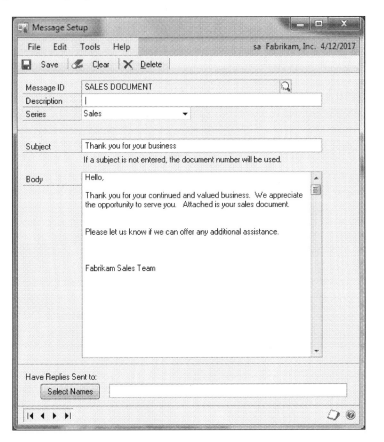

4
Harnessing the Power of SmartLists

Several of the recipes discussed so far have touched on the edges of SmartLists. In this chapter, we'll dive deeper into ways to really harness the power of Dynamics GP's Ad hoc reporting tool.

In this chapter, we will look at ways to leverage the reporting power of SmartLists in Dynamics GP including:

- ▶ Sorting data to get the information you want
- ▶ Speeding up access to information with SmartList Favorites
- ▶ Getting warnings with SmartList Alerts
- ▶ Improving information returned with SmartList Search
- ▶ Controlling data with SmartList Record Limits
- ▶ Tailoring SmartLists by adding Fields
- ▶ Controlling access by sharing or restricting SmartList Favorites
- ▶ Renaming Fields for clarity

Introduction

In previous chapters we looked at a number of recipes that touch on SmartLists. This powerful, user-friendly reporting tool has become a foundational feature in Dynamics GP. The underpinnings of most of the Lookup windows, Reminders, and Favorites throughout the system rely on SmartLists. Because SmartLists are so easy to use many users never delve deeper than the surface. In this collection of recipes we'll dig deeper into SmartLists to see how to better leverage both their simplicity and their power.

Sorting data to get the information you want

At their core SmartLists are rows and columns of data, similar to an Excel spreadsheet. They provide a powerful, friendly way to interact with information in Dynamics GP. One of the simplest SmartList features found by most users is the ability to sort a SmartList simply by clicking on a column header. However, SmartLists provide advanced sorting features that are even more powerful, just a little harder to find.

In this recipe we'll take a look at all of the sorting options for SmartLists, simple and advanced.

How to do it...

To sort a SmartList:

1. Click on the **SmartList** button (shown in the following screenshot) on the menu bar at the top or select **Microsoft Dynamics GP** from the top and click on **SmartList**:

    If the SmartList icon is not shown at the top, right-click on the blue bar next to the menu and select the **Standard** toolbar to turn it on.

2. Select **Financial** in the left pane and then **Account Summary** below it:

Year	Period ID	Account Number	Account Description	Cre
2013	0	000-1100-00	Cash - Operating Account	
2013	1	000-1100-00	Cash - Operating Account	($1
2013	2	000-1100-00	Cash - Operating Account	
2013	5	000-1100-00	Cash - Operating Account	
2013	0	000-1110-00	Cash - Payroll	
2013	1	000-1110-00	Cash - Payroll	
2013	0	000-1120-00	Cash - Flex Benefits Progr...	
2013	1	000-1120-00	Cash - Flex Benefits Progr...	
2013	0	000-1130-00	Petty Cash	
2013	1	000-1130-00	Petty Cash	

3. Simple sorting is accomplished by clicking on the column name. Select the **Debit Amount** column title to sort by debits. The arrow next to the column name shows whether the sort is ascending or descending:

ID	Account Number	Account Description	Credit Amount	Debit Amount
4	000-1100-00	Cash - Operating Account	$2,365,000.00	$1,701,250.00
4	000-1110-00	Cash - Payroll	$9,136.95	$1,600,000.00
4	000-6617-01	Operations- -Atlanta	$0.00	$125,000.00
4	000-1130-00	Petty Cash	$0.00	$100,000.00
4	000-6615-01	Operations- -Atlanta	$0.00	$100,000.00

Account Summary

4. Click on **Debit Amount** again to change the sort order.

5. For more advanced sorting select **Search** from the SmartList Toolbar and click on **Order By**. This window allows sorting by multiple fields; including fields that are included but not displayed on the SmartList:

6. Select **Year** and click on **Insert**. Set **Order By** to **Descending**.

7. Select **Period ID** and click on **Insert**. Set **Order By** to **Ascending**:

8. Select **Account Number** and click on **Insert**. Set **Order By** to **Ascending**.

9. Select **Debit Amount** and click on **Insert**. Set **Order By** to **Descending**:

10. Click on **OK** twice to return to the SmartList.

11. Notice that the SmartList has now been sorted by **Year**, **Period ID**, **Account Number**, and **Debit Amount** following the sorting rules set up in this example:

Year	Period ID	Account Number	Account Description	Credit Amount	Debit Amount
2014	0	000-1100-00	Cash - Operating Account	$0.00	$338,562.25
2014	0	000-1101-00	Cash in Bank - Canada	$0.00	$10,510.29
2014	0	000-1102-00	Cash in Bank - Australia	$0.00	$6,573.56
2014	0	000-1103-00	Cash in Bank - New Zeala...	$0.00	$8,425.79
2014	0	000-1105-00	Cash in Bank - United Kin...	$0.00	$8,887.73
2014	0	000-1106-00	Cash in Bank - South Afri...	$0.00	$5,102.55
2014	0	000-1107-00	Cash in Bank - Singapore	$0.00	$3,772.87
2014	0	000-1110-00	Cash - Payroll	$0.00	$925.44
2014	0	000-1120-00	Cash - Flex Benefits Progr...	$0.00	$345.32
2014	0	000-1130-00	Petty Cash	$0.00	$175.00
2014	0	000-1140-00	Savings	$0.00	$15,656.96
2014	0	000-1200-00	Accounts Receivable	$206.99	$1,202,937.06
2014	0	000-1205-00	Sales Discounts Available	$0.00	$206.99
2014	0	000-1210-00	Allowance for Doubtful A...	$27,371.40	$0.00
2014	0	000-1260-00	Employee Advances	$0.00	$250.00

How it works...

Complex sorting in a SmartList can often bring clarity to information by providing a better arrangement of data. Frequently, users who don't know about this feature take the extra step of exporting the data to Microsoft Excel and then sorting it there. With advanced sorting this step is unnecessary and it can eliminate the potentially time-consuming effort of sending a large amount of data to Excel just for sorting.

Additionally, even when the SmartList is selected with the intention of sending it to Excel, pre-sorting the information can speed up the analysis once the data is exported to a spreadsheet.

See also

▶ *Building analyses by Exporting SmartLists to Microsoft Excel*

▶ *Getting fine grain control of Excel Exports from SmartLists*

Speeding up access to information with SmartList Favorites

SmartLists are designed for individual users to tailor reporting to their needs. This is important because users have the ability to save their unique SmartLists and make these available to be reused over and over again.

Default SmartLists are represented by an asterisk and can be customized by moving fields around, adding or removing fields, filtering the data to be returned, and sorting data in interesting ways. However, the time and effort required to do all of that is lost if a user can't save and reuse these unique settings. Saved SmartLists are called Favorites and they are the focus of this recipe.

How to do it...

In this recipe we'll set up a SmartList and save it as a Favorite:

1. Click on the **SmartList** button on the menu bar at the top or select **Microsoft Dynamics GP** from the top and click on **SmartList**.

2. Select **Financial**, then **Accounts** from the list on the left.

3. Click on the **Account Number** column heading to sort by Account Numbers:

4. Click on **Favorites**. In the **Name** field, name the Favorite **Account Number**.
5. Leave **Visible To** equal to **System**.
6. Click on **Add** and then **Add Favorite** to save the SmartList:

How it works...

SmartList Favorites provide a way to save a group of SmartList settings much like options do for built-in reports. This provides a simple way to return to the same SmartList settings over and over. Favorites are saved under the category these are created in on the left. Consequently, our Account Number Favorite is saved under **Financial | Accounts**.

There's more...

SmartList Favorites can be also be modified, and there are even more SmartList recipes to come. Favorites provide fast access to preset SmartLists and GoTos provide a path back to the source data.

Modifying SmartList Favorites

It is possible to change a SmartList Favorite by selecting that Favorite, making changes, and clicking on **Modify** instead of **Add**.

Go To

Double-clicking on a row in a SmartList drills back to the source data. Sometimes, there is more than one possible source. For example, should a sales row drill back to the Sales Transaction or to the Customer Master Record? Well, the GoTo button in the upper right displays more drill back options beyond the default double-click selection. An example is shown in the following screenshot:

Additionally, the default GoTo can be changed in the **SmartList Options** window. This window is reached by clicking on the **Administration** button on the Navigation Pane and then clicking on **SmartList Options** in the **Administration** Area Page.

See also

▸ *Getting faster access to data with the Shortcut Bar*

▸ *Getting warnings with SmartList Alerts*

▸ *Controlling access by sharing or restricting SmartList Favorites*

Getting warnings with SmartList Alerts

In the previous recipe we saw how to save SmartLists as Favorites. Now we can look at how to use a Favorite to build a custom reminder. SmartList Favorites actually make up the core of the Reminder feature in Dynamics GP.

A custom reminder is a warning or alert generated by Dynamics GP and displayed on the **Reminders** section at login. It's used to alert a user about situations that exist in Dynamics GP. For example, reminders can display the number of invoices sixty days or more past due. These can also include the ability to drill back into the transactions that generated the reminder. The basic process takes a SmartList Favorite and builds criteria used to drive the reminder.

Built-in reminders were covered previously in the *Using Reminders to remember important events* recipe in Chapter 3. In this recipe, we'll take a look at creating custom reminders.

Getting ready

The first step in creating a custom reminder is to create a SmartList Favorite. That topic was covered in detail in the last recipe, *Speeding up access to information with SmartList Favorites*, so this should be easy for everyone. We'll keep this example simple and assume that we simply want to be alerted about debit transactions over $1 million.

How to do it...

Once a SmartList Favorite has been created it can be turned into a custom reminder using these steps:

1. Click on the **SmartList** button on the menu bar at the top or select **Microsoft Dynamics GP** from the top and click on **SmartList**.

2. Select **Financial**, then **Account Transactions**.

3. Click on **Search**. Set **Column Name** to **Debit Amount**. Set **Filter** to **is greater than** and **Value** to **1000000**:

![Search Account Transactions window showing Search Definition 1 with Column Name "Debit Amount", Filter "is greater than", and Value "1000000". sa Fabrikam, Inc. 4/12/2008]

4. Click on **OK**.

5. Click on **Favorites** to save this as a Favorite.

6. Name the Favorite **Debit > 1 mil** and leave it visible to **System**:

![Add or Remove Favorites window showing Category "Account Transactions", Name "Debit > 1 mil", Visible To "System", with Remove, Modify, Add, and Cancel buttons]

7. Click on **Add | Add Favorite and reminder**.

8. Select **Number of records**. Select **is greater than**. Leave the amount equal to zero. Select the **Display as a Cue** checkbox and click on **OK**:

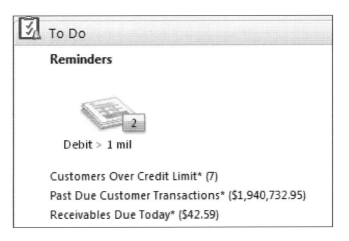

9. On the **To Do** Area Page click on the Refresh button. The Refresh button is indicated by two swirling arrows in the upper right near the **Help** button. This refreshes the current page.

10. In the **Reminders** pane you should see the **Debit > 1 mil** reminder with the number of debit transactions over a million dollars:

11. Click on the **Debit > 1 mil** line to drill back into the SmartList Favorite:

How it works...

Custom Reminders start with SmartList Favorites as their base and let users build reminders based on those results. This increases the power of Reminders because the core SmartList itself can be narrowed to provide very targeted results that can then be used to drive the alert.

Different users will need to be reminded about different things. SmartList Favorites provide opportunities to deliver relevant information to the right people in time for them to take action.

There's more...

Custom Reminders can also be modified and removed. Users aren't locked in after creating them.

Modifying and removing Custom Reminders

It is possible to change a custom Reminder by selecting **New Reminder** from the Home page, highlighting a reminder to change, and clicking on **Modify** instead of **New**. This reopens the **Custom Reminder** window allowing changes to be made.

Additionally, selecting **Remove** instead of **Modify** will delete that reminder.

See also

▸ *Improving information returned with SmartList Search*

▸ *Tailoring SmartLists by adding Fields*

▸ *Using Reminders to remember important events*

▸ *Speeding up access to information with SmartList Favorites*

Improving information returned with SmartList Search

The basic SmartLists included with Dynamics GP are great, but they really shine once companies figure out how to fine tune and filter the records that are returned. The Search feature in SmartLists does just that, making it easy to see which invoices were generated on a particular date or which transactions affected a certain general ledger account during the month.

In this recipe we'll look at how to better control the results that are returned using the Search feature in SmartLists. For our example, assume that auditors want to see any checkbook transactions over ten thousand dollars ($10,000) during the month of February. We'll use the Dynamics GP sample company for this recipe.

How to do it...

To limit the results of a SmartList with the Search feature:

1. Click on the **SmartList** button on the menu bar at the top or select **Microsoft Dynamics GP** from the top and click on **SmartList**.

2. Select **Financial**, then **Bank Transactions**.

3. Select **Search**.

4. In **Search Definition 1** set **Column Name** to **Checkbook ID**, **Filter** to **is equal to**, and **Value** equal to **First Bank**:

5. In **Search Definition 2** set **Column Name** to **GL Posting Date** and **Filter** to **is between**.

6. This opens up two date boxes. Set the dates to **2/1/2008** and **2/28/2008**:

7. In **Search Definition 3** set **Column Name** to **Checkbook Amount**, **Filter** to **is greater than**, and **Value** equal to **10000**:

```
┌─ Search Definition 3 ──────────────────────────────────────────────────┐
│  Column Name:                    Filter:              Value:            │
│  ┌──────────────────────┐ ┌────┐ ┌──────────────┐▼┐  ┌───────────────┐ │
│  │ Checkbook Amount     │ │ 🔍 │ │ is greater than│    │ 10000         │ │
│  └──────────────────────┘ └────┘ └──────────────┘    └───────────────┘ │
│       ☐ Field Comparison            ☐ Match Case                       │
└────────────────────────────────────────────────────────────────────────┘
```

8. Click on **OK**.

9. The resulting SmartList is limited to only **FIRST BANK** transactions in February 2008 with amounts over $10,000:

Checkbook ID ▲	GL Posting Date	Descri...	Source Do...	Checkbook Amount
FIRST BANK	2/28/2008		CMTRX	$150,630.10
FIRST BANK	2/28/2008		PMCHK	$11,565.76
FIRST BANK	2/28/2008		PMCHK	$22,500.00
FIRST BANK	2/28/2008		PMCHK	$86,016.41
FIRST BANK	2/28/2008		PMCHK	$10,697.38
FIRST BANK	2/28/2008		PMCHK	$46,826.77
FIRST BANK	2/28/2008		PMCHK	$105,976.21
FIRST BANK	2/28/2008		PMCHK	$19,426.88
FIRST BANK	2/28/2008		PMCHK	$66,809.85
FIRST BANK	2/28/2008		PMCHK	$105,507.71
FIRST BANK	2/28/2008		PMCHK	$126,265.67
FIRST BANK	2/28/2008		PMCHK	$13,589.76
FIRST BANK	2/28/2008		PMCHK	$19,153.02
FIRST BANK	2/28/2008		PMCHK	$55,163.88
FIRST BANK	2/28/2008		PMCHK	$45,167.91
FIRST BANK	2/28/2008		PMCHK	$11,536.00
FIRST BANK	2/28/2008		PMCHK	$19,237.74
FIRST BANK	2/28/2008		PMCHK	$12,141.53

How it works...

By default there are four available search boxes used to narrow results. However, with the 'is between' option shown in the demonstration, it's possible to effectively have more criteria than just the four boxes. 'is between' adds two options in a single search box, meaning that users don't have to use up 2 boxes with the 'greater than' and 'less than' criteria.

There's more...

The Field Comparison and Match Case settings provide additional search features and the Search Type option changes the way in which results are returned.

Field Comparison

The **Field Comparison** checkbox changes the **Value** field to a lookup field allowing the comparison of two values. This is useful for comparing fields in the system. For example, if a user wanted to find cases where the subledger posting date is not equal to the GL posting date, Field Comparisons would be a perfect tool.

Match Case

The **Match Case** checkbox makes a search case-sensitive. Sometimes, it is important to find situations where data has been entered in all caps. This is a great way to use the Match Case option.

The Match Case option can be removed, or set as the default, via the **SmartList Options** window. This window is available by selecting **Administration** from the Navigation Pane and selecting **SmartList Options** under **Setup**.

Search Type

SmartLists default to a **Search Type** of **Match All**. This returns results that meet all of the criteria. From a technical standpoint this is an 'and' search. In our example we found transactions for a specific checkbook AND between two dates AND over a certain amount.

Switching **Search Type** to **Match 1 or More** changes the search to an 'or' type search. Our example would return transactions for a specific checkbook regardless of date or amount. In short, it would return a mess. However, if I wanted transactions that were orders or invoices, **Match 1 or More** would be perfect as a document can't be both an order and an invoice.

See also

▶   *Speeding up access to information with SmartList Favorites*

Controlling data with SmartList Record Limits

When running a SmartList the number of records returned by the SmartList are shown in the lower left of the screen. By default, SmartLists have a record limit of one thousand (1,000) records.

1000 Bank Transactior	Completed	First 1000 records with no search criteria.

The idea behind this default limit is to prevent long running SmartList queries from slowing down the system. However, sometimes it makes sense for queries to return more than a thousand records. For example, if a firm knows that they have more than a thousand fixed assets then it doesn't make sense to limit fixed assets queries to a thousand as most of the time this number will need to be adjusted. Similarly, many companies easily have more than a thousand bank transactions in a given month.

There are a few options for increasing or decreasing this record limit including adjusting it on the fly, adjusting the limit for a Favorite, and setting a new default limit. We'll take a look at all of these options in this recipe:

How to do it...

To adjust Record Limits on the fly, complete the following steps:

1. Click on the **SmartList** button on the menu bar at the top or select **Microsoft Dynamics GP** from the top and click on **SmartList**.
2. Select **Financial**, then **Bank Transactions**.
3. Select **Search**.
4. Increase **Maximum Records**, located on the bottom left, to **10,000** and click on **OK**:

Adjusting limits on the fly only works for that session; the changes aren't saved. The easiest way to save new record limits is to save the SmartList as a Favorite. To adjust record limits for a Favorite:

1. Click on the **SmartList** button on the menu bar at the top or select **Microsoft Dynamics GP** from the top and click on **SmartList**.
2. Select **Financial** and then **Accounts**.
3. Select the **Account Number** Favorite set up in the *Speeding up access to information with SmartList Favorites* recipe.
4. Select **Search**.
5. Increase **Maximum Records** to **10,000** and click on **OK**:

6. Click on **Favorites**. Then click on **Modify** to save the new record limit:

7. The next time the **Account Number** Favorite is run, the record limit will be 10,000.

Finally, if the number of records returned is consistently over a thousand, it makes sense to adjust the default record limit for a particular SmartList category accordingly. To adjust the default limit:

1. Click on **Administrator** on the Navigation Pane. Then select **SmartList Options** under **Setup**.

2. Select the appropriate **Category**. For our example, select **Accounts**.

3. Change **Maximum Records** to **10,000** and click on **OK**:

How it works...

By adjusting record limits users and administrators gain improved productivity. If record limits are consistently too low, users waste time running SmartLists, adjusting record counts, and then running these again. If record limits are consistently set too high users may create unacceptably long running queries, slowing the system down for all users.

Tailoring SmartLists by adding Fields

Default SmartLists contain predefined sets of fields. However, users always want to add additional fields or rearrange existing columns. Fortunately, Dynamics GP provides this functionality out of the box.

Users can add fields to SmartLists, remove fields, or rearrange their order allowing users to fine tune SmartLists to meet their needs. In this recipe, we'll look at adding and rearranging fields in SmartLists.

How to do it...

To add a field to a SmartList:

1. Click on the **SmartList** button on the menu bar at the top or select **Microsoft Dynamics GP** from the top and click on **SmartList**.

2. Select **Financial**, then **Account Transactions** in the left pane.

3. Click on **Columns**:

Change Column Display

Display Name	Original Name
Journal Entry	Journal Entry
Series	Series
TRX Date	TRX Date
Account Number	Account Number
Account Description	Account Description
Credit Amount	Credit Amount
Debit Amount	Debit Amount

Add... Remove Default OK Cancel

4. Click on **Add**. This exposes all of the available fields for a SmartList, not just the defaults:

5. Select **Account Type** and click on **OK** to add this field to the SmartList:

To rearrange fields on a SmartList:

1. Continue on the current screen and select **Account type**
2. Click on the Up arrow button twice to move **Account Type** above **Credit Amount**:

3. Click on **Debit Amount** and click on the Up arrow button once to move it ahead of **Credit Amount**:

Change Column Display

Display Name	Original Name
Journal Entry	Journal Entry
Series	Series
TRX Date	TRX Date
Account Number	Account Number
Account Description	Account Description
Account Type	Account Type
Debit Amount	Debit Amount
Credit Amount	Credit Amount

[Add...] [Remove] [Default]   [OK] [Cancel]

4. Click on **OK** to finish

How it works...

The ability to add, remove, and rearrange fields on a SmartList gives users even more control over SmartList reporting. When users can satisfy their own custom reporting needs it significantly reduces the reporting burden for administrators.

There's more...

Sometimes users need to remove fields from SmartLists as well. Also, field changes are NOT saved from one session to another. So saving the SmartList as a Favorite after the changes are made is important. Finally, it is possible to add, remove, and rearrange fields on the default SmartLists.

Removing fields

Sometimes a SmartList just has more information than needed. To remove fields and clean up a SmartList click on **Columns**, select the column to delete, and click on **Remove**.

Favorites

Field changes to SmartLists are not saved. Clicking on another SmartList or otherwise moving off of a SmartList will cause field changes to reset. Saving the SmartList as a Favorite after the changes is the only way to preserve field changes. The recipe *Speeding up access to information with SmartList Favorites* has specifics on saving SmartLists.

Default SmartLists

The default SmartLists can also be modified to include or exclude columns and adjust the order as well. This is done by selecting **Administration** from the Navigation Pane and then selecting **SmartList Options** under **Setup**.

In this window, fields are added or removed by selecting or deselecting the checkbox next to a column. These can be reordered using the arrows at the right:

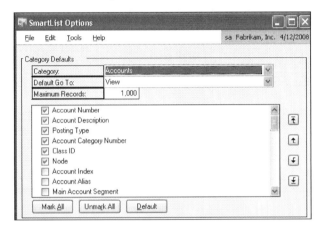

See also

▸ *Renaming Fields for clarity*

▸ *Speeding up access to information with SmartList Favorites*

Controlling access by sharing or restricting SmartList Favorites

In the recipe, *Speeding up access to information with SmartList Favorites* earlier in this chapter, we looked at the benefits of saving SmartLists as Favorites, along with how to make it happen. A key component of saving a Favorite that is often overlooked is setting the visibility of the Favorite.

The **Visible To** field defines who has access to use and modify a particular SmartList Favorite. As there are only a couple of options, it is sometimes difficult to get the visibility right. For example, consider a user who crafts a SmartList to meet their particular need but sets the visibility to **System** making the SmartList available to everyone. They could find that another user has made changes and modified the Favorite by saving those changes. Now our original user has to figure out how to put their Favorite back together.

In this recipe, we'll look at how to set the visibility of a Favorite and how to determine the right visibility to set.

How to do it...

The process to set the visibility of a Favorite is as follows:

1. Click on the **SmartList** button on the menu bar at the top or select **Microsoft Dynamics GP** from the top and click on **SmartList**.

2. Select **Financial**, then **Account Transactions**.

3. Select **Favorites** and name the Favorite **Account Trans**:

Add or Remove Favorites	
Category:	Account Transactions
Name:	Account Trans
Visible To:	System ▾
	System
	Company
Remove	User Class Add ▾ Cancel
	User ID

4. Set the **Visible To** field to **User Class** and click on **Add | Add Favorite**.

How it works...

The Visible To property of a Favorite controls who has access to both run and modify a Favorite.

There are four options for setting visibility:

- **System**: The Favorite is available to all users with access to this SmartList category across all Dynamics GP companies.

- **Company**: The Favorite is available to all users with access to this SmartList category but only for the company it was created in.

- **User Class**: The Favorite is available to all users in the same user class as the creator. With Dynamics GP 10 user classes are no longer connected to user security so it's easier to redirect user classes for other uses such as sharing Favorites. This works well for limiting access to a small group of users.

- **User ID**: The Favorite is only available to the user who created the SmartList.

Too many users default to selecting **System** every time. However, this exposes the Favorite to everyone with access to that SmartList category. In many cases, **User Class** is the best option to select because it limits access to a much smaller list and that list is most likely to be commonly shared. For critical SmartLists, selecting **User ID** will ensure that no one else can change it.

Visibility isn't the only security control on SmartLists, but it is the most commonly used and the only user-controllable option. In addition, there are some best practices for naming Favorites.

SmartList security

Dynamics GP provides security options for administrators to control access to SmartLists. This only controls who can access a SmartList category, not individual SmartList Favorites. For example, this controls which users have access to payroll related SmartLists, but a user with access to the payroll category would have access to all of the information in that SmartLists category.

Favorite naming best practices

A best practice for naming SmartLists is to include the user's initials at the beginning of the name. This doesn't prevent another user from using or renaming this Favorite, but it does remind users that they aren't the creators. It also makes it easy to change the name when modifying a Favorite. Simply change the initials to avoid overwriting the original favorite and click on **Modify**.

> ► *Speeding up access to information with SmartList Favorites*

Renaming Fields for clarity

SmartLists are full of cool features and these are great for throwing together a report quickly. However, sometimes the column names don't mean much to an average user, or the way that a company uses a field is different from its original intent.

It's not only possible, but easy to change the column description that shows up on a SmartList. In this recipe we'll look at how to do that.

To change the name of a SmartList column:

1. Click on the **SmartList** button on the menu bar at the top or select **Microsoft Dynamics GP** from the top and click on **SmartList**.

2. Select **Financial**, then **Account Transactions** from the pane on the left.

3. Click on **Columns**.

4. Click on **TRX Date** under the **Display Name** column heading. Type **Tran Date** right over the old name and click on **OK**:

How it works...

Changing the column names in a SmartList doesn't change the name in the database; it uses the new name as an alias to overlay the database name for reporting. Notice that the title in the **Original Name** column doesn't change. This means that there is no way to save the new column name to the default SmartList. However, the new column names can be saved as part of a Favorite.

Additionally, when exporting a SmartList to Excel, the new column name is passed to Excel. This means that this recipe can be a great timesaver for users who regularly export SmartLists to Excel and then rename columns.

There's more...

Column names can be changed for default SmartLists.

Default SmartList column names

The column names can be changed for the default SmartLists as well. To demonstrate how to do this:

1. Click on **Administration** on the Navigation Pane on the left.

2. In the **Administration** Area Page select **SmartList Options** from the **Setup | System** area.

3. Select **Accounts** for the **Category**.

4. Select **Posting Type** and key **PST Type** in its place:

5.   Click on **OK** to save the new default description.

See also

- ▶ *Tailoring SmartLists by adding Fields*
- ● *Speeding up access to information with SmartList Favorites*

5
Connecting Dynamics GP to Microsoft Office 2010

Dynamics GP provides tight integration with Microsoft Office 2010 across multiple integration points. Chapter 5 looks at the options for connecting Dynamics GP with Office. In this chapter we will see the following recipes:

- Getting control of Outlook features on the Home page
- Building analyses by Exporting SmartLists to Microsoft Excel
- Delivering flexibility by exporting Navigation Lists to Excel
- Improving reports by sending SmartLists to Word
- Communicating with customers using Letters from Microsoft Word
- Skipping the exports by using Prebuilt Excel Reports
- Improving performance by globally turning off Outlook integration
- Reporting on any Dynamics GP data with direct Excel Connections
- Importing data with Microsoft Word and a Dynamics GP Macro
- Getting fine grain control of Excel Exports from SmartLists
- Gaining flexibility by printing documents with Microsoft Word

Introduction

In Chapter 5 we move out of working only in Dynamics GP and look at connecting Dynamics GP with Microsoft Office 2010. Dynamics GP provides a number of interaction points with Office and we'll look at ways to connect Dynamics GP with Outlook, Word, and Excel. This chapter also covers some ways to use Office applications to improve processes in Dynamics GP.

The connection between Dynamics GP and Office 2010 provides a platform for using all of the great functionality found in Office to leverage the data in GP for analysis, reporting, and communication. Let's go play with Office!

Getting control of Outlook features on the Home page

One of the most obvious intersections between Dynamics GP and Microsoft Office 2010 is the presence of Outlook information on the Home page. Dynamics GP 2010 can display a count of unread e-mails and calendar data for a specified number of days. There are options to customize how Outlook appears on the Home page and we'll look at those in this recipe.

How to do it...

To customize the look of Outlook on the Dynamics GP Home page:

1. Select the pencil icon in the upper right of the title bar for the **Microsoft Office Outlook** section on the Home page:

2. The **Microsoft Office Outlook Details** window that opens includes a checkbox to activate or deactivate the display of unread e-mails. Ensure that the **Inbox summary** checkbox is selected.

3. The calendar control provides an option to show or hide calendar entries and control the number of days of appointments to be displayed, up to a maximum of seven (7) days. Ensure that the **Calendar** checkbox is selected. Change the value in the **Show this number of days in my calendar** field to **3** and click on **OK**:

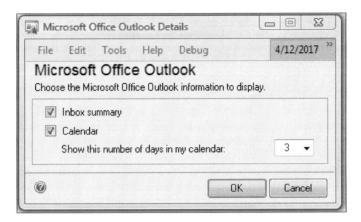

4. On the Home page select the count of **unread messages** to drill back to e-mails in Outlook.

5. Then select an Outlook appointment from the Home page to drill back to that appointment in Outlook:

Microsoft Office Outlook	
✉ **0 unread messages**	
Today	
All Day	Avis Rent A Car Reservation Confirmation Number: 46618860US1
5:30 AM - 9:39 AM	Your Itinerary: MCO-GSO, CUI605
8:30 AM - 4:30 PM	Project Task: PEC00011PRO
12:00 PM - 12:30 PM	Open Enrollment Closes today at Noon
Tuesday	
8:30 AM - 4:30 PM	Project Task: PEC00011PRO
8:30 AM - 9:30 AM	PA Core Team Meeting
11:00 AM - 12:00 PM	SQL Server Tips Webinar
10:30 PM - 1:30 AM	ORL @ LAC

How it works...

Even this basic connection to Outlook provides some great advantages for GP users. Users can see when new messages arrive without the distraction of Outlook pop-up windows. Also, users can see the day's schedule at a glance without having to leave Dynamics GP.

Deselecting both checkboxes prevents Outlook data from flowing to Dynamics GP but doesn't remove the Microsoft Office Outlook header. We'll look at how to do that later in this chapter.

See also

▸   *Improving performance by globally turning off Outlook integration*

Building analyses by Exporting SmartLists to Microsoft Excel

Continuing on a simple-to-complex theme, we move on to another straightforward process—exporting SmartLists to Microsoft Excel. Dynamics GP allows users to export any SmartList to Excel with the simple push of a button. In this recipe, we'll look at how to export SmartLists and some of the considerations around exports.

How to do it...

Exporting a SmartList to Excel is easy to do. Here is how to do it:

1.   Select the SmartList icon from the toolbar at the top or select the **Microsoft Dynamics GP** menu from the top and click on **SmartList**:

2.   Select **Financial | Account Summary** from the **SmartList** window.
3.   Once the SmartList finishes loading click on the **Excel** button:

4. Dynamics GP will export the data to Excel in the same order and with the same columns as the SmartList.

5. Once the export is complete Excel will open with the completed data:

How it works...

The simplicity of the export to Excel process belies the power of this feature. Other applications often require saving the export to a file and then opening that file in Excel. Dynamics GP provides a simple push-button connection to Excel. Each time the **Excel** button is pushed a new Excel file is created to hold the exported data.

One potential drawback to this feature is that once the data is in Excel, it is static data. Changes to the data in Dynamics GP require a new export. The Excel file is not updated automatically.

See also

▶ *Turning on more features with Dex.ini settings*

▶ *Getting fine grain control of Excel Exports from SmartLists*

Delivering flexibility by exporting Navigation Lists to Excel

The big **Excel** button on the SmartList window provides a visual cue that SmartLists can be exported to Microsoft Excel. That same blinding flash of the obvious is not available for Navigation Lists. Navigation Lists provide another way to interact with information in Dynamics GP and they can be filtered and limited like SmartLists. Navigation Lists don't have a big **Excel** button so, in this recipe, we will look at how to export Navigation List data to Excel.

How to do it...

To export a Navigation List to Excel:

1. Select **Financial** from the Navigation Pane.

2. At the top of the Navigation Pane select **Accounts** to open up the **Accounts** list.

3. Select the white checkbox next to the **Account Number** heading to select all accounts.

4. On the ribbon at the top select **Go To** and then **Send To Excel**:

5. Excel will open with the data from the list.

How it works...

Navigation Lists provide another way to work inside of Dynamics GP by blending data with a ribbon-like interface. This setup is designed to allow users to perform associated entries, inquiries, and reporting from a single screen for a series in Dynamics GP. The ability to export SmartLists from the Navigation List interface means that there is one less reason to leave these consolidated screens.

See also

▶ *Turning on more features with Dex.ini settings*

Improving reports by sending SmartLists to Word

Microsoft Excel isn't the only Office product that SmartLists can be exported to. They can also be exported to Microsoft Word. This can be useful for exporting records for inclusion into a report, financial statement footnotes, or any other type of Word document.

Like the export to Excel feature, export to Word is very easy to do. In this recipe, we'll take a look at how and why you would want to export SmartLists to Word. For our example, we'll use a very small set of records showing retained earnings beginning balances for several years from the sample company.

This type of data could be useful for inclusion in financial statement footnotes for example.

How to do it...

To send a SmartList to Microsoft Word:

1. Select the SmartList icon from the toolbar at the top or select **Microsoft Dynamics GP** from the top and click on **SmartList**.

2. Select **Financial | Account Summary** from the left pane of the **SmartList** window.

3. Click on **Search**. For **Search Definition 1** set the column name to **Period ID,** the **Filter** field to **is equal to**, and the **Value** field to **0** (zero):

4. For **Search Definition 2** set the column name to **Account Number**, the **Filter** field to **contains**, and the **Value** field to **3030** and click on **OK**.

5. Period 0 contains the beginning balances for each year and account 3030 is the retained earnings account in the sample company.

6. Click on the **Word** button to send this data to Microsoft Word.

7. Microsoft Word will open a new document with the SmartList data included in a Word table format:

How it works...

The nature of Microsoft Word makes this feature less useful than Excel for processing large amounts of tabular data. However, if users need to insert small amounts of data into a much larger document then exporting the data to Word is an easy way to get tabular data into a report. Typically, once exported to Word, the data would be cut and pasted into the larger report document, keeping the table intact.

Saving the related SmartList as a Favorite makes this process easily repeatable and provides a consistent data set.

See also

▶ *Improving information returned with SmartList Search*

▶ *Tailoring SmartLists by adding Fields*

▶ *Renaming Fields for clarity*

▶ *Getting fine grain control of Excel Exports from SmartLists*

Communicating with customers using Letters from Microsoft Word

SmartList exports to Word are useful but the Letter Writing Assistant feature is where the connection between Dynamics GP and Microsoft Word really shines. The Letter Writing Assistant uses built-in or user developed Word templates to create letters using information in Dynamics GP. Since the letters are based on the Mail Merge feature in Word, creating and manipulating templates follows the Word Mail Merge standards. Even better, the Letter Writing Assistant uses a wizard-style interface to build letters.

Dynamics GP comes with a selection of prebuilt letters for Collections, Customers, Vendors, Employees, and Applicants. In this recipe, we'll look at using the prebuilt letters to create the most common type of mailing—collection letters.

How to do it...

To use the Letter Writing Assistant:

1. From the menu bar, select **Reports | Letter Writing Assistant** to start the wizard and click on **Next** to get started.

2. Select **Prepare the letters using an existing letter** and click on **Next**:

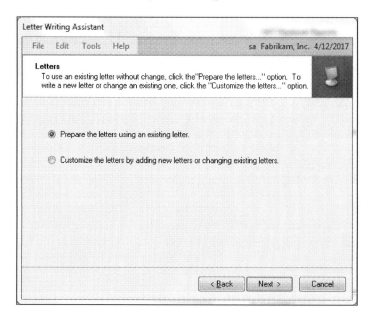

3. Select **Collection** and then click on **Next**.

4. Select the **181 and Over** checkbox and click on **Next**. Ranges of customers can also be selected here but we'll limit our example to just clients over 180 days past due for simplicity:

5. Select **Final Notice** and click on **Next**.

6. The next screen provides the ability to deselect certain customers to prevent them from getting a collection letter. Click on **Next** to continue:

7. Complete the process by adding the name and contact information for the company representative and click on **Finish**. Enter your name and contact information for our sample.

8. Microsoft Word will open and each letter will have its own page:

How it works...

The Dynamics GP Letter Writing Assistant uses a GP wizard and Mail Merge functionality to insert information from Dynamics GP into letters in Word. The wizard driven nature of this feature makes a complex process extremely simple to complete.

There's more...

In addition to our example, SmartList Favorites can be created and used to select information for letters. Additionally, users are not confined to built-in letters but can modify letters or build their own. Finally, there are other starting points for the Letter Writing Assistant, not just the **Reports** menu.

SmartList Favorites

On the **Prepare a Collection Letter** section of the Letter Writing Assistant, the selection field can be set to **SmartList Selection** allowing the use of a SmartList Favorite for letter selection and population:

Letter Writing Assistant

| File | Edit | Tools | Help | sa Fabrikam, Inc. 4/12/2017 |

Prepare a Collection Letter
Use this window to determine which customers will receive a letter.

SmartList Selection ▼

- Customers
  - Average Days to Pay*
  - Customer Balance*
  - Customer Contact List*
  - Customers on Hold*
  - Customers Over Credit Limit*
  - Inactive Customers*

First 1000 records where Average Days To Pay - Year is greater than 0.

⚠ Only customers with a bill-to address are included in the range.

< Back | Next > | Cancel

Letter Customization

Selecting **Customize the letters by adding new letters or changing existing letters** on the second screen of the wizard changes the wizard path and walks a user through modifying existing letters and creating new letters:

Other Starting Points

Reports | Letter Writing Assistant is not the only place that Letter Writing Assistant can be started from. Various windows including **Customer Maintenance**, **Vendor Maintenance**, and **Employee Maintenance** include a **Write Letters** button with the Word logo. Selecting this button drops down a set of options to start the Letter Writing Assistant at the appropriate point in the wizard:

See also

▶   *Speeding up access to information with SmartList Favorites*

Skipping the exports by using Prebuilt Excel Reports

The connections we've looked at so far between Dynamics GP and Excel have been one way and static. Data was moved from Dynamics GP to Excel. Once in Excel users could analyze and manipulate data, but when information in Dynamics GP changed, the user would need to re-export the data and re-run any analysis.

Microsoft Dynamics GP 2010 provides a new set of Excel based reports. These reports use the new Office Data Connection (ODC) to provide a live connection into Dynamics GP. Unlike exports, when data changes in Dynamics GP, these Excel reports can be easily refreshed to include the new data.

In this recipe, we look at how to deploy and use Excel reports in Microsoft Dynamics GP.

Getting ready

Prior to using Excel reports, they need to be deployed. This can be done to a simple shared file location on the company's network or to Microsoft Office SharePoint Server (MOSS). We'll look at deploying Excel reports to a shared file location:

1.   Create or select two file locations; one to hold the reports and one for the connections. Separating the connections from the reports makes it easier for users to run the Excel reports directly with less confusion. For our sample, ensure that locations `c:\xlreports` and `c:\xlconn` exist.

2.   Select **Administration** from the Navigation Pane on the left. On the **Administration** Area Page select **Reporting Tools Setup** under **Setup.** Enter the system password if prompted.

3.   Select the **Data Connections** tab and enter `c:\xlconn` in each field. Select the **Enable data connection deployment** and **Deploy data connections for all existing companies** checkboxes. Click on **Run Deployment**.

     For our example, we are deploying System and User Level Data Connections to the same place for simplicity. Also, selecting the **Deploy data connections for all existing companies** checkbox is optional but it creates the data connectors for all of the GP company databases at once saving steps and potential deployment conflicts down the road.

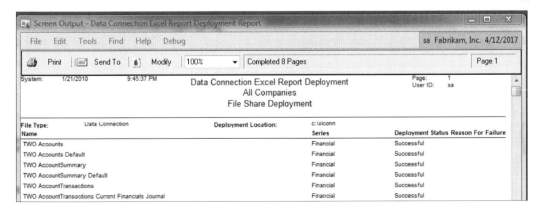

4. Click on **Yes** to view the **Deployment Report**, select the **Screen** checkbox, and click on **OK**.

5. Validate that the **Deployment Status** shows **Successful**:

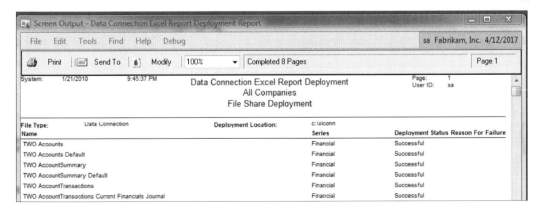

6. Select the **Reports Library** tab and enter `c:\xlreports` in each field. Select the **Enable Excel report deployment** and **Deploy Excel reports for all existing companies** checkboxes. Click on **Run Deployment**.

   As with the data connection deployment, these instructions deploy system and user level reports to the same place.

   Reporting Tools Setup

   File   Edit   Tools   Additional   Help   Debug   sa Fabrikam, Inc. 4/12/2017

   SQL Reporting Services | Data Connections | Reports Library |

   Reports Library

   Enables you to deploy and retrieve reports. The reports are viewable from within the report list automatically once the setup is complete.

   System Level Reports

   Define the location of where reports shared among multiple users will be stored.

   c:\xlreports

   User Level Reports

   Define the location of where reports available to individual users will be stored.

   c:\xlreports

   Excel Report Deployment

   ☑ Enable Excel report deployment
   ☑ Deploy Excel reports for all existing companies

   Run Deployment

   OK   Cancel

7. Click on **Yes** to view the **Deployment Report**, select the **Screen** checkbox, and click on **OK**

8. Validate that the **Deployment Status** shows **Successful**.

9. Click on **OK** when finished.

This process has now deployed both the Excel reports and the appropriate data connections. Now let's look at how to use them.

How to do it...

There are two options to run Excel reports. They can be run from within Dynamics GP or from Excel. Let's see how to do both.

To start an Excel report from within Dynamics GP:

1. Select **Financial** from the Navigation Pane. In the top section of the Navigation Pane select **Excel Reports**.

    If **Excel Reports** does not appear after deploying the reports restart Dynamics GP.

2. Double-click on the Account Summary report. (It will be preceded by the company identifier. For the sample company it's **TWO AccountSummary**):

3. Excel will open. Click on **Enable** if a security warning opens in Excel.

4. The Excel report will open with filter arrows already in place for filtering columns.

5. Right-click on one of the headings and select **Refresh** to force the report to bring in updated information from Dynamics GP.

To start an Excel report directly:

1. Open up Windows Explorer and navigate to the location where the reports were deployed. Drill into the appropriate company and module. In our example, this was `c:\xlreports\TWO\Financial`.

2. Double-click on the file named **TWO AccountSummary Default**.

3. Excel will open. If a **Security Warning** displays, select **Options | Enable this content** and click on **OK**:

4. The Excel report will open with filter arrows already in place for filtering columns.

5. Right-click on one of the headings and select **Refresh** to force the report to bring in updated information from Dynamics GP.

How it works...

Excel reports leverage Microsoft's new Office Data Connection to provide easily accessible, updateable reports. With the older style Open Database Connectivity (ODBC) connections, users had to have the connection set up on their machine. The portability of the new connectors makes sharing Excel reports based on live data much easier.

Additionally, these reports are much faster than SmartList exports. The data returns almost instantly and is presented with some basic formatting already intact.

For users who want to modify Excel reports, or build their own, these reports are still based on Excel at their core. Users can add calculations, move columns, and more, then save the reports with a new name. In most cases, the reports will maintain their connection to Dynamics GP.

There's more...

For users who want to build custom Excel reports, Microsoft offers Excel Report Builder as a part of SmartList Builder. Experienced database administrators will find a lot to like in the new Office Data Connectors and there is an easy way to avoid those security prompts.

Excel Report Builder

As part of the SmartList Builder add-on, Microsoft offers an Excel Report Builder that allows the user to select fields, order columns, add calculations, and limit records to create a unique Excel report. The process works just like SmartList Builder and the Excel Report Builder screen is almost identical to SmartList Builder. The end result, however, is a refreshable Excel report.

SQL and ODC Connections

For experienced administrators the Excel files can be modified directly by selecting **Data | Connections | Properties** from within Excel and selecting the **Definition** tab. This allows the manipulation of the underlying SQL query letting administrators add, remove, or reorder fields and, in general, manipulate the report in almost any way possible.

Once completed the changes can be saved to a new Excel file, to the original Excel file, or saved back as part of the ODC file making the changes available to all reports based on that connector.

This is not for the inexperienced, but knowledgeable database administrators will find tremendous power in the ability to manipulate the underlying SQL code.

Trust and Security

When opening Excel reports, Excel will return a Security Warning because there is a live connection back to a database. To prevent these warnings from showing:

1. Select the round main menu button in Excel and select **Excel Options**.

2. Click on **Trust Center** and then on **Trust Center Settings**:

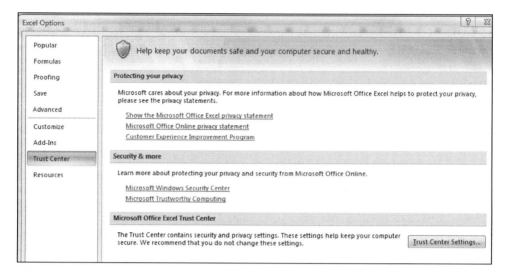

3. Click on **Trusted Locations** on the left and then on **Add new location**:

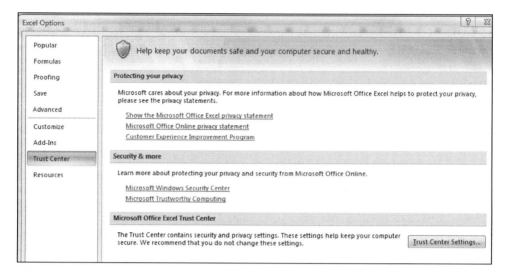

4. Add the location of the Excel Connections. In our example, this was `c:\xlconn\`:

> **Microsoft Office Trusted Location**
>
> Warning: This location will be treated as a trusted source for opening files. If you change or add a location, make sure that the new location is secure.
>
> Path:
>
> `c:\xlconn\`
>
> Browse...
>
> ☑ Subfolders of this location are also trusted
>
> Description:
>
> Date and Time Created: 12/10/2009 1:29 PM
>
> OK   Cancel

5. Select the **Subfolders of this location are also trusted** checkbox and click on **OK**.
6. Repeat this process and add the Excel Reports location, `c:\xlreports`, as well.

See also

▶   *Reporting on any Dynamics GP data with direct Excel Connections*

Improving performance by globally turning off Outlook integration

The ability to embed the Microsoft Outlook calendar and unread e-mail information on the Home page of Dynamics GP is a great feature. In some cases however, users or firms prefer not to show Outlook information on the Home page. For some it's too distracting or firms may not use Outlook as their primary e-mail and calendar tool. The most common reason, however, is that firms use Dynamics GP via Citrix or Terminal Server and often, user's profiles aren't configured to use Outlook over this connection. This issue can cause slowdowns in loading Dynamics GP and in some cases, connecting to Outlook this way can violate a license agreement.

Consequently, administrators need a way to disconnect Outlook from the Home page of Dynamics GP. This is easily done and there are actually three options. One option is for individual users, one is for administrators to turn the Outlook features off for existing users, and one is for administrators to prevent new users from connecting to Outlook.

In this recipe we'll look at all three ways to remove Outlook updates from the Dynamics GP Home page.

How to do it...

Users can remove Outlook links to their Home page by:

1. Select **Home** on the Navigation Pane.

2. Select **Customize this page** in the upper right-hand side of the Home page.

3. Deselect the checkbox marked **Microsoft Office Outlook** and click on **OK**:

Administrators can turn off Outlook connections for all existing users with an SQL script. Let's see how that works:

1. Open SQL Management Studio and connect to the Dynamics database

2. Execute the following script:

```
Update a set colnumbr = 0, seqnumbr=0, visible=0 from
Dynamics.dbo.sy08100 a where (sectionID = 2) and (DICTID=0) and
((colnumbr<>0) or (seqnumbr<>0) or (visible<>0))
```

Finally, administrators can prevent new users from connecting the Dynamics GP Home page to Outlook by:

1. Select **Administration** from the Navigation Pane.

2. On the **Administration** Area Page, select **System Preferences** under **Setup** and **System**.

3. Deselect the checkbox marked **Load Microsoft Office Outlook**.

How it works...

Users can simply deselect a checkbox to remove or activate their Outlook access, and administrators have options to globally control this setting as well. The simplicity of this recipe is important as the error messages generated by Dynamics GP can be very painful for users if GP continues to try to connect to Outlook without success.

See also

▸ *Getting control of Outlook features on the Home page*

Reporting on any Dynamics GP data with direct Excel Connections

In an earlier recipe, we looked at deploying and using the Excel reports contained in Dynamics GP. For all of the power of those dynamic reports one thing is missing—the ability to modify the type of data being returned from within Excel. Excel reports allow filtering. However, if a user only needs a subset of data, using filters can make it difficult to work with only the filtered data. Also, Excel reports bring in all of the available rows creating a much larger data set to work with, and possibly overwhelming Excel.

Fortunately, there is another option. The MS Query tool included with Excel can work with Open Database Connectivity (ODBC) to connect to live data in Dynamics GP. This process is as fast as Excel reports, allows user changeable parameters from Excel, and can be refreshed just like Excel reports. However, there are no prebuilt reports that use ODBC connections so users have to build these from scratch.

To demonstrate the power of Excel queries we'll build a simple account summary report with user selectable years in this recipe. Our ingredients are Dynamics GP and Microsoft Excel 2010.

How to do it...

To build a direct connection between GP and Excel:

1. Open Microsoft Excel 2010 and select **Data | From Other Sources | From Microsoft Query**. This will start the MS Query Wizard.

2. Select the data source used to log in to Dynamics GP. The default **Data Source** is named **Dynamics GP**. Click on **OK**.

3. Enter **sa** as the username and the sa password. Either sa or another SQL user is required here. A trusted connection can be used if properly set up. Encryption between the GP login and SQL Server prevents a regular GP login from being used for this task:

4. Click on **Options** and select the **TWO** database. Click on **OK** to start the MS Query Wizard:

5. In the **Query Wizard – Choose Columns** window scroll to the table named **GL11110**. Click on the plus (**+**) sign next to it to view the columns available:

6. Find and select the column named **ACTNUMBR_1** and click on the right arrow button (**>**) to add it to the **Columns in your query** field:

7. Repeat this process for these columns:

- ❑ **ACTNUMBR_2**
- ❑ **ACTNUMBR_3**
- ❑ **ACTDESCR**
- ❑ **DEBITAMT**
- ❑ **CRDTAMNT**
- ❑ **PERDBLNC**
- ❑ **PERIODID**
- ❑ **YEAR1**

8. The vertical arrow keys on the right can be used to reorder columns if necessary. Click on **Next** when finished.

9. In the **Query Wizard - Filter Data** window select **YEAR1**. In the **Only include rows where** section select **equals** and **2017**. Click on **Next** to continue:

10. Click on **Next** to move past the next screen and select **View data or edit query in Microsoft Query**. Click on **Finish** to open MS Query and review the details:

11. Once MS Query opens select **2017** next to **Value**. Change it to **[SumYear]** and press *Tab*:

12. Enter **2017** in the field that opens and click on **OK**. This changes 2017 from a value to a variable and then inserts 2017 as the initial value for that variable.

13. Select **File | Return data to Microsoft Office Excel**.

14. In the **Import Data** window select the **Existing worksheet** radio button and enter **=A5**. Then click on **OK**:

15. The data from Dynamics GP will now show up in Excel.

16. In cell **A1** type **Year**.

17. In cell **A2**, type **2017**:

	A	B	C	D
1	Year			
2	2017			
3				
4				
5	ACTNUMBR_1 ▼	ACTNUMBR_2 ▼	ACTNUMBR_3 ▼	ACTDESCR ▼
6	000	1100	00	Cash - Operating Account
7	000	1100	00	Cash - Operating Account
8	000	1100	00	Cash - Operating Account
9	000	1100	00	Cash - Operating Account

18. Click on the **ACTNUMBR_1** heading from the imported data. Select **Data | Connections | Properties | Definition | Parameters**:

19. Click on **Export Connection File** and save the file to create a portable Office Data Connection file with the embedded parameter.

20 Select **SumYear**. Select the **Get the value from the following cell** radio button. Key in =**Sheet1!$A$2**. Select the checkbox **Refresh automatically when cell value changes**. Click on **OK** and close all of the other open windows:

Parameters

Parameter name:

SumYear

How parameter value is obtained:

○ Prompt for value using the following string:

SumYear

○ Use the following value:

● Get the value from the following cell:

=Sheet1!$A$2

☑ Refresh automatically when cell value changes

OK   Cancel

21. Change the cell value in cell **A2** to **2016**. Press *Tab* and all of the values in the sheet will change to reflect date from 2016:

	A	B	C	D	E	F	G	H	I
1	Year								
2	2016								
3									
4									
5	ACTNUMBR_1	ACTNUMBR_2	ACTNUMBR_3	ACTDESCR	DEBITAMT	CRDTAMNT	PERDBLNC	PERIODID	YEAR1
6	000	1100	00	Cash - Operating Account	55699.93	0	55699.93	2	2016
7	000	1100	00	Cash - Operating Account	76022.07	5528.13	70493.94	3	2016
8	000	1100	00	Cash - Operating Account	233681.95	140.5	233541.45	4	2016
9	000	1100	00	Cash - Operating Account	5279.5	0	5279.5	5	2016
10	000	1110	00	Cash - Payroll	0	30697.16	-30697.16	1	2016
11	000	1110	00	Cash - Payroll	0	22346.12	-22346.12	2	2016
12	000	1110	00	Cash - Payroll	0	22103.22	-22103.22	3	2016
13	000	1110	00	Cash - Payroll	0	22119.7	-22119.7	4	2016
14	000	1110	00	Cash - Payroll	0	21623.35	-21623.35	5	2016

22. Save the Excel file. Reopening the file allows the user to simply change the year, press *Tab*, and get updated values.

How it works...

This recipe provides a live connection from Excel to Dynamics GP and the data returned is determined by selections made in the Excel spreadsheet. In this case, Excel uses an ODBC connection to return data from Dynamics GP, passing a parameter as part of the query to control the information returned. Any field in the query could be used as the parameter field and multiple parameters can be used as well. This provides incredible control for live reporting of Dynamics GP data.

The key differences between this recipe and the Excel reports covered in *Skipping the exports by using Prebuilt Excel Reports* are the type of connection and the need to build ODBC based reports from scratch. GP's Excel based reports create a portable connection automatically making them easy to share. However, they don't support user changeable parameters. Excel reports based on an ODBC connection require the user to have the appropriate ODBC connection set up on their PC for initial creation and then save a portable connection. ODBC based reports also provide greater control over the data returned. Additionally, as there are no prebuilt reports based on ODBC connections these reports need to be built from scratch making them harder to get started with.

There's more...

The biggest difficulty that comes up with this recipe is determining which Dynamics GP tables to use. Also, for experienced database administrators even more control is available.

Tables

The part that bedevils users is figuring out which table holds the data they need. Dynamics GP is full of tools to assist with that. Some of the more common tools are found under **Tools | Resource Descriptions** in the Support Debugging Tool application, which is covered in more detail in Chapter 10, and an Excel based table reference available from `http://www.DynamicAccounting.net` in the Download section.

Advanced Options

Experienced database administrators will quickly realize that they can use more complex SQL joins, views, and just about anything that they can come up with by using the SQL button in MS Query. There are some limitations though. Excel may refuse to allow parameters if the SQL query is too complex. The best option in that case is to wrap a complex query into a view or stored procedure simplifying it for Excel.

Importing data with Microsoft Word and a Dynamics GP Macro

Throughout this chapter we've looked at a number of ways to send data from Dynamics GP to Microsoft Word and Excel. With this recipe, we'll look at using Word and Excel to bring data into Dynamics GP.

Microsoft offers a number of import tools for Dynamics GP including Integration Manager, Table Import, and eConnect. In addition, there are third-party tools available such as Scribe (`http://www.scribesoft.com/microsoft-dynamics-gp.asp`) or SmartConnect (`http://www.eonesolutions.com.au/content.aspx?page=SmartConnect+for+GP`). However, these tools are not included by default and some firms don't purchase them as part of their solution. Additionally, some areas of the system simply don't have reasonable options to import data. In many cases, the combination of Microsoft Excel, Microsoft Word, and a Dynamics GP Macro can allow importing via the user interface. The basic steps are to create a macro, apply the new data to the macro using Word's Mail Merge functionality, and then run the macro to import the data. In this recipe, we'll take a look at how to do that.

Getting ready

For this example, we'll import segment descriptions for the third segment of the chart of accounts in the sample company. This is a common import requirement and somewhat difficult to do as this is normally updating information, not importing from scratch.

To set up the data to be imported:

1. Open Microsoft Excel to a new, blank Excel spreadsheet.
2. In cell **A1** enter **Segment 3**. In cell **B1** enter **Description**.
3. In cell **A2** enter '**01**. In **B2** enter **Marketing**. Be sure to put an apostrophe in front of **01** to force Excel to treat this as text.

4. Repeat this process with the data included until the spreadsheet looks similar to the example shown in the following screenshot:

	A	B	C	D
1	Segment 3	Description		
2	01	Marketing		
3	02	HR		
4	03	Plant		
5	04	Operations		
6	05	Shipping		
7				
8				

5. Save the sheet to the desktop as Segment3Import.

Now that we have our source data we can import it into Dynamics GP.

How to do it...

To set up and import data via Microsoft Word and a Macro we first create the macro like this:

1. In Dynamics GP select **Financial** from the Navigation Pane and select **Segment** in the **Setup** area:

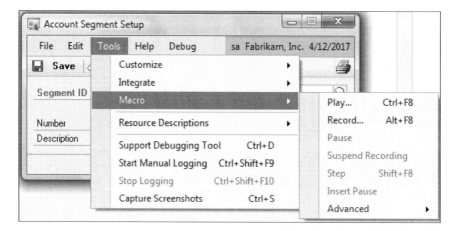

2. Select **Tools | Macro | Record**. Click on **Desktop** on the left to save the macro to the desktop. Name the Macro `Segment3.mac` and click on **OK** to save it.

3. In the **Segment ID** field click on the lookup button (indicated by a magnifying glass) and select **Segment3**. In the **Number** field type **01**. Don't use the lookup button.

4. In the **Description** field enter **Marketing** and click on **Save:**

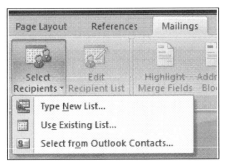

5. Select **Tools | Macro | Stop Record** to end the macro recording.

To use Word's Mail Merge functionality to add all of the data into the macro:

1. Open Microsoft Word and click on **File | Open**. Select **Desktop** on the left.

2. Change **All Word Documents** to **All Files** in the drop-down menu next to **File name**.

3. Select the **Segment3.mac** file created earlier and click on **Open**.

4. In Word select **Mailings**. Then select **Select Recipients | Use Existing List:**

5. Click on **Desktop** on the left, select the **Segment3Import** file created in the *Getting ready* section for this recipe, and click on **Open**.

6. Click on **OK** to use **Sheet1$**.

7. Find and select **01** with the left mouse button. Do NOT highlight or delete the single quotes around **01**:

```
ActivateWindow dictionary 'default'  form 'GL
'GL_Segment_Maintenance'
  TypeTo field 'Segment ID' , '01'
```

8. Select **Insert Merge Field** and then **Segment_3**:

9. This will ultimately replace **01** with the value in **Segment_3**.

```
ActivateWindow dictionary 'default'  form 'GL_Segment_Maintenance' window
'GL_Segment_Maintenance'
  TypeTo field 'Segment ID' , '«Segment_3»'
```

10. Find and select **Marketing**, but do NOT highlight or delete the single quotes around **Marketing**:

```
TypeTo field Description , 'Marketing'
MoveTo field 'Save Button'
```

11. Select **Insert Merge Field** and then **Description**. This will ultimately replace **Marketing** with the value in **Description**:

```
NewActiveWin dictionary 'default'  form 'GL_Segment_Maintenance' window
'GL_Segment_Maintenance'
ActivateWindow dictionary 'default'  form 'GL_Segment_Maintenance' window
'GL_Segment_Maintenance'
  TypeTo field 'Segment ID' , '«Segment_3»'
  MoveTo field Description
  TypeTo field Description , '«Description»'
```

12. Select **Preview Results** to see what the mail merge will send to GP.

13. Select **Finish & Merge | Edit Individual Documents** and then **OK** to have Word merge in all of the values from Excel. A new document opens with the macro code duplicated for each value in the source file.

14. Select the new document and select **File | Save As | Other Formats**.

15. Select **Desktop** on the left and change the **Save as type** to **Plain Text**. Name the file `Segment3Macro.txt` and click on **Save**. Select **OK** when prompted.

16. Close Microsoft Word.

17. Navigate to the desktop and right-click on `Segment3Macro.txt`. Select **Rename** and change the filename to `Segment3Macro.mac`. Click on **OK** when prompted.

So far we've created a base macro and populated it with our data. Next we'll look at running the macro.

1. Back in Dynamics GP select **Financial** from the Navigation Pane and select **Segment** in the **Setup** area:

2. Select **Tools | Macro | Play** and select **Desktop** on the left. Click on **Segment3Macro.mac** and click on **Open**. The macro will run and populate the description. Click on **OK** when the macro finishes:

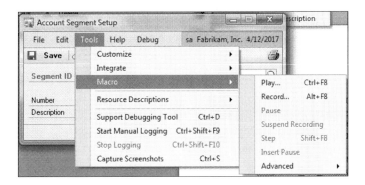

How it works...

Populating Dynamics GP via macros has a long history of use in the product. This process mimics a user's data entry so all of GP's security controls still apply. Additionally, the Dynamics GP business logic is applied as the data is integrated. Macros are primarily used for import when other options are either unavailable or prohibitively expensive in terms of either time or actual costs. Additionally, since the macro simply mimics a user's input, some firms use this process as an accepted way to avoid the paperwork that can be required for updates via SQL.

Although setting up the macro can be a little tedious, imagine how long it would take to correctly enter 200, 2,000, or 20,000 records like this by hand.

There's more...

There are some very important limitations that come with using Microsoft Word and Macros to populate Dynamics GP.

Limitations

Because Macros mimic screen input, screensavers can interfere with macro entries. I've seen employees sit and jiggle the mouse every 5 minutes for hours to prevent a group policy controlled screensaver from blanking their screen. This limitation also applies to Terminal Server and Citrix sessions. Leaving a session, even to just check e-mails, terminates the macro.

Additionally, there is no error control in Macros. If a macro fails because of data or other issues users have to delete the macro code up to just before the failure, fix the issue, and continue running it from there.

Finally, macros only work with consistent processes. If, for example, GP opens a dialogue box for one set of circumstances but not for another, a macro won't work because it can't process alternative paths.

Getting fine grain control of Excel Exports from SmartLists

In a previous recipe we looked at how to export SmartLists to Excel with the push of a button. That method creates a new Excel file each time. In many cases, users need to export the same set of data on a regular basis and build it into a formatted report via Excel. There's a way to accomplish this with SmartList exports. The feature is called ExportSolutions and it's the focus of this recipe.

Getting ready

For our recipe we'll assume that we have an Account Summary report that we want to format with a title and headers the same way every time. To begin, we need to set it up the first time:

1. Select the SmartList icon from the menu bar at the top or select **Microsoft Dynamics GP** from the top and click on **SmartList**.

2. Select **Financial | Account Summary** on the left to generate a SmartList.

3. Click on the **Excel** button to send the SmartList to Excel.

4. In Excel select the round Office button, select **Excel Options**, and ensure that the **Show Developer tab in the Ribbon** checkbox is selected. Click on **OK**:

5. Click on the **Developer** tab and select **Record Macro**. Accept the default name as **Macro1** and click on **OK**:

6. Highlight rows 1-5, right-click, and select **Insert**.

7. Highlight the titles in cells A6-F6.

8. In cell **A1** enter **Sample Excel Solution**.

9. From the **Developer** tab select **Stop Recording**.

10. Highlight and delete all of the rows.

11. Save the file in the `c:` drive with the name `AccountSummary.xlsm`.

How to do it...

To set up an Export Solution:

1. In Dynamics GP select **Microsoft Dynamics GP** and then select **SmartList**.

2. Select **Financial | Account Summary** in the left pane to generate a SmartList.

3. Click on **Favorites**. Name the favorite **Export Solution** and click on **Add | Add Favorite**:

4. Back on the **SmartList** window select **SmartList | Export Solution.** Name the solution **ExportSolution**. Set the path to **C:\AccountSummary.xlsm** and the completion macro to **Macro1**:

5. Select the checkbox next to the SmartList Favorite under **Account Summary** named **Export Solution** and click on **Save**. Then close the window.

6. Back in the **SmartList** window select the **Export Solution** favorite under **Account Summary** and click on the **Excel** button.

7. Instead of opening Excel, there are now two options. The **Quick Export** option performs a typical Excel export. The **ExportSolution** option will open the Excel file named `AccountSummary.xlsm`, export the data, and run the macro named Macro1:

8. Click on the **ExportSolution** option and watch the file open and the macro execute.

How it works...

The ExportSolution feature adds a tremendous amount of power and control to the basic Excel export functionality. The ability to run an Excel macro before and after the export opens up a host of possibilities for reporting. Additionally, once an Export Solution is set up it's very easy for an average user to run it with just a couple of clicks.

See also

> ▸ *Building analyses by Exporting SmartLists to Microsoft Excel*

Gaining flexibility by printing documents with Microsoft Word

A new feature in Dynamics GP 2010 is the ability to print sales and purchasing documents using Microsoft Word templates instead of Report Writer reports. The use of Microsoft Word to create documents provides greater flexibility in field placement, logo use, and formatting. Users can now print phenomenal looking documents such as orders, invoices, and purchase orders with Word as the backbone.

For this recipe, we'll look at how to print an invoice using Microsoft Word and the sample company. Then we'll look at some of the setup options around Word templates.

How to do it...

To print an invoice using a Word template in the GP 2010 sample company:

1. Select **Sales** from the Navigation Pane on the left.
2. On the **Sales** Area Page click on **Sales Transaction Entry** under **Transactions.**
3. Change **Type/Type ID** to **Invoice**.
4. Use the lookup button (indicated by a magnifying glass) to select invoice **INVS3014** from the sample company:

5. Click on the Printer icon in the upper-right corner.

6. Select the **Invoices** checkbox on the left and click on the **Print** button.

7. Ensure that the **Report Type** field in the center is set to **Template** and then select the checkbox next to **Screen**. Click on **OK**:

8. Microsoft Word will open and display the invoice for printing:

How it works...

By using Microsoft Word templates Dynamics GP opens up a world of formatting possibilities for documents. Currently, Word templates can be used for statements, invoices, orders, quotes, packing slips, check remittance, and purchase orders.

There's more...

Dynamics GP 2010 provides control over which documents should use Word templates instead of Report Writer documents, and users can create their own templates.

Which Report to Use

Companies upgrading to Dynamics GP 2010 may choose to slowly migrate to Word template documents meaning that they still need the old style Report Writer documents for a while.

From the main menu, selecting **Reports | Template Configuration** opens the **Template Configuration Manager** window. This window provides control over enabling templates, allowing documents to use Word templates, and allowing the use of standard documents when a Word template has been activated. It also holds the images to be sent to Word documents.

All of this is contained in an easy-to-understand window:

User Template Creation

Templates can be created by users and specific templates can be assigned to specific companies, vendors, and customers using the **Reports | Template Maintenance** selection on the main menu.

The specifics of creating a new template are beyond the scope of this recipe. However, templates can be created from scratch or copied from the default templates included with Dynamics GP 2010:

6

Exposing Hidden Features in Dynamics GP

Microsoft Dynamics GP is full of features. Users often accept the system in the way it was originally set up without understanding that there may be other features that can be activated to improve the usefulness of the system. Hidden features are the focus of this chapter including:

- ▶ Controlling Posting Dates when not posting by batch
- ▶ Reducing posting steps with better Printing Control
- ▶ Improving information with Tax Dates in transactions
- ▶ Gaining the option to Process Taxes in the General Ledger
- ▶ Tracking Tangible Personal Property Tax information for Fixed Assets
- ▶ Understanding all of the financial information about an asset with Fixed Asset Details
- ▶ Speeding up entry by Copying a Purchase Order
- ▶ Getting control of printing with Named Printers
- ▶ Speeding up month-end processing with Reconcile to GL functionality

Introduction

In this chapter, we look at some features in Dynamics GP that many users miss. Some of these features are well known to consultants but somehow users still miss the big benefits that can be gained from these recipes.

This chapter is really about leveraging features to remove obstacles. It's about those hidden settings that shave seconds off processes, seconds that build up to save hours over the course of a month. Now, it's hidden feature time!

Controlling Posting Dates when not posting by batch

Transactions in Dynamics GP can be posted individually or as part of a batch. When posting as part of a batch, the batch gets a posting date that can be different from the date of the transaction. For individual transaction posting too, the posting date can be different from the transaction but the way to accomplish this is not obvious.

When not posting in a batch the posting date on a transaction is the date that the transaction will have in the general ledger. The document date (Order Date, Invoice Date, and so on) is just that, the date of the document and it is used to calculate aging for sales and purchase transactions. Controlling posting dates is very useful when the timing of a transaction doesn't match the month it needs to be posted in. For example, my auditors once sent a bill in July for audit work done back in January. In this scenario I didn't want to post the transaction in January because January was closed. I did need the January date in Dynamics GP to ensure that we didn't wait to pay them on thirty-day terms. We probably should have made them wait for six months as it took them so long to bill us but why irritate the auditors needlessly?

In Dynamics GP I set the **Document Date** to a January date so that the bill would age and be selected for payment properly. However, the **Posting Date** was a July date putting the transaction in the current month for the general ledger.

In this recipe, we'll take a look at posting a transaction with a posting date different from the transaction date.

How to do it...

To post a transaction with different posting and transaction dates:

1. In Dynamics GP select **Purchasing** from the Navigation Pane. Select **Transaction Entry** on the **Purchasing** Area Page.

2. This opens the **Payables Transaction Entry** window. Press *Tab* to go to the **Doc. Date** field and click on the blue arrow:

3. The **Payables Date Entry** window will open to display the **Posting Date** field. Add thirty days to the date in the **Posting Date** field and click on **OK**:

4. Now, when the transaction is completed and posted with the help of the **Post** button the posting date will be thirty days later than the document date.

How it works...

This is one of those exquisitely simple items that is hidden just enough that users don't find it. The ability to separate the posting date from the transaction date is an important accounting tool that is often not present in lower-end systems. The fact that Dynamics GP supports this in both batch and transactional posting is one small difference between an Enterprise Reporting System and simple accounting software.

Reducing posting steps with better Printing Control

When posting a transaction in Dynamics GP, a series of posting reports print by default. Typically there is a posting report with full posting details, a distribution summary report, a distribution detail report, and in many cases a checkbook report.

Reports are often set to ask for the type of output (**Printer**, **Screen**, or **File**) each time. If this setting is turned on each report will open a window allowing the user to change the report destination when the report is run. This significantly increases the amount of time it takes to simply start the printing process because the user has to make a choice each time. Additionally, reports set to print to a printer will open a window allowing users to set the number of copies or limit printing to certain pages:

Report Destination window

This means it's not uncommon to have eight windows open and four reports print every time a user posts. Even worse, the summary and detail distribution reports are subsets of the posting report so some information is duplicated across three reports. With this big of a mess, users often click through the prompts without actually reading these. They print reports that they don't really need and cancel reports they should print:

Print window

There is a better way. Reports can be turned off, routed only to the screen, or sent to file. The printer prompt can be turned off as it's rarely used. All of this can save several minutes each time transactions are posted, quickly adding up to a savings of hours in the course of a month along with reduced printed waste. In this recipe, we'll see how to control printing during posting. For our example, we'll look at controlling printing when posting a payables transaction entry.

Getting ready

Prior to changing the printing of posting reports, administrators should evaluate what reports really need to be printed or saved at the time of posting. Posting reports can be reprinted at a later date as much of the data is duplicated across reports. Consequently, there is often no need to print any of the reports.

To show the range of options for our example we will send the posting report to a file, the summary report to a printer, and we'll turn off the detail report and any other reports.

How to do it...

To get control of posting reports:

1. Select **Administration** from the Navigation Pane and **Posting** under the **Posting** heading on the **Administration** Area Page to open the **Posting Setup** window.

2. In **Series**, select **Purchasing**. In **Origin**, select **Payables Trx Entry**.

3. In the lower section find the report labeled **Trx Entry Posting Journal**. Select the checkbox on the left under the **Print** heading next to **Trx Entry Posting Journal**. Deselect all of the four center checkboxes. Then, select the one under the file folder icon. Press *Tab* to go to the **Path** field and enter **c:\AP Posting.txt**.

    This process sets the AP Transaction Entry Posting Journal to default to printing to a file located in the `c:` drive and named `AP Posting.txt`. The folder icon in the top right of this section of the page can also be used to browse and select a file location.

4. Select the checkbox next to **Trx Distribution Summary** under the **Print** heading. Deselect any checkboxes in the middle and select the checkbox under the printer icon.

    This activates the Transaction Distribution Summary Report and sends it to the printer by default.

5. Deselect any other checkboxes under the **Print** heading to turn off the remaining reports and click on **Save** to continue:

Now, when a payables transaction is posted, the posting report will append to a file and the Transaction Distribution Summary Report will print to the printer.

How it works...

In most cases there is no need to print any posting reports. However, setting posting reports to ask every time these are printed is the least efficient of all of the options. As posting reports can be reprinted in Dynamics GP, once users are past the initial insecurity of using the system, posting reports should generally be turned off. However, if posting reports are required for control purposes the number and types of automatic reports should be limited and sent to a file for easy retrieval, e-mailing, and archiving.

There's more...

Printing posting reports makes less sense when users know how to reprint these on demand and there is a way to turn off the rarely used System Print Dialog.

Posting reports

Posting reports are found in the **Reports** section of each module. To continue on the theme of a payables transaction, select **Purchasing** from the Navigation Pane. Then select **Posting Journals** on the Area Page under **Reports**. The first option is the **Transaction Journal**. Other posting journals can be selected for printing with the drop-down menu:

The only exception to this is the posting report for General Journal entries. The report exists; it's just called a Cross-Reference report instead of a posting journal.

System Print Dialog

The other window that is frequently skipped during printing is the Print window. This window displays when printing to a printer. It provides the option to print more than one copy of a report or to print only certain pages of the report. This window is actually controlled via the Named Printers functionality that we'll look at in the recipe *Getting control of printing with Named Printers* found later in this chapter. For now, we'll just look at turning off this feature.

To turn off the system print dialog:

1. Select **Administration** from the Navigation Pane. Select **Named Printers** from the Area Page under **Setup**. Enter the system password if prompted.

2. Select the checkbox marked **Do Not Display System Print Dialog** and click on **OK** twice:

3. Select a default printer for Dynamics GP and click on **OK**.

4. Click on **Save** to assign the default printer to Named Printers. Then select **File | Close** to close the window:

If the Named Printers feature has already been set up, then steps 3 and 4 won't appear as an option. This process turns off print options for this printer for all users on this workstation.

See also

▸ *Getting control of printing with Named Printers*

Improving information with Tax Dates in transactions

When working with sales tax and use tax it is often useful to set the date of a transaction for tax purposes. For example, assume a February invoice subject to use tax arrives in March. This is after February has been closed and use tax submitted. The invoice still needs to be dated in February to age properly, but it needs to appear on tax reports for March to ensure that the taxing authority is paid properly. Dynamics GP includes functionality to support this but it needs to be turned on. Tax Date functionality was originally designed to support Value Added Tax (VAT), found in Europe and other parts of the world. Firms with this requirement will need to activate tax dates as well. In this recipe, we'll look at how to activate and use tax dates.

Getting ready

Prior to using Tax Dates they need to be activated. To activate Tax Dates:

1. Select **Administration** from the Navigation Pane. On the **Administration** Area Page, select **Company** under the **Setup** and **Company** headers.

2. Click on **Options** in the **Company Setup** window:

3. Select the checkbox marked **Enable Tax Date** and click on **OK** twice:

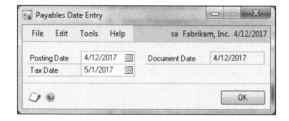

Tax Date functionality is now set up. Let's look at how to use it in a transaction.

How to do it...

To use Tax Dates in a transaction:

1. Select **Purchasing** from the Navigation Pane on the left and then select **Transaction Entry** from the **Purchasing** Area Page.

2. This opens the **Payables Transaction Entry** window. Press *Tab* to go to the **Doc. Date** field, select the blue arrow next to the date field, and enter **4/12/2017**:

3. A new **Tax Date** field appears in the **Payables Date Entry** window. Enter **5/1/2017** in the **Tax Date** field and click on **OK**:

How it works...

The Tax Date feature is required for processing Value Added Tax (VAT) but it's also very useful for sales tax and use tax reporting. Once the Tax Date feature has been activated, tax dates on transactions are available to add to the SmartLists. This makes reporting on tax dates easy and flexible.

See also

▶ *Tailoring SmartLists by adding Fields*

Gaining the option to Process Taxes in the General Ledger

There are times when companies need to process sales or use tax transactions through the general ledger rather than through a subledger such as Sales or Purchasing. Perhaps tax was incorrectly calculated or omitted on the original transaction. It's also possible that a company uses another system to feed the general ledger in Dynamics GP. For example, at one company I worked for we used a specialized accounts receivable application that was designed for our industry. Data from that application was integrated with Dynamics GP and all other transactions ran through Dynamics GP directly. This can lead to the need to process tax transactions through the GL.

Dynamics GP includes options to calculate and process taxes directly through the general ledger and that is the focus of this recipe.

Getting ready

Prior to processing tax transactions via the general ledger, this feature needs to be turned on. To activate the ability to process taxes through the general ledger:

1. Select **Administration** from the Navigation Pane. On the **Administration** Area Page select **Company** under the **Setup** and **Company** headings.

2. Click on **Options** in the **Company Setup** window:

3. Scroll down in the window and select the checkbox marked **Calculate Taxes in General Ledger**. Click on **OK** twice:

Now that tax calculations in the general ledger have been activated let's see how they work. We'll use the sample company's tax schedules for our example.

How to do it...

To calculate taxes in the general ledger:

1. Select **Financial** from the Navigation Pane. Select **General** under **Transactions** on the Area Page.

2. Select the new **Tax Entry** button on the bottom left of the **Transaction Entry** window:

3. On the **Tax Entry** window set the **Transaction Type** to **Credit**. Use the lookup button (indicated by a magnifying glass) to select or key in the sales account **000-4100-00**. Enter **$1,000.00** in the **Sale/Purchase Amount** field:

4. Use the lookup button (indicated by a magnifying glass) to select **USASTE-PS6N0** (State Sales Tax) in the **Tax Detail** field. Notice that Dynamics GP will fill in the tax amount automatically. Click on **Create** to create the transaction in the general ledger:

5. The created transaction will have the account and amount entered along with the appropriate tax. As this is only one side of the entry, enter **000-1200-00** (Other Receivables) in the next open line to balance the transaction:

How it works...

The ability to calculate taxes as part of a general journal entry provides the ability to accommodate tax adjustments and changes in tax law. It also provides flexibility to work with other systems connected to Dynamics GP.

See also

▶   *Improving information with Tax Dates in transactions*

Tracking Tangible Personal Property Tax information for Fixed Assets

In the United States Tangible Personal Property Tax is a local tax on non-real property held by businesses. It is one of the most difficult taxes to account for and process because each locality uses a different form and a different calculation. The tax can be assessed at the state, county, or city level and in some cases, at all three levels with three different forms. The small firm I worked for had to process 12 different jurisdictions for 6 locations. The number of tax returns can increase exponentially with each company location.

Dynamics GP at least provides an option to track tangible personal property locations and costs as part of Fixed Assets, but the window is not well labeled. Consequently, most users don't know that this option exists.

This recipe looks at the tangible personal property tax functions in Dynamics GP and how to use them to make the tax filing process more efficient.

Getting ready

As tangible personal property tax is based first on location, the first step is to set up locations that will ultimately be attached to Fixed Assets. To do this:

1.   Select **Financial** from the Navigation Pane and click on **Location** under **Setup**.

2.   The **Location Setup** window will open. Though it's not marked this way the **Location Setup** window is designed to hold the key location pieces for tangible personal property tax, state, county, and city.

3.   For our example, enter **SANDY SPRINGS** as the **Location ID**.

4.   In the State section enter **GA** as the **State Abbreviation**, **GA** as the **State Code**, and **Georgia** as the **State Description**.

5.   In the County section enter **FUL** as the **County Code** and **Fulton** as the **County Description**.

6. Finally, in the City portion enter **SSPR** as the **City Code** and **Sandy Springs** as the **City Description**:

Location Setup	
File Edit Tools Help	sa Fabrikam, Inc. 4/12/2017
💾 Save ✎ Clear ✕ Delete	🖨

Location ID	SANDY SPRINGS 🔍📄
State Abbreviation	GA
State Code	GA
State Description	Georgia
County Code	FUL
County Description	Fulton
City Code	SSPR
City Description	Sandy Springs|

| ◄◄ ◄ ► ►► by Location ID ▼ | 📄 ⊛ |

7. Click on **Save** to save the location. This step should be repeated to correspond to each of the firm's locations.

The second and third parts of tangible personal property tax are category and either cost or value depending on the jurisdiction's requirements. Consequently, user defined fields are the best options to hold both the tax category and the previous year's cost or value. To set up these user defined fields:

1. Click on **Financial** on the Navigation Pane and select **Company** under **Fixed Asset Setup**. Click on the blue arrow next to **User Fields** in the **User Data Options** section:

┌─ User Data Options ──────┐
│ ☑ User Data Auto Format │
│ ┌────────────────┐ │
│ │ User Fields │ → │
│ └────────────────┘ │
└──────────────────────────┘

2. This opens the **Expand User Fields** window. Set the **Prompt** for User Field 1 to **Use Tax Category**, select the **List Valid Values** checkbox, and click on the blue arrow:

Expand User Fields	
File Edit Tools Help	sa Fabrikam, Inc. 4/12/2008

User Field	Prompt	Format	List Valid Values	Valid Date
1	Use Tax Category	XXXXXX ▼	☑ ▣	☐

3. On the **User Fields List Setup** window enter **Furn** and **Veh** to represent furniture and vehicles, two common categories. Click on **OK** to close:

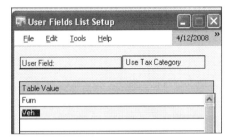

4. Back on the **Expand User Fields** window key **Use Tax Amount** in the **Prompt** field for **User Field 11**. Click on **OK** and then **Save** to finish:

As tangible personal property tax is normally based on location, category, and cost/value the first step is to attach the right location information to Fixed Assets. To attach a property tax location to an asset:

1. Select **Financial** from the Navigation Pane and then select **General** under the **Fixed Assets** header in the **Cards** section.

2. In the sample company, use the lookup button (indicated by a magnifying glass) to select asset **00001** having suffix **1**:

3. In the **Location ID** field use the lookup button (indicated by a magnifying glass) to change the location to **SANDY SPRINGS**:

4. Select the GoTo button on the top right of the window and select **User Data**:

5. Use the lookup button (indicated by a magnifying glass) next to **Use Tax Category** and set it to **Furn**. Set the value of **Use Tax Amount** to **$1,000.00**:

6. Click on **Save** twice to save the setup.

7. Now all of the based information needed for Tangible Personal Property Tax reporting can be accessed via a Fixed Asset SmartList.

How it works...

Tangible Personal Property Tax is highly local and non-standardized. Consequently, the best option is to have all of the data available to at least ease the calculation burden making reporting more of an administrative function. Using built-in location functionality allows reporting at any of the taxing entity levels.

The value of user defined fields for Tangible Personal Property Tax is such that they allow category reporting separate from other categories used for financial or federal tax reporting. As tangible personal property tax amounts are jurisdiction-specific and can be based on actual cost, a declining percentage of cost, or another value assigned by the organization, the use of a user defined value field separates this tax value from actual costs and provides a specific tax basis value.

See also

▸ *Chapter 4, Harnessing the Power of SmartLists.*

Understanding all of the financial information about an asset with Fixed Asset Details

Dynamics GP has a nice module for tracking and maintaining Fixed Assets. However, many users have trouble figuring out the history of a specific asset. Often, users find that while reviewing fixed asset general ledger postings something looks wrong, but they can't figure out where to go in the Fixed Asset module to validate how the transactions were posted.

Dynamics GP provides the ability to see every transaction for a Fixed Asset and its link back to the general ledger. This functionality can be hard to find. In this recipe, we'll look at how to trace Fixed Asset transactions.

How to do it...

To get the specifics of Fixed Asset transactions:

1. In Dynamics GP, select **Financial** from the Navigation Pane. Then select **Financial Detail** under the **Inquiry | Fixed Assets** headers.

2. Use the lookup button (indicated by a magnifying glass) to select asset **00001** having suffix **1**. Set the **Book ID** to **INTERNAL**.

3. The **Financial Detail Inquiry** window will populate to display all of the transactions for this asset:

4. The grid at the bottom displays the Fixed Asset Period, GL Batch Number, Account Type, Date, Source Document, and Amount. The key fields are **Transaction Acct. Type** and **Src Doc**. These fields provide details about the type of transaction. For example, the first two lines demonstrate the **Cost** and **Clearing** entry for the initial purchase of the asset.

5. The **Batch Number** is the batch sent to the GL. It can be reviewed using a SmartList.

6. Below that is the first depreciation entry transaction. It affected the **Depreciation** and **Reserve** accounts.

7. Select the first Depreciation entry and click on the blue **Amount** hyperlink to get more information about this transaction entry. Dynamics GP shows full details of that entry including GL batch, posting date, account, and user information. Click on **OK** to close this window:

Financial Detail Display				_ □ ▣ ⊠_	
File Edit Tools Help Debug				sa Fabrikam, Inc. 4/12/2017	

Asset ID	00001	1	Office Desk
Book ID	INTERNAL		Internal

FA Period	2015-001		Transaction Type	Depreciation

Amount		$11.90		
Source Document	FADEP		Depr. to Date	1/31/2015
Depr. from Date	1/1/2015			
			Post to GL	Yes
Fiscal Year Added	2006		GL Posting System Time	4:15:00 AM
GL Posting Batch	FATRX00000001		GL Posting Trx Date	12/31/2016
GL Posting System Date	1/1/1975			
GL Posting Account	◄ 000-6200-00	►		
Account Description	Depreciation Expense - Furniture & Fixtures			

Trans. Date Stamp	1/1/1975	4:15:00 AM	LESSONUSER1

OK

8. Back on the **Financial Detail Inquiry** screen, scroll down to the end of the transactions. Notice that there are two transaction rows without GL batches. Typically, this indicates that there is a fixed asset transaction waiting to be processed to the GL. If, however, a batch is missing for a transaction that is not at the end of the list it can indicate a transaction that was not sent to the GL:

FA Period	Batch Number	Transaction Acct. Type	Trans. Date	Src Doc.	Amount
2016-011	FATRX00000001	Reserve	1/1/1975	FAXFR-C	($273.76)
2016-011	FATRX00000001	Cost	1/1/1975	FAXFR-C	($1,000.00)
2016-011	FATRX00000001	Cost	1/1/1975	FAXFR-C	$1,000.00
2016-012	FATRX00000001	Depreciation	1/1/1975	FADEP	$11.96
2016-012	FATRX00000001	Reserve	1/1/1975	FADEP	($11.96)
2017-001	FATRX00000002	Depreciation	1/1/1975	FADEP	$11.90
2017-001	FATRX00000002	Reserve	1/1/1975	FADEP	($11.90)
2017-002		Depreciation	1/1/1975	FADEP	$11.90
2017-002		Reserve	1/1/1975	FADEP	($11.90)

How it works...

The **Financial Detail Inquiry** window provides all of the information necessary to trace all of the transactions related to a fixed asset. This is extremely useful for understanding what actually occurred. Any number of items can affect fixed assets including incorrect depreciation settings, wrong asset lives, and problems with the fixed asset calendar. Being able to understand all of the transactions that affect an asset is an important troubleshooting tool that is often overlooked.

Speeding up entry by Copying a Purchase Order

Creating purchase orders can be a time-consuming process. It's not uncommon to have a large number of line items being ordered. Validating part numbers and prices can also take time. Dynamics GP provides a mechanism to create a new purchase order by copying information from an existing purchase order. Unlike copying an inventory item, where the copy icon is on the main window, the process to copy a purchase order is not obvious. Copying a purchase order is the focus of this recipe.

How to do it...

To copy a purchase order:

1. Select **Purchasing** on the Navigation Pane and then click on **Purchase Order Entry** on the **Purchasing** Area Page.

2. Click on **Actions**. Then select **Create and Copy New PO**:

Actions ▾
Delete
Void
Copy PO Lines to Current PO
Create and Copy New PO

3. Use the lookup button (indicated by a magnifying glass) to select a **Source PO Number** to copy from. In the sample company, select **PO0997**. Dynamics GP will fill in the rest of the information:

4. Users can change various settings to fine tune the copy. To demonstrate this deselect **Copy Freight Amount from Source PO**. Also change the **Required Date** to **5/31/2017**:

5. Click on **Copy** to create a new purchase order. The new P.O. can be changed or adjusted just like one that has been entered from scratch:

How it works...

It's unclear why Microsoft chose to hide the copy functionality for purchase orders but it's great that this feature exists. The ability to selectively copy a P.O. and then adjust the end result is a huge time saver. This is a feature that definitely needs to move out of hiding.

Getting control of printing with Named Printers

In the recipe *Reducing posting steps with better Printing Control*, we touched on the edge of the Named Printers functionality by turning off the System Print Dialog. However, there is much more than that to named printers. The idea behind named printers is to allow the assignment of different printers to different functions in Dynamics GP. For example, check printing could be directed to a dedicated check printer or invoices could be automatically sent to a high-speed printer. Even better, these settings are by workstation so there is a geographical component to the setup. Users in one building can point checks to a check printer in their building without interfering with a different set of users in another building. In this recipe, we'll look at setting up Named Printers.

Getting ready

Prior to setting up Named Printers, there is some setup required:

1. Select **Administration** from the Navigation Pane. Then select **Named Printers** from the Area Page under **Setup**. Enter the system password if prompted.

2. Select the checkbox marked **Do Not Display System Print Dialog** and click on **OK** twice:

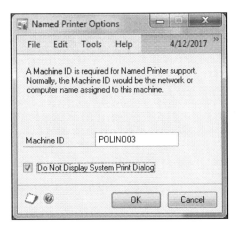

3. Select a default printer for Dynamics GP and click on **OK**.

4. Click on **Save** to assign the default printer to Named Printers:

5. Create a new **Printer ID** named **CHECKS**. Use the lookup button (indicated by a magnifying glass) to select a printer for checks. Click on **Save** and close the window:

How to do it...

To set up Named Printers:

1. Select **Administration** from the Navigation Pane. Then select **Named Printers** from the Area Page under **Setup**.

2. Notice that printers for this **Machine ID** can be set for a specific user and company. For now, we'll leave these alone. Change the **Task Series** to **Purchasing**.

3. Click on the blue **Printer ID** hyperlink to add another printer.

4. In the **Task Description** field find **Payables – Computer Checks/Cheques Printer**. Change **Printer Class** to **System**.

5. Select the printer named **CHECKS** in the **Named Printers** window that opens.

6. Click on **OK** to complete the assignment of a check printer to the check printing function:

When checks are printed via the Computer Checks function in Purchasing, from this computer and by this user, the checks will print to the designated check printer. Any other printer request combination will be sent to the default printer.

How it works...

Named Printers provides fine-grain control over printing functions in Dynamics GP. It provides the ability to control printing by the user, computer, and printer. This ability to control printing provides additional security as well as it can be used to control which reports print to shared printers in the organization. The Named Printers feature can provide huge time saving and cost benefits by preventing printing to less efficient or erroneous printers.

There's more...

Even more control is available via Printer Classes.

Printer Classes

When setting up printers in Named Printers, the option exists to select a Printer Class. Printer Classes are preset options controlling which users can select to print to a printer. For example, an expensive color printer might be limited to only certain users to prevent accidental printing to that printer. The available Printer Classes are:

▶ **System**: These printer IDs are available to all users and companies

▶ **User**: This printer ID is only available to a single user for all companies

▶ **Company**: All users of this company can access this Printer ID

▶ **User & Company**: Printer ID use is restricted to a single user and company

▶ **Any Printer ID**: Any printer available on the workstation can be used

▶ **Manual Selection**: Printer is selected by the user at the time of printing

▶ **None**: Default printer is used

See also

▶ *Reducing posting steps with better Printing Control*

Speeding up month-end processing with Reconcile to GL functionality

One process that can be extremely time consuming is balancing subledgers to the general ledger to ensure that everything in the system is balanced. An out-of-balance situation can occur if users change the GL account on a subledger transaction. For example, if a user changes the payables account on an AP subledger transaction, the AP subledger no longer matches the AP GL account.

Another common occurrence is that users post general ledger transactions to an AP or AR control account without going through the appropriate subledger. This means that the general ledger is updated but not the subledger, resulting in an out-of-balance situation.

Dynamics GP provides a feature to facilitate reconciling accounts payable and accounts receivable to the general ledger. The Reconcile to GL feature uses Microsoft Excel to provide an analysis of matched and unmatched transactions. In this recipe, we'll look at how to use the Reconcile to GL feature to balance subledger accounts to the general ledger. For our example we'll look at balancing accounts payable.

How to do it...

To use the Reconcile to GL feature:

1. In Dynamics GP select **Financial** from the Navigation Pane and select **Reconcile to GL** in the **Routines** area.

2. In the **Reconcile to GL** window set the **Module** to **Payables Management**. Use the lookup button (indicated by a magnifying glass) next to **Accounts** to select account **000-2100-00**. Repeat this process for account **000-2105-00** on the next line. As the sample company tracks discounts, we need both accounts. For the sample company don't change the dates:

3. Click on **Process** to start the reconciliation. Microsoft Excel will open up a reconciliation sheet:

B	C	D	E	F	G	H	I	J	K	L
	Payables Transactions							**General Ledger Transactions**		
	3/1/2017 - 3/31/2017							**3/1/2017 - 3/31/2017**		
										Account
										000-2100-00
			Beginning Balance:	1,807,312.99						Beginning Balance Total:
					Unmatched Transactions					
Vendor ID	Source	Voucher Number	Document Number	On Account Amount	Transaction Date	Journal Entry	Source	Orig. Control Number		Account
					Potentially Matched Transactions					
Vendor ID	Source	Voucher Number	Document Number	On Account Amount	Transaction Date	Journal Entry	Source	Orig. Control Number		Account
SIGNATUR0001	PMCHK00000057	00000000000000247	20029	(4,495.68)	3/9/2017	1333	PMCHK00000057	00000000000000247		000-2100-00
CRUGEREN0001	POIVC00000063	00000000000000446	2061	160.50	3/9/2017	1338	POIVC00000063	RCT1139		000-2100-00
ADVANCED0001	POIVC00000064	00000000000000447	2062	363.31	3/3/2017	1341	POIVC00000064	RCT1141		000-2100-00
CRUGEREN0001	POIVC00000065	00000000000000448	2063	142.30	3/15/2017	1344	POIVC00000065	RCT1143		000-2100-00
ADVANCED0001	POIVC00000066	00000000000000449	2064	455.36	3/14/2017	1347	POIVC00000066	RCT1145		000-2100-00
CRUGEREN0001	POIVC00000067	00000000000000450	2065	28.46	3/23/2017	1350	POIVC00000067	RCT1147		000-2100-00
CRUGEREN0001	POIVC00000069	00000000000000452	2067	90.25	3/31/2017	1356	POIVC00000069	RCT1151		000-2100-00
ADVANCED0001	POIVC00000070	00000000000000453	2068	183.79	3/27/2017	1359	POIVC00000070	RCT1153		000-2100-00
TELESATE0006	POIVC00000071	00000000000000454	2069	18,000.00	3/31/2017	1362	POIVC00000071	RCT1155		000-2100-00
					Matched Transactions					
Vendor ID	Source	Voucher Number	Document Number	On Account Amount	Transaction Date	Journal Entry	Source	Orig. Control Number		Account
CRUGEREN0001	PMCHK00000045	00000000000000235	20018	(1,255.26)	3/5/2017	1300	PMCHK00000045	00000000000000235		000-2100-00
CAPITALP0001	PMCHK00000046	00000000000000238	20021	(12,865.38)	3/4/2017	1306	PMCHK00000046	00000000000000238		000-2100-00
CRUGEREN0001	PMCHK00000049	00000000000000239	051792	(6,927.48)	3/17/2017	1313	PMCHK00000049	00000000000000239		000-2100-00
CRUGEREN0001	PMCHK00000050	00000000000000240	20022	(3,064.76)	3/14/2017	1314	PMCHK00000050	00000000000000240		000-2100-00
CRUGEREN0001	PMCHK00000051	00000000000000241	20023	(1,255.26)	3/15/2017	1315	PMCHK00000051	00000000000000241		000-2100-00
COMVEXIN0001	PMCHK00000052	00000000000000242	20024	(64,825.00)	3/12/2017	1318	PMCHK00000052	00000000000000242		000-2100-00
AMERICAN0001	PMCHK00000053	00000000000000243	20025	(1,063.55)	3/16/2017	1321	PMCHK00000053	00000000000000243		000-2100-00
COMVEXIN0001	PMCHK00000054	00000000000000244	20026	(368.52)	3/26/2017	1324	PMCHK00000054	00000000000000244		000-2100-00
AMERICAN0001	PMCHK00000055	00000000000000245	20027	(419.83)	3/25/2017	1327	PMCHK00000055	00000000000000245		000-2100-00
AMERICAN0001	PMCHK00000056	00000000000000246	20028	(922.50)	3/26/2017	1330	PMCHK00000056	00000000000000246		000-2100-00
AMERICAN0001	PMCHK00000058	00000000000000248	20030	(22.75)	3/30/2017	1336	PMCHK00000058	00000000000000248		000-2100-00
			Ending Balance:	1,721,971.80				Ending Balance:		
								Net Ending Balance:		
Total PM Beginning Balance:	1,807,312.99		Total PM Ending Balance:	1,721,971.80						
Total GL Beginning Balance:	97,124.69		Total GL Ending Balance:	11,673.40						
Difference:	1,710,188.30		Difference:	1,710,298.40						

4. Subledger transactions are on the left and **General Ledger Transactions** on the right. **Unmatched Transactions** are at the top followed by **Potentially Matched Transactions** and **Matched Transactions**. At the bottom is a reconciliation of the differences.

5. Finally, users would use the unmatched and potentially matched information to make adjusting entries in the GL or subledger to correct out-of-balance transactions.

How it works...

The Reconcile to GL feature for AP and AR fills an important role during month-end close. Balancing subledgers to the general ledger is an important step in ensuring the correctness of financial statements. The Reconcile to GL feature in Dynamics GP makes this easier than ever. The use of Microsoft Excel as the balancing mechanism provides a familiar, easy-to-use interface for users.

There's more...

Some firms do a poor job of monthly balancing and find that they are significantly out of balance at year end. Additionally, the Reconcile to GL feature of Dynamics GP only covers accounts payable and accounts receivable. Many companies also need this functionality for other subledgers.

Balancing the year

Whether through inexperience or a lack of oversight it is not unusual to find firms where the subledger and general ledger have been out of balance for most of the year. The best way to approach this problem is to start with the oldest out-of-balance month and work forward one month at a time. Trying to balance the entire year at once requires an overwhelming amount of data and can actually make balancing more difficult.

When AP and AR aren't enough

Although the Reconcile to GL feature of Dynamics GP works well it doesn't address any subledgers except accounts payable and accounts receivable. There is a third-party option named The Closer from Reporting Central. The Closer offers similar reconciliation functionality for AP and AR as well as Inventory, Cash, Sales Order Processing, Cost of Goods Sold, and Accrued Purchases. For companies that require more than simple AR and AP reconciliation, this is a great option. More information about The Closer is available at `http://www.Reporting -Central.com`.

7
Improving Dynamics GP with Hacks

Beyond the features present in Microsoft Dynamics GP, there are ways to use those features to accomplish things never intended—in short, hacks. In this chapter, we'll explore some useful ways to hack existing features to provide improvements, speed things up, and even add a new option or two. In this chapter, we'll look at the following recipes:

- ► Building custom help with Window notes
- ► Using Comments without needing a comment name
- ► Keeping the chart of accounts clean by reactivating Account Segment warnings
- ► Improving clarity by timing Depreciation Posting to the General Ledger
- ► Reducing licensing needs by preventing Multiple Company Logins
- ► Turning on more features with `Dex.ini` settings
- ► Entering and Tracking Use Tax with Credit Card Functionality
- ► Correcting a lost system password by resetting the System Password
- ► Warning the user if *Caps Lock* is on during login
- ► Getting greater journal entry control by clearing recurring batch amounts

Introduction

Hacking computer systems is a time-honored tradition. By hacking I mean finding ways to make a system do more and go farther than its creators ever intended, not using a system in an inappropriate way.

Microsoft Dynamics GP is incredibly flexible. Over the years users have found that there are ways to use Dynamics GP to solve business problems by applying conventional features in unconventional ways. This can include using a different feature to supply missing functionality, applying best practices to improve clarity, exposing hidden settings, or applying some simple code to add functionality to the system.

In this chapter, we'll look at ways to improve the usability of Dynamics GP by hacking the system with a few changes, some unconventional uses of features, and a little free code.

Building custom help with Window notes

Each master record and transaction in Dynamics GP includes the ability to add notes. These notes are attached to the associated record and can be accessed whenever that record is open. Dynamics GP also contains another set of notes. These notes are attached to each window in Dynamics GP and are available whenever that window is open, regardless of the record being used. Window notes are stored at the company level so different Dynamics GP companies can have different notes. Additionally, notes assigned to a window are available to all users who can access that window making them an ideal candidate for alternative uses.

The most common hack for window notes is to provide additional help or specific data entry instructions to users. For example, a note on the **Inventory Maintenance** window could be used to inform users that new nut and bolt inventory items belong to the FASTENERS Class ID, not FIXTURES. Another example would be to use a note on the **Customer Maintenance** window to remind users that new customers from Texas belong to the West region, not to the South. In this recipe, we'll look at setting up custom help using window notes.

How to do it...

To use window notes to set up custom help:

1. In Dynamics GP, select **Sales** from the Navigation Pane. Select **Customer** on the Area Page under **Cards**.

2. Click on the small, white note in the lower right-hand side corner of the window:

3. In the **Note** window enter the following:
   - ❑ **Common States and Regions:**
   - ❑ **Texas – West**
   - ❑ **Virginia – South**
   - ❑ **Tennessee – South**

❑ **Ohio – Midwest**

❑ **Pennsylvania – East**

4. Click on **Attach** to save the note.

5. Notice that the icon changes from an empty white note to a yellow one with writing on it designed to indicate the presence of information:

How it works...

Although Dynamics GP is extremely flexible and customizable there are times when customizing any system to control user behavior provides diminishing returns. Using window notes to provide customized help is one of those in-between measures that makes it easier for users to do their job correctly but requires minimal effort to implement.

The drawbacks to using window notes in this way are that they are difficult to lock down with security. Most users will have access to change notes, not just view them. Additionally, users need to actually click on the icon to view additional help. I have seen cases where custom programming was used to open the note each time the window opens. However, this has its own drawback in that it quickly becomes annoying for users who don't need the extra help.

Window notes don't eliminate the need for training and monitoring but they can make it easier for users to get data entry right.

Using Comments without needing a comment name

Many of the transaction documents in Dynamics GP provide a place for comments that can print on the document. Some common examples of these types of documents include Quotes, Sales Orders, Invoices, and Purchases Orders. Comments were originally intended to be recurring messages and were typically used to thank clients for their business, remind clients of holiday hours, or provide similar standardized messages. Consequently, each comment had a Comment ID allowing users to add a consistent comment to a document with a minimum amount of work. This worked great for standard, recurring comments. Unfortunately, the world in which we live is not standard and it's only occasionally recurring. Users really wanted to provide Ad hoc comments to clarify the specifics of a transaction.

Ad hoc comments can include clarifications to a vendor similar to "Ship the hex head version, not the Phillips head". They can provide information to customers such as "We've shipped 6 of the 10 items requested. The others will ship on Tuesday". In short, almost anything a user could come up with can end up in a comment that needs to appear on the document. The problem with this is that if each comment gets an ID the system is soon overwhelmed with Comment IDs. It becomes easier to contribute to the problem by creating a new ID for each comment than to figure which comment could be reused.

There is an option to create and use comments without assigning a Comment ID. These comments appear on a document as if an ID had been used and users have the option to modify the comment. By creating a comment without an ID this process doesn't pollute the list of actual, recurring comments that a business wants to use. Creating comments without a Comment ID is the focus of this recipe.

How to do it...

To create comments without using a Comment ID:

1. Select **Sales** from the Navigation Pane, and then select **Sales Transaction Entry** under **Transactions**.

2. Click on the right arrow in the lower left to select the first available **Sales Transaction**:

   | ◄ ◄ ► ►| by Document No.   ▼ |

3. Leave the **Comment ID** field blank and click on the blue arrow next to the **Comment ID** field:

   | Comment ID | | 🔍☐→ |

4. In the **Comment** field type **This is a comment without an ID** and click on **OK**:

> **Sales Comment Entry**
>
> File   Edit   Tools   Additional   Help   Debug   4/12/2017
>
> Comment ID
>
> Comment:
> This is a comment without an ID
>
> OK   Cancel

5. Notice that a new indicator appears between the **Comment ID** prompt and the **Comment ID** field to show that there is a comment without an ID:

> Comment ID

6. Any documents that already show comments will include comments entered without an ID. The documents don't have to be changed at all.

How it works...

This recipe is the perfect solution for Ad hoc comments without polluting comment IDs. As a plus, it continues to allow the use of traditional comments with an ID. The biggest problem with this process is that it is hidden so deeply that most users don't find it.

There's more...

This works for all Comment ID boxes including line item comments.

Line Item Comments

Our example showed a transaction-level comment that would appear at the bottom of a document. However, each line in a document such as a Purchase Order or Invoice can also use comments without an ID the same way.

Clicking on a line item in a document and selecting the blue arrow key opens up additional details about that line and exposes another Comment ID field. This works exactly like transaction-level comments except that the comments appear below each line item on the document by default, as shown in the following screenshot:

Keeping the chart of accounts clean by reactivating Account Segment warnings

Dynamics GP includes functionality to automatically name new accounts based on the account segments selected. For example, if a user creates account number 01-4000-000 and the three segments correspond to Company A, Revenue Account, and South Region, Dynamics GP can automatically name the account Company A-Revenue-South. This is a huge time saver, reducing data entry for new accounts. The specifics of this feature are covered in the Chapter 8 recipe *Preventing account selection errors with Chart Segment names*.

If, however, a user keys a segment without an associated description they get an informational message providing the opportunity to add a description. Included in that informational message is the option to turn off the message:

The actual wording of the checkbox is **Do not display this message again** and it really means it. Once this checkbox is selected for a user the feature to allow entry of a segment description on the fly is completely disabled for that user. Additionally, there is no option within Dynamics GP to turn it back on. This can be a real nightmare if the user designated to create accounts accidentally turns this off.

Since Microsoft has forgotten to include a switch to turn this feature back on, administrators will need to hack their way through some simple SQL code to make this available again. Turning Account Segment warnings back on is the focus of this recipe.

How to do it...

To re-enable Account Segment warnings:

1. Open Microsoft SQL Server Management Studio and connect to the SQL Server used for Dynamics GP. Use either a username and password or windows authentication to connect.

   Because of the way that security is implemented between Dynamics GP and SQL Server a Dynamics GP user login will not normally work here. The exception is the sa user, which is also the SQL Server system administrator login:

2. Click on **New Query** and select the appropriate company from the drop-down menu on the top left. The sample company is named **TWO**. In the query area on the right, enter the following script:

   ```
   Delete from SY01401
   where coDefaultType = 13
   ```

   This will enable Account Segment warnings for all users.

3. To turn on Account Segments for a single user add this third line and change myUserID to the appropriate user ID:

   ```
   and USERID = 'myUserID'
   ```

4. Click on **Execute** to run the script:

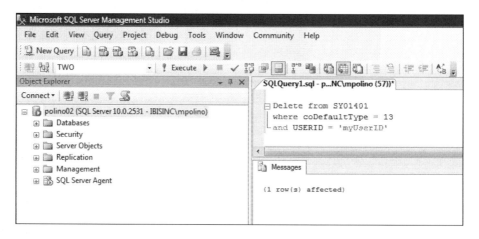

How it works...

Fixing features that the developer left out is what hacking is all about. In this case, Microsoft simply missed the option to turn this feature back on for a user and it can be very painful if the primary account entry user accidently turns it off. Fortunately, an administrator can re-enable the Account Segment warning with just a few lines of SQL code.

See also

▶ *Preventing account selection errors with Chart Segment names*

Improving clarity by timing Depreciation Posting to the General Ledger

Microsoft Dynamics provides a robust Fixed Asset module for tracking and depreciating a company's assets. Part of the Fixed Asset module includes a routine to process asset additions, retirements, and depreciation through to the general ledger. This GL Posting routine sends all of the related asset transactions to the general ledger as a single transaction in a single batch.

When firms make errors with fixed assets it is almost always in the addition or retirement of an asset. The key to preventing errors is to review fixed asset transactions prior to posting to the general ledger. Depreciation amounts are small enough in relation to the value of an asset that depreciation errors for a single asset typically won't be material to the company's financial statements. New assets, however, can represent millions of dollars in value and can affect the correctness of a firm's financials.

Typically, companies have a small number of asset additions and retirements in any given month when compared to the number of assets being depreciated. Even high-growth firms rapidly acquiring assets will quickly have more active, depreciating assets than new assets. Since Dynamics GP aggregates all of the Fixed Asset transactions into a single general transaction it can be difficult to review asset additions and retirements for correctness when they are mixed among hundreds or thousands of depreciation entries waiting to be posted.

Unfortunately, there is no magic code or hidden feature to solve this problem but there is a process that users can follow to ensure that asset additions and retirements are processed separately from depreciation. The process is to create two general ledger transactions, one for depreciation and one for everything else. This makes it much easier to verify the correctness of additions and retirements. In this recipe, we'll look at how to separate the posting of Fixed Asset additions and retirements from Depreciation.

Getting ready

The basic operation of the Fixed Asset module isn't the focus of this recipe so we'll assume that asset additions and retirement transactions have been processed, but that both depreciation and the GL Posting routine have not been run for the month.

How to do it...

To separate fixed asset additions and retirements posting:

1. Before running depreciation for the month, select **Financial** from the Navigation Pane. Select **GL Posting** under the **Routines** and **Fixed Assets** headings on the Area Page.

2. Leave the **Beginning Period** as all zeros (**0000-000**) and set the **Ending Period** to the appropriate period. Usually the Ending Period is the previous or current month. In the sample company use **2017-004**. Click on **Continue**:

3. The resulting GL transaction will have only additions, retirements, and transfers, creating a much smaller number of transactions to review prior to posting:

```
1/14/2010                 FA Posting to General Ledger              10:24:14 PM
                  Batch Number: FATRX00000003   TRX Date: 4/30/2017

                          Additions/Retirements

000-1530-00
    Fleet Vehicles

  Asset ID and Suffix  FA Yr/Period   FA Source Doc.      Amount

   1111-1                 2009/4         FAADD             $250,000.00

000-1530-00                                    Total       $250,000.00
    Fleet Vehicles
```

This process can be segregated even more by sending transactions to the general ledger after processing each type of transaction for additions, retirements, and transfers.

4. Select **Depreciate** on the **Financial** Area Page. Run depreciation as you normally would.

5. Repeat the GL Posting process to process depreciation transactions to the general ledger in a separate batch.

How it works...

Separating non-depreciation transaction posting from the posting of depreciation provides greater clarity to additions, retirements, transfers, and depreciation. Less common transactions are not mixed in with depreciation, making it easier to ensure that asset additions, retirements, and transfers post to the correct accounts.

There's more...

Though this process works consistently depreciation doesn't have to be posted after other transactions. There is another option.

Timing Depreciation posting

The key is that depreciation can be posted before or after other fixed asset transactions are entered, just not in the middle. For example, a company can run and post depreciation at the start of a new month and then enter and post asset additions, retirements, and transfers. Finally, the company can re-run depreciation at month end to depreciate only new and changed assets.

Reducing licensing needs by preventing Multiple Company Logins

Microsoft Dynamics GP is licensed on the basis of concurrent users. This means that if a company has ten user licenses, any ten users can log in at once but the eleventh user is prevented from logging in. Many firms also manage multiple companies in Dynamics GP and users have a tendency to log in to more than one company at a time to make switching between companies faster. However, each company login uses up a concurrent license. In our previous example with ten licenses, if each user logs into two companies simultaneously, only five individuals will actually get to log in.

For companies where the number of actual users is very close to the number of licenses this presents a real problem. I've seen cases where an AP clerk can't log in to print checks and a controller couldn't log in to review accounts because users were logged in to multiple companies. An obvious solution to this problem is to purchase additional licenses. However, that is also an expensive solution. A better option is to prevent users from logging in to multiple companies.

Unfortunately, there is no built-in functionality to prevent users from logging in multiple times so in this recipe we'll turn to a hack from a surprising place—Microsoft.

How to do it...

To prevent users from logging in to multiple Dynamics GP companies simultaneously:

1. Open Internet Explorer and navigate to `http://blogs.msdn.com/ developingfordynamicsgp/archive/2008/ 08/25/preventing-users-from-logging-into-multiple- companies-example.aspx`.

2. Download and save the file `Prevent User Logging In To Multiple Companies.zip` to your desktop:

Example code for v8.0, v9.0 & v10.0 is attached at the bottom of the article.

Please see the "Installation Instructions.txt" file in each version's archive for more information.

Posted: Monday, August 25, 2008 5:16 PM by David Musgrave
Filed under: VBA, ADO

Attachment(s): Prevent User Logging In To Multiple Companies.zip

3. Right-click on the downloaded file and select **Extract**. Then click on the **Extract** button.

4. After the files extract repeat this process with the new file named `v10.00 Prevent User Logging In To Multiple Companies.zip`. Despite the v10.00 designation in the filename, this file works just fine in version 2010.

5. Back in Dynamics GP select **Microsoft Dynamics GP | Tools | Customize | Customization Maintenance**.

6. Click on **Import** and then on **Browse**. Navigate to the location where you extracted the `v10.00 Prevent User Logging In To Multiple Companies.zip` file on the desktop and select the `MicrosoftActiveXDataObjects 2.8 Reference.package` file. Click on **OK** to install.

7. Repeat steps 5 and 6 using the `SwitchCompany.Package` file.

8. Apply this customization to each user's workstation using steps 5, 6, and 7.

9. Once applied, users will be prevented from logging in to multiple companies simultaneously. If they try, users will get a message and an indication of what company they are already logged in to:

Microsoft Dynamics GP

User 'sa' is already logged into company 'Fabrikaboom', login aborted.

OK

How it works...

This hack uses a free, unsupported Visual Basic for Applications (VBA) file created by David Musgrave, a developer at Microsoft. David was kind enough to release this code as a free benefit to the Dynamics GP community.

There's more...

There are some additional things to look out for when cooking up this recipe.

Additional considerations

Since this hack uses a VBA customization, companies will need to be licensed to either build or run customizations in Dynamics GP. For companies requiring a Customization Site Enabler license, it is available for a fee through a Microsoft value added reseller.

If there are any issues with installation there are additional troubleshooting steps in the included `Installation Instructions.txt` file.

Turning on more features with Dex.ini settings

Microsoft Dynamics GP contains a number of features that can't be controlled via the interface. The controls for these features reside in an initialization file known as the Dex.ini file. Dynamics GP loads settings from the Dex.ini file as it starts. The Dex.ini file settings affect only the computer on which the file is installed. This means that the system can behave differently for different users if their Dex.ini files are different.

As an example, Dex.ini file settings can be used to control the date warning that appears when midnight passes, allow the installation of update files without a warning, and dramatically speed up the export of SmartLists to Excel. If a particular setting is not present in the Dex.ini file a user can simply add it to the end of the file.

If there are errors in the Dex.ini file it can prevent Dynamics GP from opening. So users should make a copy of the Dex.ini file before making changes. In this recipe, we'll look at how to apply some of the most common and useful Dex.ini settings.

Getting ready

Before we can change Dex.ini settings we need to open up the file. To open and modify the Dex.ini file:

1. Open the Notepad utility provided with all copies of Microsoft Windows.

2. In Notepad select **File | Open**. Navigate to the **GP** folder. Typically, this is found in c:\Program Files\Microsoft Dynamics\GP.

3. Open the **Data** folder and select **Dex.ini** to open the file. (If the Dex.ini file is not visible type ***.ini** in the **File name** field to show files without a .txt extension):

```
Dex.ini - Notepad
File  Edit  Format  View  Help
[General]
Initial=FALSE
Synchronize=FALSE
AutoDisplayUpdate=TRUE
DynHelpPath=C:\Program Files\Microsoft Dynamics\GP\
DexHelpPath=C:\Program Files\Microsoft Dynamics\GP\
Word Macro File=C:\Program Files\Microsoft
Dynamics\GP\Data\Letters\wordIntegration.dot
Letters Directory=C:\Program Files\Microsoft Dynamics\GP\Data\Letters\
Workstation=WINDOWS
Workstation2=Windows
WindowMax=TRUE
BTInterface=NOLoad
Pathname=DYNAMICS/dbo/
FileHandler=SQL
SQLQueryTimeout=0
SQLProcsTimeout=0
DPSInstance=1
BuildSQLMessages=FALSE
OLEPath=C:\Program Files\Microsoft Dynamics\GP\Data\Notes\
ReportDictionaryPath=C:\Program Files\Microsoft Dynamics\GP\Data\
FormDictionaryPath=C:\Program Files\Microsoft Dynamics\GP\Data\
UpdateLogin=https://mbsupdates.microsoft.com/taxupdate/login.aspx
SQLLogSQLStmt=FALSE
SQLLogODBCMessages=FALSE
```

How to do it...

To demonstrate how to change the settings in the `Dex.ini` file we'll start by turning on an alternative setting to dramatically speed up exporting SmartLists to Excel and then we'll look at other common settings:

1. To force Dynamics GP to export SmartLists to Excel using the much faster recordset method instead of the default line-by-line process navigate to the `Dex.ini` file and add the line `SmartlistEnhancedExcelExport=TRUE` to the bottom of the `Dex.ini` file.

2. To force Dynamics GP to always open in a full screen navigate to the `Dex.ini` file, find the setting named **WindowMax**, and set it to `WindowMax=True`.

3. To suppress sounds in Dynamics GP, but not other applications, find the setting **SuppressSound** and set it to `SuppressSound=True`.

4. Prevent the warning that appears when adding new code or modules to Dynamics GP by finding **AutoInstallChunks** and setting it to `AutoInstallChunks=True`.

5. One of the problems that occur when exporting Report Writer based reports is that long sets of data wrap to the next line in the export. This makes opening and analyzing exported data in Excel difficult. To prevent text report lines from wrapping when exporting find the Dex.ini setting named **ExportOneLineBody** and set it to `ExportOneLineBody=True`.

6. In the chapter 6 recipe, *Reducing posting steps with better Printing Control*, we looked at how to turn off the print dialogue box via the interface. The same result can be accomplished by finding the **NoPrintDialogs** setting and changing it to `NoPrintDialogs=True`.

7. Finally, when the computer time passes midnight Dynamics GP displays a message indicating that the date has changed and asking the user if they want to change the date in Dynamics GP. This message can be turned off by setting `SuppressChangeDateDialog=True`. The date in the open Dynamics GP session won't automatically change to the next day, the warning is simply suppressed.

8. When finished, select **File | Save** to save the `Dex.ini` file and restart Dynamics GP to see the changes.

There's more...

These settings are just a sample of common changes that can be made via the `Dex.ini` file. There are lot more settings available.

Additional Dex.ini settings

- ▶ `OLEPath=\\server\folder\ole`: This sets the path for linked and embedded files and should be the same for all users. When using a Universal Naming Convention path, such as `\\server\`, the complete folder structure must exist. Dynamics GP will not create it with the first note. If a mapped drive is used, such as `f:\`, the folder structure does not have to be created beforehand.

- ▶ `ShowAdvancedMacroMenu=True`: This setting turns on an additional menu for working with macros.

- ▶ `DPSInstance=1`: This setting allows the use of multiple process servers on a single physical machine. Process servers can be used to move the load of certain functions, such as posting, off a user's machine and on to a central process server. More information about this setting is available to users with access to CustomerSource at `https://mbs.microsoft.com/knowledgebase/KBDisplay.aspx?WTNTZSMN WUKNTMMYVTQUUXNNZOUKYPPPYVKXPYMRVTVZYYQRKNWPNURWQWYMSQPR`

- ▶ `SampleDateMsg=False`: This setting prevents the date warning that appears when the sample company is opened in Dynamics GP. However, the sample date is still set to 4/12/2017.

- ▶ `SampleDateMMDDYYYY=00000000`: This prevents the date warning in the sample company and sets the sample company date to the current date.

- ▶ `SampleDateMMDDYYYY=03302010`: This prevents the date warning in the sample company and sets the date to the date entered in the setting. In this case, March 30, 2010.

See also

- ▶ *Troubleshooting issues with a Dex SQL log*
- ▶ *Reducing posting steps with better Printing Control*

Entering and Tracking Use Tax with Credit Card Functionality

Use Tax is a form of self-reported sales tax. Companies in the United States who purchase items not intended for resale are typically required to pay sales tax. If they are not charged sales tax at the time of purchase they are required to report and remit use tax on these items.

Dynamics GP is well equipped to deal with sales tax but use tax presents more of a challenge. Essentially, use tax needs to be applied to an accounts payable transaction but the payment of use tax is sent to a taxing authority, not to the transaction vendor. A common way to accomplish this in Dynamics GP is to use the built-in credit card functionality to shift the use tax liability from the vendor to the taxing authority.

In this recipe, we'll use the sample company and look at hacking credit card functionality to enter and track use tax.

Getting ready

Before we start we need to set up a use tax detail and a credit card for a taxing authority. To set up a use tax detail:

1. Select **Administration** from the Navigation Pane. Select **Tax Details** from the Area Page under **Setup | Company**.

2. Type **IL USE TAX** in the **Tax Detail ID** field and set **Type** to **Purchases**.

3. Set the **Account** field to **000-6630-00** and the **Percentage** to 7%. Click on **Save** to continue:

![Tax Detail Maintenance window showing Tax Detail ID "IL USE TAX", Type "Purchases", Account 000-6630-00, Description "IL State Sales Tax Expense", Based On "Percent of Sale/Purchase", Round "Up to the Next Currency Decimal Digit", Percentage 7.00000%]

Part two of the setup is creating a credit card to "pay" the use tax amount and transfer the liability for payment from the vendor to the taxing authority. To set up a use tax credit card:

1. Select **Administration** from the Navigation Pane. Select **Credit Cards** from the Area Page under **Setup | Company**.

2. Name the credit card **IL Use Tax** and select the **Used by Company** checkbox.

3. Click on **Credit Card** and set the **Vendor ID** to **ILSTATE0001**:

![Credit Card Setup window showing Card Name "IL Use Tax", Used by Company checked, Credit Card selected, Vendor ID ILSTATE0001]

4. Click on **Save** to finish the setup.

How to do it...

Now that we've completed the use tax setup let's see how to apply use tax to a transaction:

1. Select **Purchasing** from the Navigation Pane. Select **Transaction Entry** from the Area Page under **Transactions**.

2. Use the lookup button (indicated by a magnifying glass) next to **Vendor ID** to select **ACETRAVE0001**.

3. Press _Tab_ to move to the **Document Number** field and type **1234**:

Payables Transaction Entry								□ □ 🖾
File Edit Tools Options Help Debug						sa Fabrikam, Inc. 4/12/2017		
💾 Save	✕ Delete	⊷ Post	🖨 Print					
Voucher No.	00000000000000474			Intercompany	Batch ID			
Document Type:	Invoice				Doc. Date	4/12/2017		
Description								
Vendor ID	ACETRAVE0001			Currency ID	Z-US$			
Name	A Travel Company			Document Number	1234			
Address ID	PRIMARY			P.O. Number				
Remit-To ID	REMIT TO			Shipping Method	OVERNIGHT			
Payment Terms	Net 30			Tax Schedule ID	COMPANYPUR			

4. Move to the **Purchases** field and enter **$1,000.00**. Press _Tab_ to move to the **Tax** field and click on the blue arrow next to it to open the **Payables Tax Entry** window:

Purchases	$1,000.00
Trade Discount	$0.00
Freight	$0.00
Miscellaneous	$0.00
Tax	$0.00
Total	$1,000.00

5. In the **Payables Tax Entry** window use the lookup button (indicated by a magnifying glass) to select the tax detail **IL USE TAX** replacing the existing tax detail named **USEXMT+PSONO** that defaults from the vendor. Click on **OK** to return to the payables transaction:

Payables Tax Entry				□ □ 🖾
File Edit Tools Options Help Debug				sa Fabrikam, Inc. 4/12/2017
Type	Invoice			
Document Number	1234			
Pre-Tax Amount		$1,000.00		
Tax Detail ID	Total Purchases	Total Taxable Purchases		Tax Amount
Description		Account		Percent/Amount
IL USE TAX	$1,000.00		$1,000.00	$70.00
	$0.00		$0.00	$0.00

6. Now that tax has been applied to the transaction, if we leave it like this, the vendor will get paid $1,070. That won't work since we actually owe the vendor $1,000 and we owe the Illinois taxing authority $70. To fix this, press *Tab* to move to the **Credit Card** field and enter **$70.00**:

Purchases	$1,000.00		1099 Amount	$0.00
Trade Discount	$0.00		Cash	$0.00 →
Freight	$0.00		Check	$0.00 →
Miscellaneous	$0.00		Credit Card	$70.00 →
Tax	$70.00 →		Terms Disc Taken	$0.00
Total	$1,070.00		On Account	$1,070.00

7. Press *Tab* to move off the **Credit Card** field and the **Payables Credit Card Entry** window will open. Use the lookup button (indicated by a magnifying glass) to select **IL Use Tax** as the **Card Name**. Click on **OK** to continue:

Payables Credit Card Entry					
File	Edit	Tools	Options	Help	Debug

Card Name	IL Use Tax
Receipt Number	CREDIT CARD
Date	04122017
Payment Number	00000000000000475

OK

Notice that the **On Account** field is now **$1,000**. This is the amount due to the vendor. When this transaction is posted two AP vouchers will actually be created, one to Ace Travel for $1,000 and one to the Illinois taxing authority for $70. At month end when a check is generated to the Illinois taxing authority, each use tax voucher is included in the check, providing an effective audit trail for use tax transactions.

How it works...

Combining sales tax and credit card functionality to solve a use tax need is a perfect example of a useful hack. The vendor ends up being paid the right amount and so does the taxing authority. In addition, the expense side of the tax doesn't have to go to a tax expense account. The account can be changed to apply to the same account as the purchase to reflect the true cost of the transaction.

Because this is a hack it's not perfect. Payments to the vendor are overstated by the tax amount because the tax wasn't actually paid to the vendor. This could result in an incorrect 1099 for vendors due one at tax time. The 1099 amounts can be adjusted on each transaction, but this is often missed. Generally though, these issues are minor compared to benefits of applying use tax to transactions.

Correcting a lost system password by resetting the System Password

Part of the security matrix of Dynamics GP is the System Password. The system password provides another layer of protection after users have already logged in to Dynamics GP. Certain processes such as changing security settings or setup options may require an additional password known as the System Password. Even if a user has appropriate rights to set up options they can't changes those options without the system password.

Although the use of a system password is technically optional, it is typically used in Dynamics GP implementations. In many environments it is entered very infrequently and typically only by administrators. Consequently, the system password can be lost or forgotten as people leave the company or change roles. Imagine how painful it could be to explain that security can't be changed because the system password has been lost!

Fortunately, there is a process available for administrators with access to SQL Server to reset the administrator password. In this recipe, we'll look at how to do just that.

How to do it...

To reset the system password:

1. Open **Microsoft SQL Server Management Studio** and connect to the SQL Server used for Dynamics GP. Enter a username and password or use windows authentication to connect.

   Because of the way that Dynamics GP maintains security with SQL Server a Dynamics GP username can't be used here. The only exception is the SQL system administrator (sa) user.

2. Click on the **New Query** button. Select the **DYNAMICS** database from the drop-down menu on the top left. Enter the following script in the code area on the right:

   ```
   Use Dynamics
   Go
   Update SY02400 Set Password = 0X00202020202020202020202020202020
   ```

3. Click on **Execute** to run the script. This resets the system password:

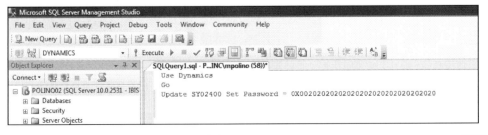

4. Open **Microsoft Dynamics GP** and select **Administration** from the Navigation Pane. Select **System Password** from the Area Page under **System**.

5. Enter a new system password. Re-enter the new system password as a confirmation and click on **OK** to save.

How it works...

The long line of strange numbers after `Set Password` simply sets the password back to blank. The password isn't encrypted, it's simply masked. With enough time, energy, and access to a company's SQL Server it would be possible to decode the masking. Then again, if a troublemaker has access to a firm's SQL Server, they don't need the system password to make a mess. This tip belongs with a company's database administrator. Ordinary users should be prevented from running queries that update information via SQL.

Warning the user if Caps Lock is on during login

Login passwords for Dynamics GP are case sensitive and limited to three tries. This means that the words "password" and "Password" are viewed as completely different when logging in because of the capital "P" in Password. After three failed login attempts Dynamics GP closes and the user has to restart before trying to login again. When a user accidently has the *Caps Lock* button on it almost always leads to failed logins and user frustration.

In recognition of this Patrick Roth, in Developer Support at Microsoft, wrote a VBA utility that checks for *Caps Lock* activation and warns the user if it is on during login. He made the utility freely available to the community via the Developing for Dynamics GP blog.

In this recipe, we'll look at deploying and using this utility to warn users if *Caps Lock* is on.

How to do it...

To warn users if *Caps Lock* is on during Login:

1. Open Internet Explorer and navigate to: `http://blogs.msdn.com/ developingfordynamicsgp/archive/2009/ 07/22/determine-if-the-caps-lock-button-is-enabled-on- password-entry.aspx`

2. Download and save the file `Login_Password_Warning.zip` to your desktop:

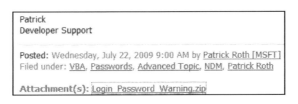

Patrick
Developer Support

Posted: Wednesday, July 22, 2009 9:00 AM by Patrick Roth [MSFT]
Filed under: VBA, Passwords, Advanced Topic, NDM, Patrick Roth

Attachment(s): Login_Password_Warning.zip

3. Right-click on the downloaded file and select **Extract**. Then click on the **Extract** button.

4. Back in Dynamics GP select **Microsoft Dynamics GP | Tools | Customize | Customization Maintenance**.

5. Click on **Import** and then on **Browse**. Navigate to the location where you extracted the Login_Password_Warning.zip file on the desktop and select the Login_Password_Warning.Package file. Click on **OK** to install:

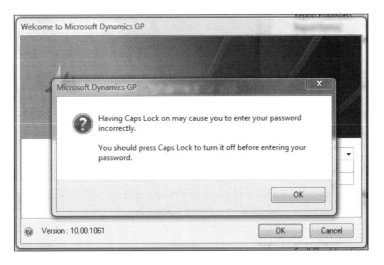

6. This customization will need to be applied to each user's workstation by repeating steps 4 and 5.

7. Once applied a user will be warned if the *Caps Lock* button is on when logging in:

How it works...

Like the *Reducing licensing needs by preventing Multiple Company Logins* recipe earlier in this chapter, this hack uses a free, unsupported Visual Basic for Applications file. The package file will need to be applied to each user's computer for the *Caps Lock* warning to appear. However, that is a small price to pay for a recipe that significantly reduces user frustration.

There's more...

There are some additional things to look out for when cooking up this recipe.

Additional considerations

Since this hack uses a Visual Basic for Applications (VBA) customization companies will need to be licensed to either build or run customizations in Dynamics GP. For companies that require a Customization Site Enabler license, it is available for a fee through a Microsoft value added reseller.

See also

> ► *Reducing licensing needs by preventing Multiple Company Logins*

Getting greater journal entry control by clearing recurring batch amounts

For years Dynamics GP has provided a feature called Quick Journal. Quick Journals allow users to set up a journal entry shell where the accounts remain the same but users can change the amounts each time they create an entry.

The Quick Journals feature is great in principal for transactions where only the amounts change regularly, but it has a number of flaws. Specifically, the transactions can't be placed in batches and they can't be controlled with batch approval. This has led many companies to choose not to use Quick Journals.

The recurring batch functionality in Dynamics GP provides the batch and approval functionality that many companies need but until version 2010 the only option to change the amounts was to overwrite each line. This process left a lot of room for user error making it an imperfect solution as well.

Dynamics GP 2010 introduces the ability to clear the amounts from a recurring batch after it is posted. This allows a user to build a journal entry but not be locked into the same amounts each time. It also allows the use of batch approval.

Let's see how to clear recurring batches in this recipe.

How to do it...

To set up recurring batches to clear after posting:

1. Select **Financial** from the Navigation Pane and then **Batches** under **Transactions**.
2. In the **Batch ID** field enter **TEST**.
3. Set **Origin** to **General Entry**.
4. Change **Frequency** to **Monthly** to set up a recurring batch.
5. Select the checkbox marked **Clear Recurring Amounts**:

6. Click on **Transactions** to add recurring journal entries.

After the recurring batch is posted the amounts will clear allowing users to enter new amounts the next time.

See also

▶   *Getting control of accruals and deferrals with Recurring GL batches*

8
Preventing Errors in Dynamics GP

Microsoft Dynamics GP is a robust **Enterprise Resource Planning** (**ERP**) system. However, any software system is vulnerable to the possibility of errors. Errors can be caused by user actions, software bugs, network issues, hardware failures, or other sources. In this chapter, we'll look at some ways to prevent errors in Dynamics GP by:

- Preventing posting errors by managing Batch dates
- Reducing out-of-balance problems with Allow Account Entry
- Ensuring entry in the correct company by warning about Test Companies
- Protecting Dynamics GP with key security settings
- Providing clean vendor information by properly closing Purchase Orders
- Protecting against information loss by printing Fixed Asset Reports
- Preventing account selection errors with Chart Segment names
- Ensuring proper year-end closing by checking Posting Types
- Preventing sales of Discontinued Inventory
- Correcting errors by backing out, correcting, and copying Journal Entries

Introduction

The longevity and popularity of Microsoft's Dynamics GP Enterprise Resource Planning software is a testament to the system's robustness. However, any system is vulnerable to errors. There are times when users make entry mistakes, network outages occur, and computer hardware fails. Any of these events can cause errors in Dynamics GP. For a Dynamics GP administrator, some of the most common and most controllable errors are those related to user activities. For example, an administrator can't control when a network switch is going to fail but they can ensure that proper security is in place to prevent users from deleting tables.

Preventing errors frees up administrator and user time so they can focus on more important things. In this chapter, we'll look at some common setup and procedural changes that administrators and users can make to help prevent errors in Dynamics GP. Additionally, we'll take a look at how to fix erroneous transactions that managed to make it to the general ledger.

Preventing posting errors by managing Batch dates

In most modules, Microsoft Dynamics GP provides the option to post transactions individually or to collectively post a group of transactions in a batch. The common best practice when implementing Dynamics GP is to use Batch Posting, not individual transaction posting.

The reasoning behind this preference is that batches and batch posting provide a number of benefits over transactional posting. These benefits include the ability to save transactions without posting them, improved error handling, and the ability to post multiple transactions or multiple batches at once. Additionally, batches can be used to control the date that transactions are posted on making it easy to ensure that transactions are posted in the right period.

In this recipe, we will look at batch naming and posting techniques along with error handling options designed to minimize posting errors.

Getting ready

To set up the process to post transactions by batch:

1. In Dynamics GP select **Administration** from the Navigation Pane. Select **Posting** under the **Posting** heading in the **Setup** section on the **Administration** Area Page.

2. Select the **Series** to change the settings for. For our example, select **Purchasing**.

3. Select a posting **Origin**. In this example, select **Payables Trx Entry** to control posting settings for accounts payable voucher entry:

[Posting Setup window]

Posting Setup

File   Edit   Tools   Additional   Help   Debug   sa Fabrikam, Inc. 4/12/2017

Series: Purchasing ▼   Origin: Payables Trx Entry ▼

Create a Journal Entry Per:

☑ Post to General Ledger   ◉ Transaction
☑ Post Through General Ledger Files   ◯ Batch   ☐ Use Account Settings

☐ Allow Transaction Posting   Posting Date From: ◉ Batch   ◯ Transaction
☐ Include Multicurrency Info   If Existing Batch: ◯ Append   ◉ Create New

4. Deselect the **Allow Transaction Posting** checkbox to force posting to the general ledger by batch.

5. Select the **Transaction** radio button under **Create a Journal Entry Per** to avoid rolling up transactions in the general ledger.

   Sending batches of subledger transactions to the general ledger as a single transaction has its roots in ledger paper accounting. This practice moved to software when disk space was at a premium. It is almost never needed now and complicates tracing subledger transactions through the general ledger.

6. Click on **Save**, then on **OK** to finish.

How to do it...

To set up a batch using best practices:

1. Select **Purchasing** from the Navigation Pane. Select **Batches** under the **Transactions** section on the **Purchasing** Area Page.

2. Name the batch with your initials followed by that day's date. My example batch is named **MDP-2010-02-17**:

[Payables Batch Entry window]

Payables Batch Entry

File   Edit   Tools   Help   Debug   sa Fabrikam, Inc. 4/12/2017

💾 Save   ✎ Clear   ✖ Delete   📥 Post   🖨

Batch ID   MDP-2010-02-17 🔍📄   Origin: Payables Trx Entry ▼
Comment

Frequency: Single Use ▼   Posting Date   2/17/2010 📅
                                      Check Date   0/0/0000

Recurring Posting   0
Days to Increment   0   Checkbook ID   UPTOWN TRUST 🔍
                                      Currency ID

- ❏ By naming batches this way users searching for a batch will see the available batches sorted in order by user initials and then date.
- ❏ Typically, firms either let users post their own batches or they use a designated individual/group to post batches from multiple users:
  - ❏ If users post their own batches, start the batch name with your initials followed by the date such as MDP-2010-02-17. This will cluster a user's batches together when posting, making it easier to post multiple batches for a single user.
  - ❏ If a different individual posts transactions for multiple users, start the batch name with the date followed by the initials such as 2010-02-17-MDP. This clusters batches together by date making it easier to select the right batches across multiple users.
- ❏ Dates in batch names should start with the year and then the period such as 2010-02. This naming convention clusters batches together when approaching year end or period end. For example, it's typical at period end to have some left over transactions from the previous period and new transactions for the current period. Starting dates with the year and period helps ensure that users select the correct batch to post.
- ❏ Single-digit periods and days should use a zero in front as Dynamics GP sees batch names as text. Not using a leading zero will cause a batch for period 10 to come before a batch for period 9.

3. Select **Payables Trx Entry** in the **Origin** field.

4. Set **Frequency** to **Single Use** for our example. Recurring batches have a frequency other than single use (monthly, weekly, and so on). They are designed to be posted multiple times. For recurring batches, the following recommendations apply:
   - ❏ Start recurring batches with the letter 'z' to cluster them at the bottom of lookup windows. It may make sense to date recurring batches with their end date instead of creation date to make it easy to identify when this batch will stop recurring.
   - ❏ Provide a complete description and notes for recurring batches since the rational for the recurring batch may fade from memory over time.
   - ❏ If there are multiple transactions in a recurring batch ensure that they are all designed to stop repeating at the same time.

5. Enter the **Posting Date** for the batch following these recommendations:

    □ **One period per batch**: Users shouldn't mix transactions from multiple periods in a single batch. This makes it impossible to post the transactions in the proper period since the entire batch will post in one period.

    The only exception to this is the general ledger (GL) batches. General ledger batches always use the date on the transaction for posting. There is no option to post GL batches by date.

    □ **Post using the batch date**: Posting using the batch date ensures that all of the transactions in the batch post using the same date and the date is visible with a glance at the batch. This contrasts with individual posting where the posting data could be different on each transaction.

    For transaction posting the true posting date is hidden behind an expansion arrow on the date field making it difficult to validate the posting date on multiple transactions.

6. Click on the **Transactions** button to add transactions to a batch.

7. Once transactions are entered batches can be posted from the same window. When posting batches:

    □ Non-recurring batches should disappear when posted. In the event that this doesn't happen users need to select the printer icon in the upper right to print the batch edit list either to paper or to the screen. Printing the batch edit list prior to posting is a best practice but this process can be impractical for batches with a large number of transactions.

    □ The Transaction Edit List will show batch-level errors at the top and transaction-level errors below any problem transactions. The most common batch-level error is a closed fiscal period preventing batches from posting. For transaction-level errors missing accounts or account related problems are seen most often.

❑ Batches that contain errors may fail posting and end up in Batch Recovery. The **Batch Recovery** window is found in the **Administration** Area Page under **Routines**. Batch Recovery will either resolve minor errors and continue the posting or return the batch to a state where a Transaction Edit List can be printed and reviewed for corrections:

How it works...

Following these batch-level posting techniques simplifies batch management by providing a standard process and naming convention for all users. Posting errors are reduced by managing posting dates at the batch level and ensuring that batches only cover a single period.

Years of experience have shown consultants and advanced users that transactions posted in a batch have a better chance of recovery in the event of a catastrophic posting error such as a network outage during posting. This isn't acknowledged explicitly in any of the software documentation but there is a wealth of painful stories illustrating that transactions posted by batch recover from errors better than individually posted transactions.

See also

▶ *Getting control of accruals and deferrals with Recurring GL batches*

▶ *Controlling Posting Dates when not posting by batch*

▶ *Preventing entry of wrong dates by Closing Periods*

Reducing out-of-balance problems with Allow Account Entry

Balancing subledgers such as accounts payable or accounts receivable to the general ledger (GL) can be a time-consuming process at period end. A common reason that a subledger doesn't match the corresponding account in the general ledger is that a user has made an entry directly to the general ledger.

Transactions in Dynamics GP generally flow down from subledgers into the general ledger. With rare exceptions, transactions made in the general ledger do not flow back upstream to a subledger. This means that when users make an entry directly to a general ledger account the information doesn't flow back up to a related subledger, resulting in an out-of-balance situation.

A scenario like this is easily prevented by disabling an often overlooked feature known as Allow Account Entry. Disabling the Allow Account Entry setting prevents entries directly to the general ledger for certain accounts. When this feature is deactivated for an account transactions must flow from a subledger. Direct entries to that account from the general ledger are blocked by the system.

In this recipe, we will look at how to deactivate the Allow Account Entry feature and we'll see how it works in practice.

How to do it...

To require transactions to flow through a subledger for a particular account:

1. Select **Financial** from the Navigation Pane and then select **Accounts** under the **Cards** section.
2. Use the lookup button (indicated by a magnifying glass) to select account **000-2100-00**, the Accounts Payable account in the sample company.
3. Deselect the checkbox marked **Allow Account Entry** and click on **Save** to finish:

To illustrate what happens when this feature is deactivated for an account:

1. Back on the **Financial** Area Page select **General** under **Transactions**.

2. Use the lookup button (indicated by a magnifying glass) in the **Account** field to select account **000-2100-00** in the account field on the bottom of the window.

3. Dynamics GP responds with a message that **Account 000-2100-00 does not allow account entry.**

How it works...

This feature is simple to implement but extremely powerful. A simple checkbox can dramatically improve the process of balancing transactions at period end. There are a number of accounts that can benefit from turning off Allow Account Entry. Common accounts that are prime candidates for preventing direct general ledger entry include Cash, Accounts Payable, Accounts Receivable, Inventory, Payroll Accounts, Fixed Assets, Accumulated Depreciation, and Depreciation Expense.

There's more...

There can be valid reasons for adjusting some of these accounts in the general ledger so administrators need to understand the process to accomplish this.

Adjustments

There are times when an adjustment to one of these accounts is needed in the general ledger. Perhaps a network outage happened during posting that resulted in a transaction properly posting to the subledger but not moving to the general ledger. In a scenario like this, an administrator can temporarily select the checkbox to allow account entry and deselect the checkbox as soon as the correction is posted. This is an occasional inconvenience when compared to the benefits of smoother monthly balancing. Because of the potential effects on balancing, the ability to adjust this setting should be limited to select users.

See also

▶ *Speeding up month-end processing with Reconcile to GL functionality*

Ensuring entry in the correct company by warning about Test Companies

Most companies using Dynamics GP set up a test company. This is normally a copy of the live, production GP database and may reside on its own server. A test company may be used for testing things such as new processes, modules, or even test upgrades if it resides on a separate server.

A test company is used in addition to the sample company because it contains a copy of the firm's actual data. Consequently, they have different uses. For instance, the sample company is great for learning about new modules that a firm is not yet licensed for since unlicensed modules aren't available in a test company. A test company is great for trying out the process to close a year or providing training to new users.

A common problem occurs when a user mistakenly logs into the test company and enters a transaction. When they find their mistake they have to enter it again in the production database. Even more problems can occur if a user mistakenly enters a test transaction in the production company.

Dynamics GP provides a feature to help prevent these scenarios from occurring. There is a small trick that can be used to warn users when they log in to a test company. This is similar to the message that users get when they open the sample company. Warning users when entering a test company is the focus of this recipe.

How to do it...

To warn users that they are opening a test company:

1. Sign in to a test company in Microsoft Dynamics GP. This recipe will not work with the sample company because of the way it is set up.

2. In Dynamics GP select **Administration** from the Navigation Pane. Select **Company** under the **Setup** and **Company** headings on the **Administration** Area Page.

3. Next to the company name in the **Company Name** field type **<TEST>** in all caps:

Company Setup				
File Edit Tools Help Debug			sa Fabrikaboom <TEST> 2/3/2010	
Company Name	Fabrikaboom <TEST>		Company ID	THREE
Address ID	PRIMARY	Q *i* ⅋	User Defined 1	

4. Click on **Save** to save the setting.

5. Restart Microsoft Dynamics GP and log in to the same test company.

6. A warning message will appear alerting the user that this is a test company:

```
Microsoft Dynamics GP

  (i)    This company is set up for testing only. Do not use this company
         when processing live data.


                              [ OK ]
```

How it works...

Warning users about test companies is a great way to prevent errors. I've seen it be a real life saver when a user realized that they didn't see the warning and were entering test data in the production company. This recipe is so simple to implement that everyone should use it.

See also

▸   *Coloring windows by company*

Protecting Dynamics GP with key security settings

Security is an important part of any ERP system and Dynamics GP provides a robust security model that rolls up individual item access into tasks and tasks into roles. Roles can then be applied to individual users, providing fine grain control of security with minimal work after the initial setup.

While the setup and maintenance of security in Dynamics GP could fill a book by itself, there are a couple of critical settings that every administrator needs to be aware of.

Dynamics GP security contains a master switch that turns all security on or off. The original purpose of this switch was to allow setup and testing of the system while security was still being configured. Then, like Chevy Chase's Christmas lights in the movie National Lampoon's Christmas Vacation, a master switch could be flipped and security would be active. As Dynamics GP has matured it has become easier to add users to a Power User role, giving them access to everything in the system during setup and testing while leaving security active. The master security switch still remains and administrators need to ensure that it is on.

Located below the security master switch is an Account Security switch. Often users think that if security is on, turning on account security must mean more security. What account security does is it limits access to accounts based on an organizational structure that needs to be set up first. If an organization structure is not set up all users are denied access to the chart of accounts and it appears that the chart of accounts has been deleted. Few checkboxes in Dynamics GP can induce the stomach-dropping fear that comes with inadvertently selecting the **Account Security** checkbox. This is easily one of the most panicky support calls I see and certainly it is the one with the easiest fix.

Setting up security and account security aren't recipes, they are more like Thanksgiving dinners. For this recipe, we'll trim it down to a snack and show how to ensure that security is on and account security is off.

How to do it...

To activate security and deactivate account security in Dynamics GP:

1. Select **Administration** from the Navigation Pane. Select **Company** under the **Setup** and **Company** headers on the **Administration** Area Page.

2. Select the **Security** checkbox on the lower right to activate security. If it is already marked, security is on; congratulations!

3. Below that is the **Account Security** checkbox. Simply deselect the checkbox to ensure that account security is off.

How it works...

These are two very basic settings that often trip up administrators. It's maddening to see a very detailed security model with a lot of work put into it and then find the **Security** checkbox deselected. Don't even think about the effect on an administrator's career if an auditor finds this checkbox deselected. It's also career limiting to have the CFO asking where the chart of accounts has disappeared to because someone accidently turned on account security. Don't misunderstand, account security is a great feature; it's just not one that should be turned on lightly.

There's more...

Given the power of these checkboxes, access to them should be secured as well. For complicated security setups and additional security features consider third-party solutions.

Security for Security

The **Security** and **Account Security** checkboxes are powerful. Once they are set up correctly, it is important that security be restricted to the **Company Setup** window to prevent a user from disabling security entirely by simply deselecting a checkbox.

Security Solutions

There are several third-party solutions that build on Dynamics GP security making security management easier and adding additional features. For example, FastPath's Config AD product synchronizes user passwords with Windows Active Directory passwords to allow multiple single sign on options. Additionally, Config AD provides an interface outside of Dynamics GP to assign security roles to users. This allows a central security manager to assign Dynamics GP security to users without using up a Dynamics GP license or providing excessive access to the security manager. More information is available at http://www.gofastpath.com.

Providing clean vendor information by properly closing Purchase Orders

It's not unusual for a Purchase Order to be left open in Dynamics GP due to a vendor's inability to deliver goods. However, when the time comes to close an incomplete Purchase Order, too many users simply change the P.O. line quantity to match the quantity delivered and close the P.O. The problem with this process is that it reduces visibility into the performance of a vendor. By changing the quantity ordered there is no way to track the fact that the vendor didn't deliver the goods.

A better way to close a Purchase Order is to put any undelivered amounts in the **Quantity Canceled** line. This makes performance information available to SmartLists and Excel reports, making it possible to analyze the performance of a vendor over time. As an example, an analysis may show that it may make sense for a firm to pay a little more to a reliable supplier instead of dealing with the frustration of product outages.

In this recipe, we'll look at the right way to close a partially received Purchase Order using the sample company.

How to do it...

To properly close a partially received Purchase Order:

1. Select **Purchasing** from the Navigation Pane. Select **Purchase Order Entry** under the **Transaction** section on the **Purchasing** Area Page.

2. Use the lookup button (indicated by a magnifying glass) to select Purchase Order **PO1016**. Change the **Quantity Canceled** to **5** to zero out this P.O:

3. Click on **Save** to save the changes. The P.O. closes automatically when the last line is cancelled.

How it works...

Properly closing Purchase Orders in Dynamics GP allows a company to make intelligent sourcing decisions about which vendors are able to meet the firm's needs. Companies gain the data necessary to analyze vendor performance and make decisions based on factors beyond just price. After all, having a cheaper product to sell isn't very helpful if it never arrives.

Protecting against information loss by printing Fixed Asset Reports

Microsoft Dynamics GP provides a robust Fixed Asset module for managing Fixed Asset additions, retirements, and depreciation. However, it has one significant shortcoming. The year-to-date depreciation amounts for previous fiscal years are not kept in Fixed Asset Management. This means that companies should print any reports that contain year-to-date depreciation prior to closing the year in the Fixed Asset module. The information in the year-end reports is important for auditing and year-to-year comparisons so it's important to retain this information.

Year-end reports don't need to be printed to paper. They can be printed to a file for easy archiving and searching. In this recipe, we'll look at which fixed asset reports to print at year end and how to print them.

How to do it...

To archive fixed asset reports at year end:

1. Select **Financial** from the Navigation Pane. Select **Activity** from the **Financial** Area Page under the **Reports** and **Fixed Assets** sections.

2. Select **New** to create a new report option. Name the **Option** as **Corporate** and set the **Book** to **INTERNAL**:

3. Select **Destination**. Select the **File** checkbox. Add a location to save the file to and set the format to **Text file**. Click on **OK** to close.

4. Select **Print** to print the report to a file.

5. Repeat this process with each of the company's asset books using a different name for the different books.

6. Follow these basic instructions for the additional recommended reports:

- ❑ Select **Transactions** on the **Financial** Area Page under **Reports** and **Fixed Assets** to print the **Additions**, **Retirements**, and **Transfers** reports

- ❑ Select **Depreciation** on the **Financial** Area Page under **Reports** and **Fixed Assets** to print the **Depreciation Ledger** report

- ❑ Select **Inventory** on the **Financial** Area Page under **Reports** and **Fixed Assets** to print the **Property Ledger** report

- ❑ Select **Activity** on the **Financial** Area Page under the **Reports** and **Fixed Assets** sections to print the **Fixed Assets to General Ledger Reconciliation** report

- ❑ Finally, select **Comparison** on the **Financial** Area Page under **Reports** and **Fixed Assets** to print the **Book to Book Reconciliation**

How it works...

Printing fixed asset reports prevents an accidental loss of year-to-date depreciation data due to users not understanding that this information is not retained when the Fixed Asset closing process is run. Printing these reports is not difficult and printing them to files provides easy storage and archiving, even for companies with a large number of fixed assets.

There's more...

For companies with a large number of fixed assets there is a third-party fixed asset analysis cube available for Dynamics GP.

Fixed Asset Analysis Cube

Microsoft Dynamics GP partner and solutions developer I.B.I.S., Inc. has developed a predefined analysis cube based on Dynamics GP Fixed Asset data. The analysis cube stores data using SQL Server Analysis Services and provides pivot table-like analysis functionality for all of a firm's Dynamics GP fixed asset data. This is one of the few ways to compensate for the lack of year-to-date historical reporting in Dynamics GP. The Fixed Asset Analysis Cube is available from I.B.I.S. for a fee. More information is available at http://www.ibis.com.

Preventing account selection errors with Chart Segment names

Given the typical meticulous tendencies of most accountants, it's a little bit of a surprise that the descriptions in an average chart of accounts are a complete mess. Most charts of accounts are initially very pristine but as accounts are added by various people over time, their descriptions become inconsistent. This makes it very difficult to ensure that users select the right account.

As an example, assume that the first segment in the chart of accounts represents the company, the second is the natural account, and the third is a department. An account description would ideally be something like "ABC Co.-Cash-Marketing" or "ABC Co.-Accounts Payable-Operations". In reality, accounts tend to look like "Marking Cash, ABC" or "AP Ops". This makes it hard for users to find and select the right account.

Dynamics GP provides a mechanism to ensure that new accounts follow a set naming pattern. Rather than adding a description to the chart of accounts every unique option in each segment is given a name in a setup screen. When that item is selected Dynamics GP provides the name of that segment from the setup. This builds the name of the resulting account on the fly and creates a consistent naming convention for the chart.

We'll use the sample company to set up and use Account Segment descriptions to cook this recipe.

Getting ready

To set up account segment descriptions:

1. Select **Financial** from the Navigation Pane. Select **Segment** under the **Setup** section.

2. Set **Segment ID** to **Segment1**. Use the lookup button (indicated by a magnifying glass) in the **Number** field to find number **100**. Add or change the description to **Sales**. Click on **Save**:

3. Set **Segment ID** to **Segment2**. Use the lookup button (magnifying glass) in the **Number** field to find number **1100**. Add or change the description to **Accounts Receivable**. Click on **Save**.

4. Set **Segment ID** to **Segment3**. Use the lookup button (magnifying glass) in the **Number** field to find number **01**. Add or change the description to **Marketing**. Click on **Save**.

How to do it...

To create an account description using account segments:

1. Select **Financial** from the Navigation Pane. Select **Accounts** under the **Cards** section.

2. In the **Account** field enter **100-1100-01** and press *Tab*.

3. The name will be automatically built in the **Description** field from the descriptions of the three segments in the account number:

Account Maintenance	☐ ☐ ✕
File Edit Tools Help Debug	sa Fabrikam, Inc. 4/12/2017

| 💾 Save | ✎ Clear | ✕ Delete | |

Account	‹ 100 -1100 -01 › 🔍📄→🔛 ☐ Inactive
Description	Sales-Accounts Receivable-Marketing
Alias	☑ Allow Account Entry

How it works...

Having consistent account descriptions prevents errors by providing clear and consistent account naming, making it easy for users to select the right account. This recipe also makes it easy for users who create accounts. They no longer have to wrestle with the right naming order. Unfortunately, it does not provide a mechanism to fix existing accounts. Users will have to cook up that recipe on their own.

See also

▸ *Keeping the chart of accounts clean by reactivating Account Segment warnings*

▸ *Importing data with Microsoft Word and a Dynamics GP Macro*

Ensuring proper year-end closing by checking Posting Types

When setting up accounts in the Chart of Accounts, users are required to select a posting type of either Balance Sheet or Profit and Loss. These selections correspond to their respective financial statements, the Balance Sheet and the Profit and Loss statement, also known as the Income Statement. Asset, Liability, and Equity accounts should have a posting type of Balance Sheet. Revenue and Expense accounts need the Profit and Loss Posting Type. This is important because the Posting Type controls the behavior of year-end closing for these accounts.

The year-end closing routine in Dynamics GP zeros out the accounts with a Posting Type of Profit and Loss and updates the selected Retained Earnings account. This process resets the Profit and Loss accounts to prepare for a new year and uses the ending balance in Balance Sheet accounts to create the beginning balance in the new year.

If accounts are incorrectly set up as Profit and Loss accounts their year-end balance will be erroneously cleared to Retained Earnings. Similarly, accounts incorrectly set up as Balance Sheet accounts will not get cleared to Retained Earnings to reflect prior year's net income. In short, if the Posting Type is not correct during year-end closing, companies end up with a mess that can be difficult to fix. Correcting entries can possibly be made if the number of accounts is very small but even that can be time consuming and difficult to get right. There is no way to roll back a year-end closing without reverting to a pre-closing backup or an expensive consulting engagement with Microsoft.

Because of this, validating that the Posting Type is set correctly is an important step prior to closing the year. There are two typical processes to validate Posting Types, using a SmartList to view exceptions and using a report to review all accounts. In this recipe, we will cook up both options.

Getting ready

The two main options for validating Posting Types are an exception based SmartList and a built-in Dynamics GP report. Many firms use a standard, generalized numbering system for their chart of accounts based on the first digit of the natural account. When a schema like this is followed it makes it possible to double-check that accounts have the correct posting types. A typical scenario uses accounts starting with one, two, or three as balance sheet accounts representing assets, liabilities, and equity respectively. Those starting with four or higher are used for the profit and loss statement.

The benefit of this type of setup is that users can create a SmartList that only shows the exceptions. This makes it very easy to find and correct errors. If there is no pattern or identifier designed into the account structure, a report built into Dynamics GP can still be used to review account Posting Types.

Once incorrect posting types have been identified they can be corrected using the **Account** selection on the **Financial** Area Page under **Cards**.

For our example, we use the sample company which is set up with the last Balance Sheet account as 3999 and the first Profit and Loss account as 4000.

How to do it...

To review Account Posting Types with a SmartList:

1. Click on the SmartList icon to open the SmartList window.

2. Select the **Accounts** SmartList under the **Financial** section.

3. Click on the **Search** button.

4. For **Search Definition 1** set the column name to **Account Number**, **Filter** field to **is less than**, and **Value** to **000-4000-00**.

5. For **Search Definition 2** set the column name equal to **Posting Type**, **Filter** field to **is equal to**, and **Value** to **Profit and Loss**:

6. Click on **OK** to display low-numbered accounts that are improperly listed as Profit and Loss accounts.

7. Press the **Print** button to print this report to make the appropriate corrections in the **Account Maintenance** window later.

8. Click on **Favorites** and save this SmartList as a Favorite named **YE BS Errors**.

9. Click on **Search** again.

10. For **Search Definition 1** change the **Filter** field setting to **is greater than** and **Value** to **999-3999-99**:

11. For **Search Definition 2** change the **Value** field setting to **Balance Sheet**

12. Click on **OK** to display high-numbered accounts that are improperly listed as Balance Sheet accounts.

13. Click on the **Print** button to print this report and allow a user to make the appropriate corrections in the **Account Maintenance** window later.

14. Click on **Favorites** and save this SmartList as a Favorite named **YE PL Errors**.

If a firm's chart of accounts is not set up in a way that makes identifying exceptions possible, a user still needs to print the chart of accounts and review the account Posting Types individually prior to year end.

To print and review the chart:

1. Select **Financial** from the Navigation Pane. Select **Accounts** from the **Financial** Area Page under the **Reports** and **Financial** sections.

2. In the **Report** field type **Posting**. Click on the **New** button.

3. In the **Option** field select **Posting Type**:

Chart of Accounts Report Options

File Edit Tools Help Debug   sa Fabrikam, Inc. 4/12/2017

💾 Save ✎ Clear ✕ Delete 🖨 Print 📇 My Reports

Option: Posting Type   ▼   Report   Posting

Sort By: Segment ID   ▼   Segment ID   Segment1   🔍

4. Click on **OK** to finish.

5. Select the **Print** button and review the report for Posting Type corrections:

System: 2/3/2010 9:31:28 PM	POSTING ACCOUNTS LIST			Page: 1
User Date: 4/12/2017	Fabrikam, Inc.			User ID: sa
	General Ledger			

Ranges:	From:		To:			Sorted By: Segment1	
Account:	First		Last			Include:	
Account Description:	First		Last				
Category:	First		Last				

Account	Description		Alias	Category	Active	Account Type	Posting Type	Typical Balance
User-Defined 1		User-Defined 2		User-Defined 3			User-Defined 4	
000-1100-00	Cash - Operating Account		Op	Cash	Yes	Posting Account	Balance Sheet	Debit
000-1101-00	Cash in Bank - Canada		1101	Cash	Yes	Posting Account	Balance Sheet	Debit
000-1102-00	Cash in Bank - Australia			Cash	Yes	Posting Account	Balance Sheet	Debit
000-1103-00	Cash in Bank - New Zealand			Cash	Yes	Posting Account	Balance Sheet	Debit

How it works...

Reviewing Posting Types prior to running year-end close is a simple solution to preventing an embarrassing situation. Firms that are able to use exception based reporting get a fast, easy validation that Posting Types are correct. Even when exception reporting is not available, reviewing Posting Types is an important procedure to prevent a year-end disaster.

See also

Chapter 4, Harnessing the Power of SmartLists

Preventing sales of Discontinued Inventory

Companies frequently discontinue inventory items. Perhaps an item's sales volume is too low, it has been replaced with a new model, or the item is no longer available from a supplier. By default, in Dynamics GP, discontinued inventory items can still be sold. The reasoning is that companies would still want to sell these items and clear out inventory if the opportunity arose but they don't want to purchase more of a discontinued item.

The problem comes when companies need to prevent the sale of discontinued items. There could be a safety or health issue contributing to the importance of not selling a particular item. The typical advice in cases like this is to write off the discontinued inventory to prevent the sale. However, this removes visibility to inventory that might be returnable for credit in the case of a safety recall. Additionally, in the event of a health issue the inventory may need to be retained for inspection or proof of proper disposal. Writing the items off or moving them to a different item number may not be appropriate in these cases.

There is a mechanism to reduce errors by preventing the sale of discontinued inventory. In this recipe we'll look at how to do just that.

How to do it...

To prevent Dynamics GP from allowing sales of discontinued inventory:

1. Select **Sales** from the Navigation Pane. Select **Sales Order Processing** under the **Setup** section on the **Sales** Area Page.

2. Click on the **Options** button.

3. In the bottom grid, scroll down and deselect the **Allow Sale of Discontinued Items** checkbox. Click on **OK** to Finish:

When a user enters a discontinued item in Sales Order Processing the system presents an error message asking the user to select an active item as a replacement.

How it works...

Preventing the sale of discontinued inventory items is easy but since the setting is buried in Sales, not Inventory, most administrators never find it. One important point about this setting is that it is universal for a company. If the sale of discontinued items is prevented, it's prevented for all discontinued items. There is no per item control.

Correcting errors by backing out, correcting, and copying Journal Entries

This chapter is dedicated to preventing errors but for this recipe I want to look at fixing errors. Specifically, the Correct Journal Entry functionality in Dynamics GP. The occurrence of errors is inevitable. The recipes in this chapter are designed to help users and administrators minimize errors, but once an error occurs, quickly fixing it is the next priority.

A common problem arises when users post journal entries to an incorrect period. They create and post a transaction using the current date forgetting that it belongs in a previous period.

Dynamics GP includes functionality to fix journal entry errors by backing out a journal entry and optionally presenting a duplicate journal entry for the user to change and repost. This same functionality allows copying a journal entry for users who forgot to use a recurring batch.

In this recipe, we'll use the sample company to look at fixing errors by backing out, correcting, and copying journal entries.

How to do it...

To back out and correct a journal entry:

1. Select **Financial** from the Navigation Pane. Select **General** under the **Transactions** section.
2. Select **Correct** from the top right.

3. In the **Action** field select **Back Out a Journal Entry and Create a Correcting Entry**. Set the year to **2013** and enter **802** as the **Original Journal Entry**. Click on **OK** to continue.

4. Click on **OK** to acknowledge that this is a recurring entry and click on **Select** to choose the only option. The sample company has a very limited number of journal entries that didn't originate in a subledger and this is the best example.

5. The back out transaction will open in the **Transaction Entry** window with the debit and credit amounts switched. This reverses the effect of the original entry.

6. Dynamics GP also provides a connection to the original entry in the **Reference** field:

7. In the **Batch ID** field enter **CORR** and press *Tab*. Select **Add** to add the batch and **Save** to save the batch. Click on **Save** to save the transaction. Dynamics GP will create the correcting entry once the back out entry is saved.

8. Change the date on the correction transaction to **11/30/2017** to simulate correcting a transaction posted in the wrong period. At this point, transaction lines could be added or deleted and amounts can be changed. Users can adjust any part of the transaction to correct the entry:

9. Click on **Save** to save the transaction. Both the back out transaction and the correction are now in the **CORR** batch waiting to be posted.

10. Because this is a general journal entry, the entry is posted based on the transaction date so mixing different dates in a single batch is OK.

The process for copying a journal entry is similar and works like this:

1. On the **Transaction Entry** window, select **Copy**.

2. Set the year to **2014** and enter **27** as the **Original Journal Entry**. Click on **OK** to continue:

3. The user now has a copy of the original journal entry that can be changed or adjusted as necessary.

How it works...

Backing out and correcting journal entries provides an easy mechanism to fix errors. Because the original transaction is retained and a reversing transaction is used, it's easy to audit the process and address questions about these corrections. Since copying a journal entry starts with a posted entry these transactions are also less likely to contain errors.

There's more...

For our example we used an entry that originated in the general ledger. There is also a setting that allows the correction of entries that originated in subledgers.

Subledger Corrections

Generally, corrections to a subledger transaction should be made in the originating module. For example, AP transactions should typically be voided and re-entered in Purchasing, not just corrected in the general ledger. However, if a transaction needs to have only the general ledger portion corrected, subledger transactions can be backed out, corrected, and copied via this method as well. In order to make this work there is a setting that must be activated. To activate the ability to back out, correct, and copy transactions that originated in a subledger:

1. Select **Financial** from the Navigation Pane. Select **General Ledger** under the **Setup** section.

2. Select the checkbox marked **Voiding/Correcting of Subsidiary Transactions** and click on **Save**:

9
Maintaining Dynamics GP

Maintaining Dynamics GP is an important part of keeping the system healthy. In this chapter, we will look at some common maintenance items including:

- Preventing entry of wrong dates by Closing Periods
- Improving performance by adjusting AutoComplete settings
- Cleaning up Accounts Receivable with Paid Transaction Removal
- Providing correct tax information by Updating 1099 information
- Maintaining updated code by rolling out Service Packs with Client Updates
- Improving stability by Managing Dictionaries
- Safeguarding data by Backing Up everything
- Resolving errors with the Check Links utility
- Validating balances with the Reconcile utility
- Troubleshooting issues with a DexSQL log
- Speeding security setup with User Copy

Introduction

Basic maintenance is important to keep Dynamics GP healthy and secure. No complex system runs well without regular maintenance to prevent errors and improve system performance. A significant amount of maintenance isn't normally required for a Dynamics GP implementation, but there are some areas where regular maintenance can provide significant benefits in terms of safety and performance. In chapter 9 we will look at recipes designed to help maintain a healthy Dynamics GP system. Most of these recipes will typically be performed by an administrator or power user as these recipes can have adverse consequences if improperly performed.

Preventing entry of wrong dates by Closing Periods

An important step in maintaining any accounting system is controlling access to financial periods. Financial period balances control how financial statements are presented. Once financial statements are complete they shouldn't change except in very specific, controlled circumstances. If a firm doesn't properly control access to financial periods the company's past financial statements will continue to change. In addition to the frustration of trying to compare results to a moving target, continually changing financial statements can cause Securities and Exchange Commission (SEC) issues, audit problems, and a loss of confidence in the firm's financial reporting.

The way to control access to financial periods in Dynamics GP is to close financial periods that are not being used. In some systems, closing a period is a time-consuming and irreversible process. This is not the case with Dynamics GP. Dynamics GP provides an easy way to close periods and reopen them for adjustments prior to finalizing financial statements.

Typically, companies have the current period open for transaction entry. As transactions arrive for the next period, firms typically open the next period as well to allow entry of next period's transactions. This leaves two periods open at around month-end close but otherwise, only one period is open at a time. Once a period is complete it's important to close that fiscal period to prevent further transactions.

In this recipe, we will look at the process to close fiscal periods in Dynamics GP.

How to do it...

To close a fiscal period in Dynamics GP:

1. Select **Administration** from the Navigation Pane. Select **Fiscal Periods** under the **Setup** and **Company** sections on the **Administration** Area Page.

2. Select the checkbox next to the period and module to close. Typically, the **Financial** series, which includes the General Ledger, is the last series to be closed:

Fiscal Periods Setup

File   Edit   Tools   Help   sa Fabrikam, Inc. 4/12/2008

✓   OK   │ 🏢   Calculate │ 🗗   Redisplay │

Year: 2008   ▾   First Day   1/1/2008   🏢   ☐ Historical Year
                        Last Day   12/31/2008 🏢   Open All   Close All
Number of Periods   12

			Series Closed					
Period	Period Name	Date	Financial	Sales	Purchasing	Inventory	Payroll	Project
1	Period 1	1/1/2008 🏢	☑	☐	☐	☐	☐	☐
2	Period 2	2/1/2008 🏢	☐	☐	☐	☐	☐	☐
3	Period 3	3/1/2008 🏢	☐	☐	☐	☐	☐	☐
4	Period 4	4/1/2008 🏢	☐	☐	☐	☐	☐	☐
5	Period 5	5/1/2008 🏢	☐	☐	☐	☐	☐	☐
6	Period 6	6/1/2008 🏢	☐	☐	☐	☐	☐	☐
7	Period 7	7/1/2008 🏢	☐	☐	☐	☐	☐	☐
8	Period 8	8/1/2008 🏢	☐	☐	☐	☐	☐	☐

Mass Close

3. Deselecting the checkbox under a series reopens the period for subsequent adjusting of entries.

How it works...

Closing the period is an important monthly maintenance procedure. It is critical to preventing transactions from posting in the wrong period and it's an important step to ensuring the correctness of the financial statements.

There's more...

By default, the **Fiscal Periods Setup** window controls posting transactions to a period for all transactions in a module. Sometimes though, the module level is too high and companies need the ability to allow certain types of transactions to post while preventing others.

Mass Close

Closing fiscal periods based on series is easy. However, there are times when a company isn't ready to close an entire series, but does need to prevent the posting of certain transaction types. This can be accomplished using the **Mass Close** button on the **Fiscal Periods Setup** window.

For example, if accounts payable needs an extra day to finish cutting checks but the company wants to prevent the entry of new payable vouchers in the period, the **Mass Close** button presents a list of all of the posting transaction types and allows a user to close the period, not for a series, but for one or more transaction types within that series.

To demonstrate closing only a particular transaction type:

1. In the **Fiscal Periods Setup** window click on **Mass Close**.

2. Set the **Series** to **Purchasing**.

3. Scroll to **Payables Trx Entry** and select the checkbox next to it:

4. Click on **Save** to close the period for that transaction type.

5. Notice that the entire series is marked as closed. There is no visual cue that only part of this module has been closed.

Improving performance by adjusting AutoComplete settings

Microsoft Dynamics GP provides AutoComplete functionality that remembers previous entries and displays them to users during subsequent data entry. Users can select the appropriate item without having to type the entire text. This is a great feature but the entries are stored per user and per field. This means that each time the system saves a vendor number that has been keyed it's saved as one entry for that user. By default, Dynamics GP is set up to hold ten thousand entries, per user, for each field.

As you can imagine, over a long period of time, and in organizations with heavy entry volume, the number of entries can build up slowing down AutoComplete performance significantly. Additionally, the number of choices presented to users can become unwieldy. For this recipe, we will look at a two-part solution to this problem. First we will set up a maintenance routine to clean out any entries not used over the last sixty days and then we will reduce the number of results being saved per field to a more manageable one thousand.

How to do it...

To get control over AutoComplete entries:

1. Select **Home** from the Navigation Pane. Select **User Preferences** in the Shortcut Bar.
2. Click on the **AutoComplete** button.
3. Set **Remove Unused Entries After** to **60** days. Click on **OK** to finish.
4. Change the **Max. Number of Entries to Store per Field** setting to **1,000**:

![AutoComplete Setup dialog window. Menu bar: File Edit Tools Additional Help, with date 4/12/2008. Checkbox checked for "Show AutoComplete Suggestions". Field "Remove Unused Entries After" set to 60 Days. Field "Max. Number of Entries to Store per Field" set to 1,000. Buttons: Remove Entries, OK.]

5. The new settings will take effect once the user logs out and back in.

How it works...

Companies can help prevent system slowdowns by controlling the volume of entries that Dynamics GP uses for AutoComplete. This setting is a per user setting so each user needs to make the change for their own login.

There's more...

Administrators can change this setting for all users with an SQL command.

Making the change for all users

Some users obviously make greater use of the AutoComplete feature than others. Consequently, companies may not want to set all users to the same settings. If a firm wants to globally set the number of days to remove unused entries after and the maximum number of entries to store per field, they can do that by executing the following code in SQL Management Studio against the Dynamics database:

```
Update Dynamics..sy01402
Set syUSERDFSTR='TRUE-60-1000'
Where syDefaultType=30
```

The middle line turns AutoComplete on with the TRUE setting, removes unused entries after 60 days, and sets the maximum number of entries to store per field to 1,000.

See also

▸ *Cleaning up the mess by fixing AutoComplete errors*

Cleaning up Accounts Receivable with Paid Transaction Removal

An important maintenance item that is often overlooked is Accounts Receivable Paid Transaction Removal. Perhaps it is overlooked because the name is somewhat misleading. Paid Transaction Removal only removes receivable transactions for companies that are not keeping receivables history. Most firms do keep history, and in that case Paid Transaction Removal moves Accounts Receivable transactions to history. This significantly reduces the number of transactions to be processed by Dynamics GP when running Accounts Receivable Aging and it can provide tremendous speed improvements to the aging process because the aging routine no longer has to work through the pile of completed paid transactions.

Once Paid Transaction Removal is run companies can no longer unapply payments to a receivables invoice. Additionally, once a check is moved to history via Paid Transaction Removal, it can no longer be marked as Non-Sufficient Funds (NSF). With these restrictions it's commonly recommended that the Paid Transaction Removal process be run with a date in arrears. A misapplied invoice will typically be picked up within an invoicing cycle or two. Using a delay provides a buffer to allow for easy corrections of recent transactions while still providing the efficiency of removing completed transactions.

Companies typically run Paid Transaction Removal monthly. The routine is set to remove paid transactions older than a set date and most firms set this date 30 to 90 days before the current date. I've seen firms use time frames of six months or longer when they have significant issues with misapplied payments. The key to an efficient AR aging process isn't in the interval used; it is in running the process regularly to control the number of open receivables that keeps the AR aging process efficient. In this recipe we'll look at how to process Paid Transaction Removal.

Getting ready

To ensure that history is being kept prior to running Paid Transaction Removal:

1. In Dynamics GP select **Sales** from the Navigation Pane. Select **Receivables** under the **Setup** section on the **Sales** Area Page.

2. Select the **Print Historical Aged Trial Balance** checkbox to ensure that transaction history is kept regardless of other customer history options.

3. Click on **OK** to save:

How to do it...

To run Paid Transaction Removal in Dynamics GP:

1. In Dynamics GP select **Sales** from the Navigation Pane. Select **Paid Transaction Removal** under the **Routines** section on the **Sales** Area Page.

2. The process can be limited to certain customers and classes but most firms run the process for all of their customers.

3. In the sample company change the **Cut Off** date next to **NSF** to **2/12/2017**.

4. This cutoff date applies to all of the items from **NSF** down to the next cutoff date. This includes:

   - **NSF**

   - **Void**

   - **Waived**

   - **Paid Transactions**

5. Change the cutoff date next to **Checks** to **2/12/2017**.

6. Select the **Print Register** checkbox to print the transactions being moved to history:

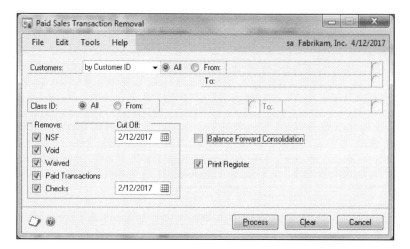

7. Click on **Process**. Choose to print the report to the screen and click on **Yes** to remove paid transactions.

8. A report will print with the specific transactions moved to history by the customer.

How it works...

Regularly running Paid Transaction Removal reduces the workload on Dynamics GP when processing receivables aging. Reports based on open receivables transactions will also run faster. All of these improvements allow receivable employees to spend less time waiting for information and more time collecting open invoices.

There's more...

This process behaves differently for companies tracking receivables using the Balance Forward method.

Balance Forward

For companies using the Balance Forward balance type there are only two aging buckets— current and non-current. Most firms do not use the Balance Forward setting for receivables. For those firms that do use the Balance Forward method the **Paid Sales Transaction Removal** window is used to consolidate balances and move current transactions to the non-current bucket.

To consolidate balances for Balance Forward customers:

1. Select the **Balance Forward Consolidation** checkbox.

2. Deselect the other checkboxes and click on **Process**:

Providing correct tax information by Updating 1099 information

A common problem arises at year end in the United States with vendors that were not properly set up as 1099 vendors. 1099 vendors are vendors who are required to be sent a 1099 tax form from the company. The types of transactions that can require a 1099 include rent, legal payments, and contract labor among others. The requirement is broad enough that most vendors who are not incorporated (proprietors, partnerships, and so on) may be due a 1099 if they are paid more than six hundred dollars in a year.

Recent changes to the U.S. law have dramatically increased the number of 1099 forms that will need to be sent in the future. Essentially, all payees who receive more than $600 in payments will need to receive a 1099 in the future. As part of this legislation the fines for 1099 reporting errors have also been increased significantly. Correctly reporting 1099 information is more important than ever and this recipe can save companies a lot more than just lunch money.

The specifics of 1099 requirements often meant that vendors were incorrectly set up and the amounts required for tax reporting on 1099 forms were not collected for that vendor in Dynamics GP. The preferred solution is to use SmartLists or built-in reports to determine what the correct 1099 amount should have been. These amounts are then added to the vendor record so that they will print correctly on the 1099 form.

The specifics of figuring out what should be on a vendor's 1099 form are beyond the scope of this recipe. For this recipe, let's look at how to serve up correct 1099 forms in the sample company once the right amounts have been obtained.

How to do it...

To correct 1099 amounts for a vendor:

1. Select **Purchasing** from the Navigation Pane. Select **1099 Details** under the **Cards** section of the **Purchasing** Area Page.

2. In the **Vendor ID** field enter **COMPUTER0001** and click on *Tab*.

3. Set the **Tax Type** to **Miscellaneous** and the **Display** to **Month**.

4. Change the **Month** to **December**.

5. In the **Amount** field, next to **7 Nonemployee Compensation**, key in **$1,100.00** to represent the 1099 amount:

1099 Box	Description	Amount
1	1 Rents	$0.00
2	2 Royalties	$0.00
3	3 Other Income	$0.00
4	4 Federal Tax Withheld	$0.00
5	5 Fishing Boat Proceeds	$0.00
6	6 Medical Payments	$0.00
7	7 Nonemployee Compensation	$1,100.00
8	8 Substitute Payments	$0.00

Vendor ID: COMPUTER0001
Name: Computer Training Systems
Tax Type: Miscellaneous
Display: Month / Year
Month: December   Year: 2017

6. Entries must be made at the **Month** level. Selecting **Year** won't allow users to make an entry in the amount field. When catching up vendor 1099 amounts companies can make an entry per period but most simply put the catch-up amount in the last month of the year.

How it works...

Maintaining 1099 vendors and amounts is something that many companies do a poor job with. This maintenance recipe will at least correct things for year end and provide correct 1099 amounts for tax filing. Ultimately though, better vendor setup is the answer to reducing this maintenance requirement.

There's more...

A better option to correcting 1099 amounts at year end is to get vendor setup right in the first place.

1099 Vendor Setup

The preferred alternative to correcting 1099 amounts is to improve vendor setup. Often the problem is that vendor setup is rushed and insufficient information is provided. As a result of this, vendor's requirement for a 1099 comes to light later, after invoices have already been processed.

The key is to get control of the vendor process by placing all new vendors on hold until the vendor record contains specific information such as the vendor's tax ID number, whether or not this is a 1099 vendor, and the type of 1099 expenses to be incurred. Most of the required information can be gathered by obtaining a completed W-9 form from the vendor. Vendors are happy to provide the necessary documentation if they know up front that their invoice won't be paid without it. Communicating and enforcing this policy is a step to better 1099 reporting.

Even with proper vendor setup discipline, it is possible for someone to erroneously remove the 1099 amount from a payables voucher. However, the number of vendors that would need to be corrected in this case would be less and this maintenance recipe becomes a simple year-end process, not an onerous one.

Maintaining updated code by rolling out Service Packs with Client Updates

Using service packs for Dynamics GP is an important part of maintaining the system. Service packs provide bug fixes, close potential security holes, and improve system performance. Some service packs, known as Feature Packs, even add new functionality. Service packs should normally be tested on a test server prior to applying them to a production environment. Service packs can negatively affect modified forms, modified reports, customizations, and third-party products so it's important to test them first.

Once service packs are tested they should be applied to the company's server first. After that comes the burdensome process of installing service packs on each user's computer as users won't be able to log in after the service pack has been applied to the server. A better alternative is to use the Client Update functionality for service packs in Dynamics GP 2010.

That's right; Dynamics GP provides a mechanism to make the service packs available on the server. When a user without the appropriate service pack logs in Dynamics GP notifies the user, downloads the service pack from the server, and installs it on the user's machine, all without the intervention of an administrator. As rolling down service packs is the focus of this recipe, let's look at how to do it.

Getting ready

Prior to rolling out service packs to users:

1. Download the service pack from CustomerSource (`http://www.microsoft.com/dynamics/customersource.mspx`) and save it to a network location accessible to Dynamics GP users.

2. Apply the service pack to the server and test to ensure that the system operates as expected.

3. For our example, we'll assume that this is service pack 2 and that we've downloaded it to a network location as `\\myserver\GPServicePacks\MicrosoftDynamicsGP-KBXXXXX-v11-ENU.msp`.

How to do it...

To roll out a service pack to Dynamics GP users:

1. Select **Administration** from the Navigation Pane. Select **Client Updates** under the **System** section of the **Administration** Area Page.

2. In **Update Name** enter **Service Pack 2** to separate this from other updates.

3. Select the checkbox marked **Update clients at next use**.

4. Enter the update location as `\\myserver\GPServicePacks\MicrosoftDynamicsGP-KBXXXXX-v11-ENU.msp`.

   Note that this requires the location to be formatted using a **Universal Naming Convention** (**UNC**). A typical `c:\mylocation` style path will not work even though the lookup button allows that:

Manage Automated Client Updates		sa Fabrikam, Inc. 4/12/2017

   File   Edit   Tools   Help   Debug

   💾 Save   🖉 Clear   ✖ Delete

   Update Name | Service Pack 2 |

   ☑ Update clients at next use

   UNC path to the update file
   `\\myserver\GPServicePacks\MicrosoftDynamicsGP-KBXXXXX-v11-ENU.msp`

5. Click on **Save** to activate the rollout. Users will get a prompt to start the update the next time they log in.

Companies can set up the client update during testing and simply refrain from selecting the **Update clients at next use** checkbox. This saves the update until testing is complete. After that, it's easy to select the checkbox and start updating clients.

How it works...

Rolling out services packs automatically is a huge time saver in a traditional desktop environment. Administrators need to properly plan and communicate that clients will be updated as the application of a service pack can be very time consuming. A lot of complaints result when users show up on a Monday morning expecting to be productive only to find that they have to wait an hour or more for a service pack to apply.

This feature isn't as important in a Citrix or Terminal server environment. As only the Citrix or Terminal servers need to be updated in addition to the SQL Server components, the Client Update feature doesn't provide a big time saving over manual updates.

There's more...

It's also important to avoid the common error of removing a service pack from the server without deselecting the **Update clients at next use** checkbox.

Service Pack Errors

It's not unusual for someone to delete a service pack installation file from the server without deselecting **Update clients at next use**. When this happens Dynamics GP displays an error the next time that a client computer without the service pack installed tries to log in. In that scenario either the service pack installation file needs to be returned to the download location or the **Update clients at next use** checkbox should be deselected and the client computer updated manually:

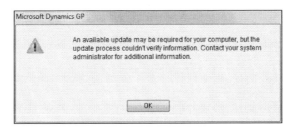

Improving stability by Managing Dictionaries

Microsoft Dynamics GP uses dictionary files to hold application code, forms, and reports. Form and report modifications in Dynamics GP don't modify the underlying item; instead, modified forms and reports are modified copies of the original that are stored in the reports and forms dictionaries.

The key question facing companies is the placement of the dictionaries because this can impact the availability of custom forms and reports. Improper placement may mean that users don't get necessary customizations, so dictionary locations need to be set up properly with each client install of Dynamics GP.

We will look at how to set up dictionary locations in this recipe.

How to do it...

To change the location of a user's forms and reports dictionary:

1. Select **Administration** from the Navigation Pane. Select **Edit Launch File** under the **Setup** section on the **Administration** Area Page.

2. Enter the system password if prompted.

3. Click on the product having ID **0** and name **Microsoft Dynamics GP**. This is the main Dynamics GP application. At the bottom of the window are three dictionary locations for the **Application, Forms**, and **Reports**:

Edit Launch File						
File	Edit	Tools	Help	Debug		4/12/2017

Launch File:	C:\Program Files\Microsoft Dynamics\GP$PERS

Product ID	Product Name
0	Microsoft Dynamics GP
258	Project Accounting
309	Fixed Assets
414	Human Resources
949	FieldService
1,042	Interfund Management

Dictionary Location ID: Windows

Dictionary Locations:

Application	C:\Program Files\Microsoft Dynamics\GP$PERS
Forms	C:\Program Files\Microsoft Dynamics\GP$PERS
Reports	C:\Program Files\Microsoft Dynamics\GP$PERS

OK

4. Changing the location of the application dictionary is not recommended as this is where the core business logic is stored and moving this file can negatively impact performance.

5. Select the **Forms** field and scroll to the right to see the full location. This is the location for custom forms. Changing this to a new location will create an empty custom forms file in the new location. If an existing custom forms field is in a different location, either enter the new location or use the file lookup to identify the new location. The same process applies to change the location of the **Reports** dictionary.

6. Each installed product outside of the core Microsoft Dynamics GP dictionary has its own application, forms, and reports dictionaries.

7. Select the **Fixed Assets** product and notice that the dictionaries have names specific to the Fixed Asset module ID.

8. Click on **OK** to save any changes.

How it works...

Dictionary control is an important piece of maintaining Dynamics GP. As new users are added and more instances are installed, it's important to ensure that the dictionaries are pointed to the right place. Without this, companies end up with an incoherent mess of customized windows and reports.

The two most common placements are locally on each user's machine or centrally on a file share. Local placement was preferred for a long time as this resulted in significantly fewer incidents of dictionary corruption. Typically, a master copy of the forms and reports dictionaries was maintained and copied to user machines via a network login script.

Over time the problem of corrupt dictionaries was significantly reduced. Improvements in Dynamics GP and network reliability made dictionary corruption extremely rare. This made centrally managing dictionaries much more feasible.

There are pros and cons to each approach. Locally managing dictionaries provides a type of backup. In the event of damage to the dictionary file, the file can be replaced by another user's copy. Conversely, locally managing dictionaries lets users have different customizations from their peers as each user's files can be unique. Finally, locally managing dictionaries permits forms and reports to be customized while Dynamics GP is in use.

Local placement of dictionaries does cause additional IT overhead as it involves creation and management of login scripts to update dictionaries with changes. Also, if users leave Dynamics GP logged in over several days dictionary updates won't propagate to their machines during that time period. Finally, users could customize forms and reports locally only to have them overwritten the next day when central dictionaries are rolled down via a login script.

Central management of dictionaries provides a consistent experience for users as everyone gets the same set of customizations in their dictionaries. Backup can be centrally managed as well. Customizations can't be made directly while other users are in the system. However, forms and reports customizations can be exported locally, modified, and then applied to a central dictionary.

There's more...

For administrators there is another option for setting dictionary locations outside of the interface.

Dynamics.set file

Installed dictionaries and their locations are held in the `Dynamics.set` file. The recipe explained previously shows how to set dictionary locations via the interface. This process changes the `Dynamics.set` file. The same changes could be made in the file with Notepad instead of via the interface. The `Dynamics.set` file could also be copied to a user's computer (assuming that they have the same modules and dictionary locations). This process is faster and easier than changing each user's `Dynamics.set` file via the interface.

Safeguarding data by Backing Up everything

Data backup may be the single most important maintenance item related to Dynamics GP. Backing up data is crucial to ensuring the long term integrity of the system. Dynamics GP provides a basic backup process designed to protect data and schedule full backups.

The built-in Dynamics GP backup routine is not intended to be a one-size-fits-all backup process. For example, it doesn't provide a mechanism for transaction log backups via the interface. Most companies prefer to use SQL tools to manage their backup process. Ultimately, each company should determine a recovery plan and then work with IT professionals to create an appropriate backup process.

However, the Dynamics GP backup process is an acceptable option, especially as a preference to no backup at all. The focus of this recipe is on setting up a backup process using the Dynamics GP backup routine.

How to do it...

To set up a Dynamics GP backup routine:

1. Select **Microsoft Dynamics GP** at the top. Select **Maintenance | Backup** from the **Microsoft Dynamics GP** menu. Enter the system password if prompted.

2. Select the company to back up. For our example, select **Fabrikam, Inc**. and set a backup file location. The backup location needs to exist or be created using the file lookup button to the right of the field:

Back Up Company

File   Edit   Tools   Help   sa Fabrikam, Inc. 4/12/2008

Select the company to backup.

Company Name: Fabrikam, Inc.

Database Name: TWO

Select the backup file:

C:\Program Files\Microsoft Dynamics\GP\backup\TWO_Apr12-200|

Schedule   OK   Cancel

3. Click on **Schedule** to set up recurring backups.

4. Name the schedule **FABRIKAM**.

5. Select the checkbox for each day to provide daily backups.

6. Set the backups to delete after **4 Weeks**:

Schedule Backup

File   Edit   Tools   Help   Debug   sa Fabrikam, Inc. 4/12/2017

Schedule Name: FABRIKAM   ☐ Suspend

Company Name: Fabrikam, Inc.

Database Name: TWO

Enter path for backup file:

C:\Program Files\Microsoft Dynamics\GP$PERSONAL\backu

Select the days to perform a backup:

☑ Monday   ☑ Tuesday   ☑ Wednesday   ☑ Thursday
☑ Friday   ☑ Saturday   ☑ Sunday

Backup Start Time: ◄ 12:00:00 AM ►   Next backup:
                                             3/3/2010 12:00:00 AM

☑ Delete backup files older than   4 Weeks ▼

Save   Delete   Cancel

7. Click on **Save** to save the backup routine.

8. Repeat this process for other company databases and the **System Database**.

Backing up data is the single most important maintenance function. Companies may need to go beyond the built-in backup routine to intra-day transaction log backups for true point-in-time recovery. The built-in routine does provide at least a daily backup option for protection.

There's more...

In addition to the databases, other files need to be backed up as well.

Additional Backups

Backing up the company and system databases provides the ability to restore a firm's information. However, it's important to back up the infrastructure around that information as well. Dictionary files hold customized forms and reports that can be extremely time consuming to restore. This also applies to financial statement layouts in the FRx Sysdata folder and integration definitions in the IMD file that stores integrations. Key items to back up include:

- Any file with a DIC extension.
- Any file with a VBA extension.
- Any file with an IMD extension from Integration Manager.
- The entire Sysdata folder from FRx.
- Exports of VBA code, Custom Forms, and Custom Reports as an additional backup. These are created with the **Export** button found in the **Microsoft Dynamics GP** menu under **Tools | Customization Maintenance**.

Resolving errors with the Check Links utility

Check Links and Reconcile are the two most commonly used utilities in Dynamics GP. Despite their common usage, their roles and outcomes are regularly misunderstood. We will look at Check Links in this recipe and move on to Reconcile for our next dish.

Check Links is a utility designed to review links between related tables for data consistency. For example, if there is a detail record there should be a header record. The Check Links utility is able to compare header and detail records and potentially rebuild damaged or missing data. When transaction data is unrecoverable, running Check Links will remove the damaged records, possibly requiring re-entry.

A transaction record can be damaged in any number of ways including lost network connectivity, poorly imported data, database level changes, and power outages. Most transactions in Dynamics GP include a header record with information about the transaction and a detail record with transaction specifics. Imagine an invoice for example. The invoice header contains things common to the whole invoice such as the invoice number, customer, and date while the invoice detail record holds the specifics of each item being purchased.

In many cases, if a header record is damaged much of it can be repaired from the information in detail records. When possible, running the Check Links utility will rebuild header records. Users may still need to make some adjustments but most of the data will be recovered. However, if a detail record has been damaged, often there is not enough information for the Check Links utility to recover the details. In those cases the Check Links utility can and will delete data so it is a good idea to run a backup prior to running Check Links.

Depending on the number of transactions being checked, Check Links can take a long time to run. As the reports generated by running Check Links are not reprintable it's a good idea to send them to a file as well as the screen. The reports can be very large so blindly sending them to a printer is usually not a good idea. With this background, let's cook up some Check Links.

How to do it...

To run Check Links for Sales Order Processing transactions:

1. Ensure that a current backup has been created.
2. Select the **Microsoft Dynamics GP** menu and from there select **Maintenance | Check Links**.
3. In the **Series** field select **Sales**.
4. Select **Sales Distribution** and click on **Insert** to add this item.
5. Repeat this process with **Sales History** and **Sales Work** and click on **OK**:

6. Select **Screen** and **File** in the **Report Destination** window. Enter a location for the file and format it as a text file.
7. Click on **OK** to run Check Links.
8. A report will print to the screen with the results including any additions or deletions made by the utility.

How it works...

The Check Links utility works throughout Dynamics GP to validate data and connections between tables. There is still plenty of debate about whether Check Links should be run regularly to maintain the health of the system or only when an issue has been identified. There are good arguments on both sides. As a practical matter I've always preferred to run Check Links only when necessary.

As System and Company setup tables don't have dependent links in the same way that transaction tables do, Check Links typically won't solve issues with those tables. The Reconcile utility checks for data consistency among unlinked but still associated tables. Consequently, Reconcile should be used with System and Company tables in place of Check Links.

See also

▸   *Validating balances with the Reconcile utility*

Validating balances with the Reconcile utility

Next to Check Links, the Reconcile utility is the most commonly used utility in Dynamics GP. The job of the Reconcile utility is to replace or remove erroneous data that is related but isn't necessarily linked. For example, to improve reporting speed Dynamics GP stores the summary totals of each account in a table. Unlike Check Links these tables aren't related to each other, they simply hold the same information in different formats, one in detail and one in summary.

The summary total of an account should equal the sum of all of the detail transactions for an account. If it doesn't the Reconcile utility will recalculate the totals from the detail and replace the summary total.

Like Check Links, the Reconcile utility can remove data and should be run after a backup. Additionally, any reports that are available to be printed should be printed to the screen and to a file. There is no option to reprint these reports. In this recipe, we'll look at the most common use for Reconcile—ensuring that financial summary data matches the detail.

How to do it...

To reconcile financial totals:

1.   Make a backup of Dynamics GP.

2.   Select **Financial** from the Navigation Pane. Select **Reconcile** under **Utilities**.

3.   Select the **Year** checkbox, the **Open** radio button, and select **2017** from the drop-down menu:

4. Unlike other Reconcile processes no report prints when reconciling the year. Using the Reconcile utility on other parts of the system will result in a report showing changes.

How it works...

The Reconcile utility is designed to help ensure data integrity in Dynamics GP by correcting mismatched data and updating totals for summaries, batches, and headers. It is a powerful utility and shouldn't be used without a good backup. Like Check Links, there is disagreement in the Dynamics GP community over whether or not Reconcile should be run regularly. As with Check Links, my slight preference is to run it only when there is suspicion of a problem.

See also

▶ *Resolving errors with the Check Links utility*

Troubleshooting issues with a DexSQL log

When trying to troubleshoot issues a common request from Microsoft support and from their Partners is to run a DexSQL log. A DexSQL log is a file that logs commands made from Dynamics GP to the database to help understand performance issues. After creation, this file is sent to the company's partner or to Microsoft for assistance in troubleshooting.

When creating a DexSQL log the key is to capture only the amount of data related to the problem. In this recipe, we will look at creating a DexSQL log to provide more information to Microsoft support.

For our example, we will assume that the problem relates to creating a financial batch; so that is the process that will get captured in the DexSQL log.

How to do it...

To create a DexSQL log:

1. Ensure that Microsoft Dynamics GP is closed.

2. Open the Notepad utility in Windows.

3. Select **File | Open** in Notepad and navigate to the location where the `Dex.ini` file for Dynamics GP is installed. By default, this is `c:\Program Files\Microsoft Dynamics\GP\Data\Dex.ini`.

4. Once the `Dex.ini` file is open in Notepad, find these two lines in the file:

   `SQLLogSQLStmt=FALSE`

   `SQLLogODBCMessages=FALSE`

5. Change both lines to a value of `TRUE` and save the file. This turns on logging in Dynamics GP:

   ❑ The first line, `SQLLogSQLStmt=TRUE`, logs all SQL statements that are sent to the server by the application.

   ❑ The second line, `SQLLogODBCMessages=TRUE`, logs all ODBC messages returned to the application by ODBC:

   ❑ Either line or both lines can be set to `TRUE`. Typically, Microsoft support asks that both lines be set to `TRUE`.

6. Start Microsoft Dynamics GP and log in. This creates a file named `DexSQL.log` in the same location as the `Dex.ini` file.

   ❑ Results will be logged to the `DexSQL.log` file regardless of which lines are set to `TRUE`.

   ❑ Any ODBC messages are prefixed by [Microsoft].

7. Select **Financial** from the Navigation Pane on the left. Select **Batches** under **Transactions**.

8. The DexSQL log now holds all of the information related to logging in and everything done so far in this GP session. The log now needs to be cleared prior to recording the actual problem scenario.

9. To clear the DexSQL log, find the `DexSQL.log` file in the same directory as the `Dex.ini` file. Using File Manager, select and delete the file. Once activity starts in Dynamics GP, a new file is created.

10 Return to Dynamics GP. In the open **Batch Entry** window type **TEST BATCH** in the **Batch ID** field. Set the **Origin** field to **General Entry** and save the batch. Now the `DexSQL.log` file needs to be renamed to avoid adding unrelated data:

Batch Entry	

File Edit Tools Help Debug — sa Fabrikam, Inc. 4/12/2017

■ Save   ✎ Clear   ✕ Delete   ⊞ Post

Batch ID	TEST BATCH	Origin:	General Entry
Comment			

Frequency:	Single Use
	☐ Break Down Allocation

Recurring Posting	0	Last Date Posted	0/0/0000
Days to Increment	0	Times Posted	0

	Control	Actual
Journal Entries	0	0
Batch Total	$0.00	$0.00

	User ID	Approval Date	
☐ Approved		0/0/0000	Transactions

11. Return to the `DexSQL.log` file in File Manager. Right-click on the `DexSQL.log` file and rename it to `DexSQL-Batch.log`.

12. Once the DexSQL log has been renamed it's important to close Dynamics GP and turn off logging. If this doesn't happen, Dynamics GP can significantly slow down and the DexSQL log can grow to consume all of a computer's hard drive space.

13. To turn off logging, close Dynamics GP, and reopen the `Dex.ini` file.

14. Find these lines in the `Dex.ini` file and change `TRUE` to `FALSE`:

    ```
    SQLLogSQLStmt=TRUE
    SQLLogODBCMessages=TRUE
    ```

15. Save the `Dex.ini` file and delete the leftover `DexSQL.log` file that was created when closing Dynamics GP.

16. What is left is the `DexSQL-Batch.log` file that holds specifics from right before and after the problem area. This file can be opened using Notepad to see what information is being sent to Microsoft or the company's Dynamics GP partner.

How it works...

Creating a DexSQL log is an important maintenance process for companies to understand. Microsoft and Microsoft Partners often ask for this information when troubleshooting errors. Being able to generate a DexSQL log to facilitate problem resolution is important for maintaining a healthy Dynamics GP system.

See also

▸ *Logging transactions for troubleshooting*

Speeding security setup with User Copy

Setting up security for individual users can be a time-consuming task. Dynamics GP 2010 provides a mechanism to copy the access from an existing user to a new user including tasks, roles, and company access. This feature provides a great way to quickly set up new users and ensure that their security is consistent.

This recipe looks at how to copy security settings from an existing user to a new user.

Getting ready

This recipe requires logging in as 'sa', the system administrator. Log in to the sample company as 'sa' to start this recipe.

How to do it...

To copy security settings to a new user:

1. Select **Administration** from the Navigation Pane. Under **Setup** and **System** on the **Administration** Area Page, select **User**.

2. In the **User ID** field, type **JDOE**.

3. Type **John Doe** in the **User Name** field.

4. Type **Pass@word1** in the **Password** and **Confirm Password** fields:

![User Setup window showing User ID JDOE, User Name John Doe, Password and Confirm Password fields filled with dots, empty Class ID and Home Page Role fields]

5. Click on **Copy Access** and then on **Yes** when asked to save changes.

6. Use the lookup button (indicated by a magnifying glass) to look up and select the **LESSONUSER1** user:

7. Click on **OK** to finish.

User JDOE now has the same roles, tasks, and company access as LESSONUSER1.

10

Extending Dynamics GP with Free Software

Microsoft Dynamics GP has a rich environment of third-party software designed to enhance the product. Some of those additional products are even free. Free Dynamics GP add-ons can offer great benefits to firms. In this chapter, we'll look at recipes designed to be the rich dessert that completes the meal.

- ▶ Checking Dynamics GP spelling with Willoware
- ▶ Preventing date errors with DocDateVerify
- ▶ Executing SQL from the Support Administrator Console
- ▶ Extending Dynamics GP with the Support Debugging Tool
- ▶ Coloring windows by company
- ▶ Capturing Screenshots and sending an E-mail for support
- ▶ Logging transactions for troubleshooting
- ▶ Executing SQL from within Dynamics GP
- ▶ Getting information about Security Resources

Introduction

The ecosystem around Microsoft Dynamics GP is huge. There are a significant number of third-party applications for Dynamics GP designed to provide additional functionality, address industry-specific requirements, and improve efficiency. A few of these applications are even free. Certainly some of these free applications are designed to generate interest in the vendor's other offerings, but that doesn't mean that they aren't valuable. Also, some of these applications require registration but if that's the only price, it's close enough to free in my opinion.

Many of these free tools come from leading vendors in the Dynamics GP ecosystem and some of them come directly from Microsoft.

In this chapter, we'll take a look at functionality offered by various free, third-party applications. I don't have any kind of monetary arrangement with any of these vendors. I'm just a sucker for free software and more features.

Checking Dynamics GP spelling with Willoware

Independent software vendor Willoware provides a spell-checking application for use inside of Microsoft Dynamics GP. SpellCheck for Dynamics GP requires registration to download and is available from Willoware at `http://willoware.com/spellcheck/`.

Once installed, a user will need to select the fields that need to be spell checked. Once setup is complete, spell checking begins as soon as the user leaves the field.

In this recipe, we will look at setting up SpellCheck and checking spelling in a note field.

Getting ready

Follow the instructions included with the download to install Willoware in Dynamics GP. Microsoft Word and the Office Proofing Tools are required on the client computer as Willoware's product uses Microsoft Word for the spell checking. The Office Proofing Tools are typically installed by default with Microsoft Word. A user will need to log in to Dynamics GP as 'sa' the first time to complete the installation.

Once installed users will need the SPELLCHECK security task added to their role. Details of the security requirements are covered in the SpellCheck installation instructions.

Finally, before checking spelling, the application needs to be set up by assigning various fields for automated spell checking. To set up the note fields in Dynamics GP for spell checking:

1. In Dynamics GP select **Administration** from the Navigation Pane.
2. On the **Administration** Area Page under **Company** click on **SpellCheck Setup**.
3. Set **Product** to **Microsoft Dynamics GP** and **Series** to **System.**
4. Set **Form Name** to **Note** by selecting the first **Note** option in the list.
5. Set **Window Name** to **Note** and **Field Name** to **Text Field**:

6. Click on **Save**.

7. Repeat this process for the remaining four note fields in Dynamics GP by selecting the next note down each time in the **Form Name** field. The number of each note field shows to the right of the **Form Name** field. These five note fields cover all of the locations for record and user-level notes.

8. Close the window with the **X** in the upper-right corner.

How to do it...

To check spelling in Dynamics GP:

1. Select **Financial** from the Navigation Pane. Select **Transaction Entry** under the **Transactions** section on the **Financial** Area Page.

2. Click on the white note next to the **Journal Entry** field.

3. Type **Dynamis** in the comment window. That's right; intentionally misspell it:

4. Click on **Attach**.

5. Willoware will open Microsoft Word and use the built-in Word spell check functionality to check the spelling.

    For users with Office 2010, Word may open underneath Microsoft Dynamics GP. If that happens simply select Microsoft Word from the taskbar:

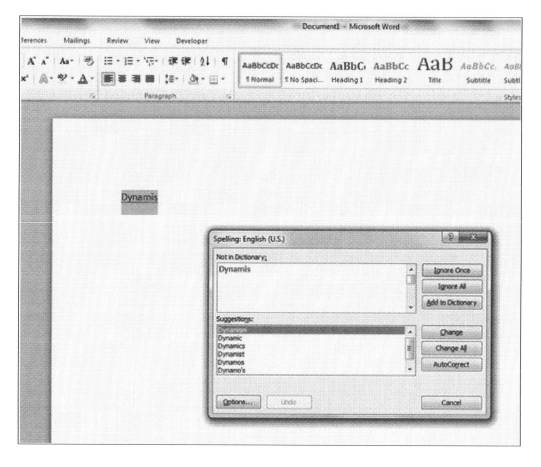

6. Select the correct spelling in the lower section and click on **Change.** Microsoft Word will close and apply the correct spelling in Dynamics GP.

How it works...

Spell checking is great for comments, descriptions, and those oddly-spelled words that always seem to stump people. The beauty of this setup is that companies can control which fields to spell check. With the proliferation of legal comments, company requirements, and other messages now being included in documents such as invoices and purchases orders, correct spelling is important. With SpellCheck from Willoware users can avoid embarrassing goofs in Dynamics GP documents.

Preventing date errors with DocDateVerify

Microsoft provides a small add-on for Dynamics GP called DocDateVerify. This little application does one thing and it does it well. DocDateVerify prevents users from entering dates in subledgers for fiscal periods that have not been set up.

Without DocDateVerify it is possible to accidently date a payables transaction with the year 2100 instead of 2010. As Payables Document Dates are often different from general ledger posting dates, the transaction could post just fine but would never be selected for payment because of the odd year. It's also hard to fix because other parts of Dynamics GP do validate against the fiscal period and prevent users from voiding some of these incorrectly dated transactions. DocDateVerify rectifies this by preventing the entry of dates that don't exist in fiscal periods that have been set up.

DocDateVerify works in core financial and distribution modules to validate date entry. This Microsoft module is available through an authorized Dynamics GP partner on request. It is free, but it's not available for download. In this recipe, let's look at how it works.

Getting ready

DocDateVerify is a file with a CNK extension, commonly called a 'chunk file'. Chunk files are installed by dropping them in the location where Dynamics GP is installed and restarting the application. Dynamics GP may need to be launched with Administrator privileges on some versions of Windows to allow the installation to proceed. Dynamics GP may ask if it's okay to install new code. Users must answer 'yes' for DocDateVerify to be installed. After installation the 'sa' user may need to log in first to allow the installation to complete.

How to do it...

To see how DocDateVerify protects dates in Dynamics GP:

1. After DocDateVerify has been installed select **Purchasing** from the Navigation Pane. Select **Transaction Entry** under the **Transactions** section on the **Purchasing** Area Page.

2. In the **Doc. Date** field enter **4/12/2100**.

3. Dynamics GP responds with a message that **A fiscal period for this date has not been set up**. Users must change the date to continue with the transaction.

How it works...

DocDateVerify provides some peace of mind for core financial and distribution transactions. Other modules, such as the Contract portion of Field Service, actually need to put dates out beyond the existing fiscal periods because of the nature of the transaction. For financial and distribution modules DocDateVerify does not work with Quotes and Orders, as it is reasonable that those transaction types could affect fiscal periods not yet set up. DocDateVerify does need to be installed on each workstation. It cannot be rolled down via Client Update.

Executing SQL from the Support Administrator Console

There are times when the best way to confirm that information in Dynamics GP is correct is to simply look at the records in the SQL Server. Typically, this is done by executing an SQL command in SQL Server Management Studio. However, SQL Server Management Studio is not typically installed on an average user's machine. Also, the user's machine can be a long way from a computer with Management Studio installed. Finally, Management Studio contains a lot more features than is necessary to simply execute a query.

Microsoft again provides a free tool, this time in the form of the Support Administrator Console. Originally, this tool was designed for versions of Dynamics GP that ran on a light version of SQL Server that didn't include SQL Server Management Studio. Nevertheless, the Support Administrator Console works just fine with Dynamics GP 2010 and provides a lighter option in place of using SQL Server Management Studio for quick queries.

The Support Administrator Console is a free download for customers with access to Microsoft's CustomerSource site. The version for Dynamics GP 10 also works in Dynamics GP 2010. It's available at `https://mbs.microsoft.com/downloads/customer/SptCon.zip`.

In this recipe, we will take a look at how the Support Administrator Console works.

Getting ready

The Support Administrator Console needs to be downloaded and installed on a user's machine prior to using.

To get the Support Administrator Console:

1. Download the file from Microsoft at `https://mbs.microsoft.com/downloads/customer/SptCon.zip` and save it to the desktop.

2. Right-click on the `SptCon.zip` file, select **Extract All**, and follow the prompts to unzip the file.

3. In the new `SptCon` folder double-click on **Setup** and follow the installation prompts.

How to do it...

To use the Support Administrator Console:

1. On the Windows Start menu find the **Microsoft Support Administrator Console** folder added in **All Programs**. Select **Support Administrator Console** in that folder to start the tool.

2. Select the appropriate server for Dynamics GP and log in with an SQL username and password. The GP username and password will not work but the 'sa' password will.

3. In the window at the top select the sample Dynamics GP database named **TWO**.

4. Type **Select * from GL00105** and click on the arrow-like Play icon:

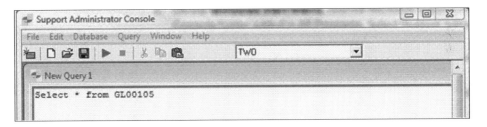

5. The basic Chart of Accounts information is returned to the screen in the tab marked **Result** at the bottom:

6. To modify the query select the **SQL** tab.

7. Select **File | Export** to export the data to a comma-delimited file.

8. Click on **File | Save** to save the query to use at a later time.

How it works...

The Support Administrator Console is a great, quick way to check data in Dynamics GP. It loads faster and with less overhead than SQL Server Management Studio. However, it is a powerful tool and should still be controlled with care.

See also

▸ *Executing SQL from within Dynamics GP*

Extending Dynamics GP with the Support Debugging Tool

It has been said that bacon is the meat that makes other meat taste better. Along those lines, the Support Debugging Tool is the bacon of the Dynamics GP world. It makes working with Dynamics GP better in so many ways.

The Support Debugging Tool is a free utility from Microsoft with enough features to fill several recipes. We'll do just that and spend the next several recipes looking at specific Support Debugging Tool features. The Support Debugging Tool is free but because of its power, it has to be obtained from a Microsoft partner; it cannot be downloaded directly.

The Support Debugging Tool is the creation of Microsoft Escalation Engineer and all-around dexterity guru David Musgrave. David, along with help from some folks in the Dynamics GP community, created the Support Debugging Tool to improve error tracing. The tool has morphed into an extremely handy utility for Dynamics GP.

One of the benefits of the Support Debugging Tool is that it works with Dynamics GP security. The Support Debugging Tool comes with two predefined security roles. One role, MBS DEBUGGER USER, provides access to standard mode features such as logging and support requests. This role can safely be given to average users.

The Support Debugging Tool also includes a more advanced MBS DEBUGGER ADMIN role that provides access to the more advanced sections of the tool. Finally, GP security can be used with the associated tasks to fine tune these security options.

Before we can dig into the Support Debugging Tool we need to install it. We will do that here and turn on the Administrator mode so that we don't have to revisit this with each new recipe.

How to do it...

To install and set up the Support Debugging Tool to activate company-based color schemes:

1. Obtain the `DEBU_1100.zip` file from Microsoft via a Microsoft partner.

2. With Dynamics GP closed, right click the `DEBU_1100.zip` file, select **Extract All**, and follow the prompts to unzip the file.

3. In the new `DEBU_1100` folder copy the CNK file to the location where Dynamics GP is installed. By default this is `c:\Program Files\Microsoft Dynamics\GP\`.

4. Start Microsoft Dynamics GP and agree to the Add New Code message. Dynamics GP may need to be run as an administrator with some versions of Windows.

5. In Microsoft Dynamics GP select the **Microsoft Dynamics GP** menu option and then **Tools | Support Debugging Tool**.

6. To turn on Administrator settings select **Debugger | Dex.ini Settings**.

7. Select the **Enable Debugger Advanced Mode Features** checkbox and enter the system password if prompted:

> **Support Debugging Tool Options**
> ☑ Enable Debugger Advanced Mode Features
> ☐ Enable Debugger Setup Mode (Do not automatically start Triggers)

8. Click on **OK** to finish.

The Support Debugging Tool is now installed and we're ready for some juicy treats.

See also

- ▸ *Coloring windows by company*
- ▸ *Logging transactions for troubleshooting*
- ▸ *Capturing Screenshots and sending an E-mail for support*
- ▸ *Executing SQL from within Dynamics GP*
- ▸ *Getting information about Security Resources*

Coloring windows by company

Many companies use several company databases in Dynamics GP. This may be because they have multiple entities to account for or because they want a test and a production database. Invariably, data entry mistakes are made because users inadvertently key information to the wrong company. For some time, users have asked for a way to visually tell one company from another. One feature of the Support Debugging Tool is designed to do just this.

The Support Debugging Tool allows a user to change the window background color for a specific company. This provides a consistent visual cue to identify the company being used.

In this recipe, we will look at how to assign colors to specific companies to distinguish them from each other.

Getting ready

The Support Debugging Tool needs to be installed on each user's machine and users need access to the MBS DEBUGGER USER security role for the company-based color schemes to work. Additionally, the Administrator mode needs to be activated within the tool.

How to do it...

To use color to identify specific companies:

1. In Microsoft Dynamics GP select the **Microsoft Dynamics GP** menu option and then **Tools | Support Debugging Tool**.

2. In the **Support Debugging Tool** window select **Debugger | Administrator Settings**.

3. Enter the system password if prompted.

4. Select the **Company** tab.

5. Select the drop-down menu next to **Select Theme Colors** and set the theme to **Blue**. This provides a preset blue theme throughout this company:

![Administrator Settings window showing the Company tab with Activate Company based Color Schemes option and Select Theme Colors set to Blue]

6. Click on **Apply** to see the changes. The window colors change to blue to match the theme. This setting is retained for this company.

7. Repeat this process by opening other companies and changing their window colors.

8. Colors can be controlled individually for the Toolbar, Background, and Window Heading with the selections below the theme.

How it works...

This feature of the Support Debugging Tool started out as a simple Visual Basic for Applications (VBA) add-on. Eventually, it was incorporated into the Support Debugging Tool.

Changing the background color is a great way to prevent data entry errors. I've even seen firms match the color of a company's check stock to the color of the company database to prevent check printing errors.

See also

- ▸ *Ensuring entry in the correct company by warning about Test Companies*
- ▸ *Extending Dynamics GP with the Support Debugging Tool*
- ▸ *Logging transactions for troubleshooting*
- ▸ *Capturing Screenshots and sending an E-mail for support*
- ▸ *Executing SQL from within Dynamics GP*
- ▸ *Getting information about Security Resources*

Capturing Screenshots and sending an E-mail for support

When it comes to support, few things are better for troubleshooting than a snapshot of what went wrong. One of the great features available in the free Support Debugging Tool from Microsoft is the ability to grab screenshots and environment files, such as the `Dynamics. set` file, and e-mail them for support. This e-mail doesn't have to go to Microsoft. It can go to a company's Microsoft Partner, an internal support team, or almost anyone else who could help. It's also nice to be able to grab screenshots from within the Dynamics GP interface rather than relying on an external tool such as the Windows Snipping Tool.

We looked at installing the Support Debugging Tool in this chapter's *Extending Dynamics GP with the Support Debugging Tool* recipe, but I'll mention again that this free tool is available from Microsoft Dynamics partners on request.

Installing the Support Debugging Tool adds a camera icon to the Standard toolbar. Additionally, the *Ctrl* + *S* key combination can be used, making it easy to grab an error message and send out for help.

In this recipe, we'll look at the Screen Capture functionality included in the Support Debugging Tool.

How to do it...

To use the Screen Capture feature of the Support Debugging Tool:

1. Select **Financial** from the Navigation Pane. Select **General** under **Transactions**.

2. In the **Transaction Entry** window click on the blue arrow next to **Batch ID** to open the **Batch Entry** window as well.

3. Use one of these three options to capture the screenshot:

    ❑ Click on the camera icon on the Standard toolbar

    ❑ Press *Ctrl + S* on the keyboard

    ❑ Select the **Microsoft Dynamics GP** menu followed by **Tools | Capture Screenshots**.

4. The **Support Debugging Tool ScreenShot** window will open with attached screenshots of both of the open windows. The checkboxes on the left allow specific windows to be included or excluded in a support e-mail:

![Support Debugging Tool ScreenShot window showing Save Path C:\Program Files\Microsoft Dynamics\GP$GP11BETA\Data\, with two open windows listed: Microsoft Dynamics GP Batch Entry GL_Batch_Entry001.bmp Original window, and Microsoft Dynamics GP Transaction Entry GL_Transaction_Entry001.bmp Original window]

5. Next to **Attach optional files to email** select the checkboxes to **Include Current Launch File** and **Include Dex.ini Settings File.** These settings will attach the Dynamics.set file and Dex.ini file used to launch Dynamics GP.

6. Click on the **Email** button. The user's e-mail application will open with the files attached and information included in the body of the e-mail:

Support Debugging Tool System Summary (3/18/2010 12:49:24 PM)

Registration Information

Product Name: Microsoft Dynamics GP Standard
Site Name: PreviewKeys
Number of Users: 10
Language-Country: English-US

Login Information

User ID: sa
Company Name: Fabrikam, Inc.
Database Name: TWO

Environment Information

User Name: mpolino
Computer Name: POLINO02
Operating System: Windows Vista
Temporary Folder Path: C:\Users\mpolino\AppData\Local\Temp\
Database Type: SQL Server
SQL Version: Microsoft SQL Server 2008 (RTM) - 10.0.1600.22 (Intel X86)
SQL Server: POLINO02\GP11BETA
SQL Server NetBIOS Name: POLINO02
SQL Session ID: 6

Users simply need to add the e-mail address of the recipient and send the e-mail.

How it works...

The Screen Capture feature in the Support Debugging Tool is a godsend for anyone who has had to deal with uncaptured error messages or misquoted error text. Furthermore, it provides a consistent output result for support personnel to use to review data.

There's more...

In addition to the basic settings of the Screen Capture feature there are some defaults that can be set to make it even more useful.

Default Settings

In the *Extending Dynamics GP with the Support Debugging Tool* recipe in this chapter we looked at turning on Administrator settings for the Support Debugging Tool. Once Administrator settings have been activated new default settings can be created for capturing screenshots.

To change the default settings for capturing screenshots:

1. In the **Support Debugging Tool** window select **Debugger | Administrator Settings**.

2. Enter the system password if prompted.

3. In the **General** tab select the checkboxes next to **Include Current Launch File** and **Include Dex.ini Settings File** to include these files by default when a user takes a screenshot:

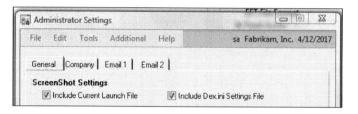

4. Click on the **Email 1** tab. Add an e-mail ID to the **Administrator Email** field to provide a default e-mail recipient for support requests and click on **Apply**. Do not add my e-mail address. I can't support everyone!

5. Click on the **Email 2** tab. The **Email Mode** field is used to control the type of e-mail mode. The options include using Outlook to send e-mail, using the SQL Server, or using a generic MAPI client to send support e-mails. If the SQL Server is used, other fields are exposed to allow additional setup options:

6. Finally, below the **Email Mode** field are three settings fields. The three fields and their uses are:

   ❑ **Preview**: A preview window opens in Dynamics GP to review the e-mail before it goes out. If **Auto Send** is off users may have the opportunity to review the e-mail again in their mail client.

   ❑ **Auto Send**: Sends the e-mail without the user having to press send in their e-mail client. However, this does not override the **Preview** button if it is selected.

   ❑ **Send HTML**: Sends the e-mail in HTML format instead of text format.

See also

▶ *Extending Dynamics GP with the Support Debugging Tool*

▶ *Coloring windows by company*

▶ *Logging transactions for troubleshooting*

▶ *Executing SQL from within Dynamics GP*

▶ *Getting information about Security Resources*

Logging transactions for troubleshooting

In the Chapter 9 recipe, *Troubleshooting issues with a DexSQL log*, we looked at creating a DexSQL log file for use in troubleshooting. That recipe didn't require any special software, but it did take a lot of back and forth to limit the contents of the file to the specific process to be logged. The free Support Debugging Tool from Microsoft not only makes this much easier, but it also adds a host of features and logging options to get more information for support.

How to do it...

To create a DexSQL log:

1. In Microsoft Dynamics GP select **Tools | Support Debugging Tool** from the **Microsoft Dynamics GP** menu.

2. In the center of the screen in the **SQL Logging** section, click on **Turn On**:

Microsoft SQL Server Options

SQL Logging: Note: Shared by all users on workstation   [Turn On]

- ● Default (DEXSQL.LOG)
- ○ Based on date and time
- ○ Specified: C:\Program Files\Microsoft Dynamics\GP$GP11BETA\I

3. Select **Financial** from the Navigation Pane. Select **General** under **Transactions**.

4. Reopen the **Support Debugging Tool** window from the Windows Taskbar and click on **Turn Off**. The DexSQL log file now exists under the `Data` folder where Dynamics GP is installed.

That's it. That is the minimum amount of work necessary to create a DexSQL log with the Support Debugging Tool. Sixteen steps from the Chapter 9 recipe reduced to four steps with the Support Debugging Tool.

As that is too easy, there are some additional options available on the main page to improve DexSQL logging.

To use the additional logging features:

1. Return to the **Support Debugging Tool** window.

2. Prior to starting a DexSQL log, two additional options can be selected in the **SQL Logging** area.

3. Select the **Based on date and time** radio button to add a date and time stamp to the DexSQL log filename. This allows for the creation of multiple logs over time.

4. Alternatively, select the **Specified** radio button to place the log file in a different location, and specify the filename:

Microsoft SQL Server Options

SQL Logging: Note: Shared by all users on workstation   [Turn On]

- ○ Default (DEXSQL.LOG)
- ○ Based on date and time
- ● Specified: C:\Program Files\Microsoft Dynamics\GP$GP11BETA\I

5. Below the **SQL Logging** option are two similar logging options—**Dexterity Script Logging** and **Dexterity Script Profiling**. **Dexterity Script Logging** logs Dexterity events. **Dexterity Script Profiling** tracks Dexterity calls and the time it takes them to complete. Both are useful but less commonly applied than **SQL logging**:

Microsoft Dexterity Options

Dexterity Script Logging: [Turn On]
- ◉ Default (Script.log)
- ○ Based on User, Company, date and time
- ○ Specified: C:\Program Files\Microsoft Dynamics\GP$GP11BETA\|

Dexterity Script Profiling: [Turn On]
- ◉ Default (Profile.txt)
- ○ Based on User, Company, date and time
- ○ Specified: C:\Program Files\Microsoft Dynamics\GP$GP11BETA\|

There's more...

On-demand logging just scratches the surface. The Support Debugging Tool can even log events automatically.

Automatic Logging

The Support Debugging Tool can log events automatically based on the type of event to be logged.

Automatic logging is set up under **Options | Setup Automatic Debugger Mode** on the **Support Debugging Tool** screen:

Support Debugging Tool Setup

File   Edit   Tools   Script   Additional   Help   sa Fabrikam, Inc. 4/12/2017

[Save   Clear   Delete   Duplicate   Options   Users]

Trigger ID	[ ] □ Disabled □ Start Trigger Automatically on Login
Trigger Description	[ ] □ Do not activate Logging Mode
Trigger Type	Select Trigger Type ▼
Trigger Event	Select Trigger Event ▼ Trigger Attach Select Attach Mode ▼

Product Name [ ] ▼   ID [0]
Form Name
Window Name
Field Name

Dialog Message [ ]
When Condition is met.   □ Display Message   □ Send Email   □ Export Table Record   □ Reject Script

The number of options available for automatic logging is too much to cover in this recipe but this process is great for tracking down errors that are hard to reproduce. The Support Debugging Tool manual has full coverage of this feature.

See also

▶ *Extending Dynamics GP with the Support Debugging Tool*

▶ *Capturing Screenshots and sending an E-mail for support*

▶ *Executing SQL from within Dynamics GP*

▶ *Getting information about Security Resources*

Executing SQL from within Dynamics GP

Earlier in this chapter we looked at executing SQL code from a user's machine with the free Support Administrator Console from Microsoft. Another option to execute SQL code from a user's machine is with the Support Debugging Tool.

Microsoft makes the Support Debugging Tool available to users via Dynamics GP partners. The tool is free; you just have to ask.

An advantage of the Support Debugging Tool over the Support Administrator Console is that the Support Debugging Tool is integrated into Dynamics GP and Dynamics GP security. This means that the Support Debugging Tool can be safely installed on a user's machine and access to it restricted via GP security roles. Also, as several other recipes in this chapter have shown, the Support Debugging Tool does much more than run SQL code.

It does run SQL code quite well though and in this recipe, we will look at how to accomplish that.

How to do it...

To execute SQL code via the Support Debugging Tool:

1. With the Support Debugging Tool installed, select **Tools | Support Debugging Tool** from the **Microsoft Dynamics GP** menu.

2. Select the **Options** button on the main window and select **SQL Execute.**

3. Enter the system password if prompted.

4. Change **Execute Query in which SQL Database** to **Fabrikam, Inc**.

5. In the large white field in the center type **Select * from GL00105** and click on the **Execute** button on the lower-right to see the chart of accounts:

6. Click on the **Export** button to export the results to a file or e-mail. The format of the export can be changed with the **Export Mode** field to the right.

7. Click on the Printer icon in the upper-right to print the results.

8. By default only twenty records are returned to prevent long running queries that might slow the system down. This can be changed in the **Limit results set to fixed number of lines** field. A setting of zero (0) indicates no limit.

9. In the **Script ID** field enter **CHART**, and in the **Script Name** field type **Chart of Accounts**. Clicking on **Save** will save this script for reuse and clear the screen.

10. Use the lookup button (indicated by a magnifying glass) next to **Script ID** to reopen the **CHART** script. Click on the **Duplicate** button to make a copy of this script and allow changes.

11. When creating scripts, click on the **Tables** button to explore Dynamics GP tables to assist in writing SQL scripts:

How it works...

The ability to view Dynamics GP data in the database is an important part of troubleshooting. Not having to find a machine with SQL Server Management Studio is important for leaving on time at night as it prevents running back and forth between machines to review query results. By integrating SQL query features into the Support Debugging Tool, troubleshooting becomes faster and easier.

See also

- ▶ *Extending Dynamics GP with the Support Debugging Tool*
- ▶ *Logging transactions for troubleshooting*
- ▶ *Capturing Screenshots and sending an E-mail for support*
- ▶ *Getting information about Security Resources*

Getting information about Security Resources

Understanding security is a key piece of working with Microsoft Dynamics GP. The free Support Debugging Tool provides options to resolve security issues easily with its Security Profiler feature. The Security Profiler portion of the Support Debugging Tool provides security resource specifics about any window in Dynamics GP including who has access to a resource and what role and tasks this window is assigned to.

We've covered features of the Support Debugging Tool in the last several recipes. Because of its power, the Support Debugging Tool has to be requested from a Dynamics GP partner, even though it's free.

Let's look at how to explore security with the Support Debugging Tool.

How to do it...

To understand Security Profiles with the Support Debugging Tool:

1. With the Support Debugging Tool installed, select **Tools | Support Debugging Tool** from the **Microsoft Dynamics GP** menu.

2. Select the **Options** button on the main window and select **Security Profiler**:

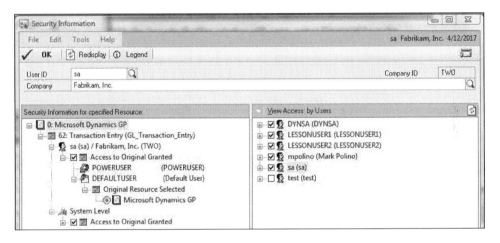

3. With the **Security Profiler** window still open, select **Financial** from the Navigation Pane. Select **General** from the **Financial** Area Page under **Transactions**. Opening a window populates the **Security Profiler** window.

4. In the **Security Profiler** window highlight the line where the technical name is **GL_Transaction_Entry** and click on **Security**:

5. The **User ID** and **Company ID** fields are displayed at the top.

6. The left-hand side pane holds Role and Task information. The right-hand side pane holds User IDs of who can access this resource. This is extremely useful when trying to set up a user to match the access of someone else.

7. Click on the **Legend** button to get an explanation of the icons on this window:

8. The GoTo button in the upper-right opens the various security windows allowing security settings to be changed on the fly, assuming that the logged in user has the appropriate access of course:

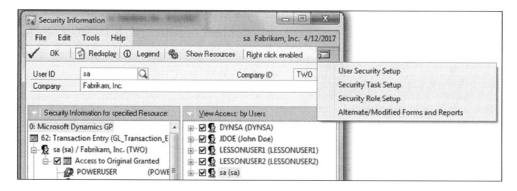

How it works...

It's not uncommon to find frustrated users trying to set security but unsure of what settings give access to a specific window. The Security Profiler feature of the Support Debugging Tool can make this process much clearer.

There's more...

The Security Profiler feature doesn't just provide resource information on request. Security information can be exported and sent by e-mail to a security administrator. Also, the Security Profiler can pop up the appropriate information automatically when access to a resource is denied. This makes it easy for an administrator to adjust access at the point of the problem.

Automatic Security Profiles

The Security Profiler can be set up to automatically display when access to a resource is denied. To apply this, the Support Debugging Tool must be installed and Administrator access turned on.

To allow the Security Profiler to be activated automatically users have to be added to the MBS DEBUGGER USER role in security, otherwise access to the **Security Profiler** window itself is denied.

To turn on automatic display of the Security Profile when access is denied to a resource:

1. In the **Support Debugging Tool** window select **Debugger | Administrator Settings**.

2. Enter the system password if prompted.

3. In the **General** tab set the **Automatic Open Mode** field under **Security Profile Settings** to either **Open on Errors Only** or **Open on Errors & Warnings** and click on **OK**.

Security Profiler Settings
Automatic Open Mode: Open on Errors & Warnings ▼

Now when access to a window is denied, the Security Profiler activates with more information on the denied resource. This makes validating security and, if appropriate, providing security to that resource much easier:

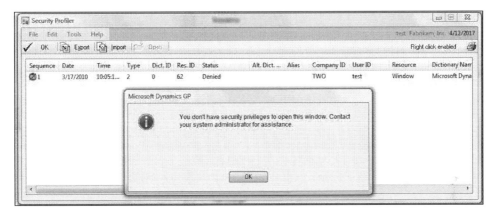

Export/Import Security Logs

On the **Security Profiler** window is an option to Export a profile to a file or e-mail. Once exported, this file can be sent to a security administrator. The administrator can then use the **Import** button to bring in the file and drill back to security to adjust the settings.

A common scenario looks like this: an employee is denied access to a resource. They export the automatically opened Security Profiler information and e-mail it to their security administrator. The administrator imports the file and then drills back to security to review. If access should be granted, the administrator can grant the appropriate rights to the user or update the role for all related users right from that screen.

See also

▶ *Extending Dynamics GP with the Support Debugging Tool*

▶ *Logging transactions for troubleshooting*

▶ *Capturing Screenshots and sending an E-mail for support*

▶ *Executing SQL from within Dynamics GP*

Index

Letter Writing Assistant, using 133
SmartList, exporting 131, 133

MOSS 50

My Reports
about 20
dates, setting up 22
report, adding 21, 22
reports without options 22

N

Named Printers
about 192
Printer Class, selecting 195
setting 194
setup 193, 194
working 195

Navigation List
exporting, to Microsoft Excel 130, 131

Navigation Pane
about 18
cleaning up 18, 19
rearranging 18
working 19

O

ODC 138
Office Data Connection. *See* **ODC**

P

Paid Transaction Removal
about 254
prior history, maintaining 254
running, in Dynamics GP 255, 256
working 256

period, closing
Fiscal Periods Setup window 251
Mass Close button, using 251
particular transaction type, closing 252
steps 250, 251
working 251
wrong date entry, preventing 250

posting dates
about 170
transaction, posting 170, 171
working 171

posting reports
about 172, 173
controlling 173
destination 172
location 175
printing changes, requirements 173
setup 174
system print dialog. turning off 175, 176
Transaction Journal 175
working 174

Posting Type
reviewing 243
reviewing, SmartList used 241-243
validating 240

Purchase Order
closing, properly 235
copying 190-192
entry, speeding up 192

Q

Quick Journal 220

Quick Links
data access, speeding up 16
Navigation Lists, adding 16, 17
working 18

Quick Links Details box 17

R

Reconcile to GL feature
about 196
month-end processing, speeding up 196, 197
using 196, 197
working 197
year, balancing 198

Reconcile utility
about 268
financial totals, reconciling 268, 269
working 269

Record Limits, SmartList
adjusting 114, 115
data, controlling 113
working 116

Recurrence button 25

recurring batches
best practices 94
clearing 221

Thank you for buying
Microsoft Dynamics GP 2010 Cookbook

About Packt Publishing

Packt, pronounced 'packed', published its first book "Mastering phpMyAdmin for Effective MySQL Management" in April 2004 and subsequently continued to specialize in publishing highly focused books on specific technologies and solutions.

Our books and publications share the experiences of your fellow IT professionals in adapting and customizing today's systems, applications, and frameworks. Our solution based books give you the knowledge and power to customize the software and technologies you're using to get the job done. Packt books are more specific and less general than the IT books you have seen in the past. Our unique business model allows us to bring you more focused information, giving you more of what you need to know, and less of what you don't.

Packt is a modern, yet unique publishing company, which focuses on producing quality, cutting-edge books for communities of developers, administrators, and newbies alike. For more information, please visit our website: www.packtpub.com.

About Packt Enterprise

In 2010, Packt launched two new brands, Packt Enterprise and Packt Open Source, in order to continue its focus on specialization. This book is part of the Packt Enterprise brand, home to books published on enterprise software – software created by major vendors, including (but not limited to) IBM, Microsoft and Oracle, often for use in other corporations. Its titles will offer information relevant to a range of users of this software, including administrators, developers, architects, and end users.

Writing for Packt

We welcome all inquiries from people who are interested in authoring. Book proposals should be sent to author@packtpub.com. If your book idea is still at an early stage and you would like to discuss it first before writing a formal book proposal, contact us; one of our commissioning editors will get in touch with you.

We're not just looking for published authors; if you have strong technical skills but no writing experience, our experienced editors can help you develop a writing career, or simply get some additional reward for your expertise.

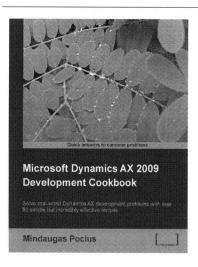

Microsoft Dynamics AX 2009 Programming: Getting Started

ISBN: 978-1-847197-30-6   Paperback: 348 pages

Get to grips with Dynamics AX 2009 development quickly to build reliable and robust business applications

1. Develop and maintain high performance applications with Microsoft Dynamics AX 2009

2. Create comprehensive management solutions to meet your customer's needs

3. Best-practices for customizing and extending your own high-performance solutions

Programming Microsoft Dynamics NAV 2009

ISBN: 978-1-847196-52-1   Paperback: 620 pages

Develop and maintain high performance NAV applications to meet changing business needs with improved agility and enhanced flexibility

1. Create, modify, and maintain smart NAV applications to meet your client's business needs

2. Thoroughly covers the new features of NAV 2009, including Service Pack 1

3. For experienced programmers with little or no previous knowledge of NAV development

Please check **www.PacktPub.com** for information on our titles